Designing Cultures of Care

Designing Cultures of Care

Edited by
Laurene Vaughan

BLOOMSBURY VISUAL ARTS
LONDON • NEW YORK • OXFORD • NEW DELHI • SYDNEY

BLOOMSBURY VISUAL ARTS
Bloomsbury Publishing Plc
50 Bedford Square, London, WC1B 3DP, UK
1385 Broadway, New York, NY 10018, USA
29 Earlsfort Terrace, Dublin 2, Ireland

First published in Great Britain 2018
Paperback edition published 2023

Cover design: Lou Dugdale

A catalogue record for this book is available from the British Library.

A catalog record for this book is available from the Library of Congress.

ISBN: HB: 978-1-3500-5538-4
PB: 978-1-3503-5353-4
ePDF: 978-1-3500-5537-7
eBook: 978-1-3500-5536-0

Typeset by Deanta Global Publishing Services, Chennai, India
Printed and bound in Great Britain

To find out more about our authors and books visit www.bloomsbury.com and sign up for our newsletters.

Contents

List of Images

Contributors

Shana Agid is an artist/designer, teacher and activist whose work focuses on relationships of power and difference in visual and political cultures. S/he is an assistant professor at Parsons School of Design. S/he holds an MFA in Printmaking and Book Arts and MA in Visual and Critical Studies from California College of the Arts (CCA) and a PhD in Design from RMIT. Their writing on design, politics, and pedagogy has been published in *Design and Culture, Design Philosophy Papers, Lateral: The Journal of the Cultural Studies Association* and in the proceedings of the Participatory Design Conference. Shana's collaborative design practice focuses on exploring possibilities for self-determined services and campaigns through teaching and design research.

Charles Anderson, PhD, is an artist and registered landscape architect with over thirty years' experience making and exhibiting work in Australia and around the world. He has a distinguished reputation as an artist and designer, and has received numerous awards for his work, from both within and outside of the landscape architectural profession. A founding partner of Stutterheim/Anderson Landscape Architecture (SAALA), Anderson is currently a senior lecturer in the School of Architecture and Design at RMIT University where he is also a member of a number of research clusters, including the Augmented Landscapes Lab (ALL), the X-Field Research Group, and the Spatial Information Architecture Laboratory (SIAL).

Rachel Clarke is an interaction-design researcher and artist supporting relational and diverse cultural community practices for the design of technology. She completed an interdisciplinary PhD in 2014 at Culture Lab, Newcastle University, UK, working across the School of Computing Science and the International Centre for Cultural Heritage Studies on long-term participatory design with an international women's center. She is currently a visiting research fellow at Northumbria University adapting participatory design approaches with nonprofit advocacy organizations working on trust, austerity, and digitally mediated representation.

Angeliki Dimaki-Adolfsen is a designer currently pursuing her PhD in play, migration, and design at HDK in Goteborg, Sweden, and a former colleague at AHO.

Mick Douglas is a transdisciplinary artist and academic working across performance, art, design, and social practice. He supervises creative practice doctoral research at RMIT University with a particular interest in performative approaches. He can be reached via email at www.mickdouglas.net.

Neal Haslem is a communication designer, design educator, and a practice-led researcher in communication design. He is Associate Dean, Communication Design at RMIT University. His practice investigates enabling futures through communication design action with people. Neal's practice-led design research investigates the intersubjective action of communication design practice with a focus on the non-instrumental aspects of design practice. His research on the conjunction of communication design and intersubjective action is articulated through projects, writing, teaching, and discourse. Ultimately he aims, through design research, education, and discourse, to initiate an "intersubjective turn" within communication design practice and research.

Brad Haylock is a designer, publisher, and academic. He is an associate professor of Design at RMIT University, Melbourne, Australia. His research spans typography, independent publishing, critical sociology, and sociologies of critique. He is founding editor of Surpllus, an independent, para-academic imprint focusing on critical and speculative practices across art, design, and theory.

Niels Hendriks is a lecturer and researcher at the LUCA School of Arts (University of Leuven, Belgium). His interest domains are participatory design and design for health. He is the founder of the Dementia Lab—a collective of researchers and designers working on design for, and together with, persons with dementia. Niels Hendriks's research and the work of the Dementia Lab focus on the exploration of artifacts and methodologies supporting design for, and together with, persons with dementia. Each year the Dementia Lab organizes a gathering for researchers and design practitioners to share and reflect on their experiences (see www.dementialab.com).

Lily Hibberd is an artist and writer and DECRA Research Fellow at National Institute of Experimental Arts, UNSW, Sydney. She is creative director and co-founder with Bonney Djuric of Parramatta Female Factory Precinct Memory Project. Together they develop and facilitate creative projects with former residents of Parramatta Girls Home. Lily curates Memory Project's on-site exhibitions and public programs and produces collaborative video and performance works with Parragirls. She is coauthor with Djuric of numerous publications. Lily Hibberd is the recipient of an ARC Discovery Early Career Researcher Award Scheme to research new digital media representations with Parragirls. This research led Lily to co-produce the 3-D immersive cinema project *Parragirls Past, Present* at UNSW EPICentre for The Big Anxiety: festival of arts+science+people, 2017, in collaboration with Parragirls and UNSW media artists.

Guy Johnson is the inaugural Unison Housing Chair of Urban Housing and Homelessness. He leads the Unison Housing Research Lab at RMIT University, a unique education and research collaboration between RMIT University and Unison Housing, Victoria's largest social housing provider. The lab was established in 2017 and is funded for five years to undertake an innovative research program informed by the experiences of service users and providers. Prior to his appointment, Johnson was director of the Centre for Applied Social Research (CASR) at RMIT University. Professor Johnson has been involved in the area of housing and homelessness for over two decades. His research investigates theoretical and applied questions relating to the dynamics of homelessness and housing.

Chuan Khoo is an interdisciplinary digital media artist and designer. Blurring the lines between art and design, Chuan's practice questions computing's consequences and its non-binding ethereal ties, designing interactive things that inhabit human identity, emotion, and belonging. Chuan headed the Diploma in Interaction Design program at Nanyang Polytechnic's School of Interactive & Digital Media, Singapore. He taught at the Rhode Island School of Design, the Guangzhou Academy of Fine Arts, and the Royal Melbourne Institute of Technology. He graduated with an MFA in Digital+Media at RISD. Chuan is currently a PhD candidate at RMIT's School of Architecture & Design.

Marcus Knutagård is a researcher, senior lecturer, and deputy head at the School of Social Work, Lund University. He is a member of the Nordic

Network of Homelessness Research and a member of an ongoing COST-action, "Measuring homelessness in Europe." He is currently working on a research project, implementing Housing First in Sweden. His research interests include housing policy, homelessness, and the importance of place for how social work is organized—its moral geography. Knutagård's research interests also concern social innovation from a welfare perspective, with a particular focus on service user influence in practice research. Together with a colleague at Lillehammer University College he has written a book, *Innovation in Social Welfare and Human Servic*es, with a special focus on social innovations.

Jordan Lacey is a vice-chancellor's postdoctoral research fellow in the School of Design at RMIT University, researching the interface of the sonic arts and urban design. His recently published book *Sonic Rupture: A Practice-led Approach to Urban Soundscape Design* (Bloomsbury 2016) proposes the diversification of everyday life through the installation of networks of sounding artworks. He is presently lead researcher in several industry-based projects, which explore new ways that urban planning and design strategies might include sound design to enhance urban livability and creative encounter. Jordan has also produced several innovative public sound installations and gallery works.

Janike Kampevold Larsen is an associate professor at the Institute of Urbanism and Landscape at the Oslo School of Architecture and Design. She is project leader for *Future North*, a research project observing and mapping changes in settlements and territories in the Arctic and Subarctic regions. She has worked as program developer and coordinator for the Tromsø Academy of Landscape and Territorial Studies since 2011, and is on the *JoLA* editorial team since 2015. Her recent publications include "Global Tourism Practices as Lived Heritage: Viewing the Norwegian Tourist Routes" in *Future Anterior* (2012), "Imagining the Geologic" in *Making a Geologic* Now (Punctum Book 2013), and *Future North: The Changing Arctic Landsca*pes (Routledge 2018).

Yanki Lee is cofounder of Enable Foundation, a nonprofit social design agency with expertise in designing social innovation ecosystems. She received her MA in Architecture from the Royal College of Art (RCA) and PhD in design participation from Hong Kong Polytechnic University. She has been a research fellow at the Royal College of Art's Helen Hamlyn Centre for Design since the year 2000 and founded Exhibit at Golden Lane Estate CIC in London. In the year 2013 she was invited by the Hong Kong Vocational Training Council to return to her hometown to set up the HKDI DESIS Lab after she received RCA Honorary Fellowship and China-UK Fellowship of Excellence for her works in design research and social innovation. She can be reached via email at www.yankilee.com.

Keely Macarow is an associate professor in the School of Art, RMIT University. Keely has worked as a creative producer, artist, curator, and writer for film, video, performance, and exhibition projects which have been presented in Australia, the United Kingdom, the United States, and Europe. She is currently working on interdisciplinary projects with art, design, housing, and medical researchers based in Sweden and Australia to explore how art and design interventions and thinking can be applied to healthcare, political and housing settings, and for public exhibition. She views her research as a matter of social, spatial, and health justice and is committed to developing new ideas, artifacts, tools, and thinking for community benefits.

Claire McAndrew is director of research at the UCL Institute for Digital Innovation in the Built Environment in The Bartlett UCL's Faculty of the Built Environment. Combining social science insight and design-led thinking, Claire's research focuses on the possibilities of design and digital innovation within the built environment for transformative social and cultural effects. She has collaborated on national and international digital innovation projects that traverse communication and interaction design, social science, and the built environment. In 2014 she was awarded an AHRC UnBox LABS Fellowship on Future Cities. She joined The Bartlett in 2011, receiving her Chartered Psychologist status the same year.

Ross McLeod is a senior lecturer in the Master of Design, Innovation and Technology program at RMIT University. His research examines the relationship between physical phenomena and sensorial perception in the design of architectural spaces. In this research the act of design is not only concerned with conceiving the physical structure of the built environment but is seen as a shaping of the spatial experience of the user. His design practice mcleodstudio engages in the production of experimental urban installations that test the parameters of human perception. He is the editor of three books related to this design theory and practice, *Interior Cities* (1998), *Intersection* (2002), and *The Sensuous Intellect* (2006).

Andrew Morrison is director of the Centre for Design Research (www.designresearch.no) at the Oslo School of Architecture and Design (AHO). His research covers multiliteracies, research mediation, transdisciplinary design, and doctoral design education. Collaborative research is central to Andrew's work on the network city, future cultural landscapes of the arctic and communication design between products, services, interactions, and systems design. His recent publications span critiques of the smart city, speculative inquiry, design fiction, design and additive manufacturing, doctoral design pedagogies, and genre innovation. Concerning design and futures literacies, Andrew is on the organizing committee of Anticipation 2017 conference and co-chair of Nordes 2017 (www.nordes.org). He has published widely from critical discourse analysis to urbanism and technology, multimodal communication, and discursive, speculative, and exploratory design.

Itai Palti is a practicing architect and researcher focusing on designing with the human experience in mind. He is a cofounder of The Centric Lab, the first cognitive neuroscience research lab for the built environment. In 2015, Itai founded the Conscious Cities movement, proposing a new field of research and industry for building people-centric environments that are aware and responsive. He is a fellow at The Centre for Urban Design and Mental Health, and a member of research and policy groups including Harvard's Frontiers of Innovation and The Brookings Institution's Learning Landscapes Committee. Itai's writing on the intersection of design and science has been featured in leading publications such as *The Guardian* and *Quartz*, and he is a co-curator of the conscious cities publications and conference series.

Sarah Pink is a distinguished professor in the School of Media and Communication at RMIT University and International Guest Professor at Halmstad University, Sweden. Her recent books include *Anthropologies and Futures: Researching Emerging and Uncertain Worlds* (2017), *Making Homes: Ethnography and Design* (2017), and *Academic Scholarship and Applied Practice* (2017).

Maria Bertheussen Skrydstrup is a member of the family owners of the Grand Hotel in Vardø and a staff member on projects and a guide at the Vardø branch of the Våranger Museum.

Cathy Smith is an architect, interior designer, and academic. With professional and research qualifications in architecture and interior design, she has taught in the subject areas of design, history, and theory and construction at several

Australian Universities including the University of Newcastle (current), the University of Queensland, and the Queensland University of Technology. Her scholarly research is published in a number of international journals including *Architectural Histories*, *Interstices*, *Architectural Theory Review*, and *IDEA*. In 2018, she will also take up a position as the inaugural Turnbull Foundation Women in the Built Environment scholar at the University of New South Wales.

Shanti Sumartojo is a vice-chancellor's research fellow in the School of Media and Communication at RMIT University. Her research explores how people experience their spatial surroundings, including both material and immaterial aspects, with a particular focus on the built environment. Recent books include *Commemorating Race and Empire in the Great War Centenary* (2017) and *Refiguring Techniques in Digital Visual Research* (2017).

Cameron Tonkinwise is the professor of design at the University of Technology Sydney. He has previously held positions at Carnegie Mellon University's School of Design and Parsons, The New School for Design. Cameron has a background in continental philosophy and continues to research what design practice can learn from material cultural studies and sociologies of technology. Cameron's current focus, in collaboration with colleagues at CMU and an international network of scholar-practitioners, is Transition Design—design-enabled multilevel, multistage structural change toward more sustainable futures.

Albert Tsang is the founding member of HKDI DESIS Lab for Social Design Research. Tsang is a design researcher and educator with a focus on social design, particularly concentrating on participation through design, co-design, as well as action research as a way of gaining knowledge.

Laurene Vaughan is professor of Design and dean of the School of Design at RMIT University. Laurene is design researcher and writer, who is internationally recognized as a leader in interdisciplinary and applied design research. Laurene was invited to the position of Nierenberg Chair, Distinguished Professor of Design, at Carnegie Mellon University, 2012–2013. Her research spans exploratory and applied contexts with a particular interest in the intersections between design and the experience of place.

Noel Waite is currently senior lecturer in the Master of Communication Design program and member of the Design Futures Lab in the School of Design at RMIT University, Melbourne. He has worked with local government, museums, and galleries, and third-sector organizations to develop and implement strategic plans, utilizing scenario building and participatory design methods to ensure a human-centered outcome. He was a member of the Steering Committee which successfully achieved UNESCO Creative City status for Dunedin, New Zealand, in 2014.

SueAnne Ware is a professor and head of the School of Architecture and the Built Environment at the University of Newcastle, Australia. She is a key founder of out(fit) and a self-confessed design activist. She holds a master's degree in landscape architecture from the University of California, Berkeley, and a PhD from RMIT University, Melbourne. Her most recent books include *Sunburnt: Australian Practices of Landscape Architecture*, edited with Julian Raxworthy (Sun, 2011) and *Taylor Cullity Lethlean: Making Sense of Landscape*, edited with Gini Lee (SpaceMaker, 2014). Her research outputs as creative works have won international awards from Australian Institute of Landscape Architecture (SIEV X memorial, the Road as Shrine, The Anti-Memorial to Heroin Overdose Victims).

Acknowledgments

This edited collection emerged from a one-day international research symposium held at RMIT University in 2016. Framed as *Designing Future Cities of Care*, this symposium brought together a disciplinary mix of scholars and practitioners who together contemplated different models and approaches to care, and how this manifests in our lived experiences of cities. This collection is the result of the conversations that were held on that day and a number of the authors in this collection were part of it. Over the course of development of the book the focus on cities was transformed to become cultures. This shift in focus was to enable us, as a community of design researchers and writers, to articulate broader propositions of *situated care*.

As is always the case, edited collections only emerge from the labor and contributions of a range of people, and I would like to take this opportunity to thank and acknowledge those who have contributed to this one. First of all I would like to thank the authors whose chapters make up the collection for these are fundamental to the realization of this project. I would also like to acknowledge and express my gratitude to Brad Haylock who, along with Anna Farago, played a key role in the 2016 Design Futures Lab symposium that led to this book. Brad also played a pivotal role in the initial development of the conceptual framework and proposal for this publication.

In undertaking this project I have been fortunate to work with students within the Bowen Street Press, a student-focused initiative of the Masters in Editing and Publishing at RMIT. I would specifically like to thank Oscar Jonsson and Suzan Calimli for their behind-the-scenes logistical work that editing requires. In particular I thank Oscar for his extraordinary and professional commitment to seeing the project through to completion. My gratitude also goes to Tracy O'Shaughnessy, the publisher of the Bowen Street Press, for taking this project on and seeing the potential of it as a learning experience for the students enrolled in that degree. I would also like to thank Rebecca Barden and Claire Constable from Bloomsbury Academic for their support and for taking this project on as part of their Design Publications List.

Finally, I must express my gratitude to Emma Hegarty for her ongoing support and editorial contribution to the completion of the chapters that make up this collection. Emma's contribution to the publication was through the support of the School of Media and Communication research team at RMIT University.

Thank you all, and take care.
Laurene Vaughan

1

Introduction

Laurene Vaughan

Contingent with our evolving understanding of design and its capacity to contribute to the social, cultural, and technological aspects of society has been an evolving body of scholarship that interrogates the nature of design practice and the emotional and affective attributes of these practices and outcomes. This discourse has been speculative, experimental, theoretical, and enacted, and is realized through projects with living communities. The catalysts for these projects are the challenges of our time: impending environmental disasters, mass migration, population growth, aging populations, and increasing disparity in wealth distribution.

One outcome of this has been the increasing interest in, and publications on, the intersections between design and care. Typically such publications frame care as a context of design and social practices, particularly as they relate to the health and aged-care sectors. Care is understood as something that is institutional, or manifest, in particular systems, services, or "things" *that* care, within professional or "lay" contexts. The outcome of this can be seen in a number of publications presenting case studies, models, and accounts, many of which are referred to in the following chapters.

The aim of this book is to expand this discourse on the relationship between design and care through a frame of culture and cultures. It is proposed that through a framework of culture we are able to envision and realize a more expansive interrogation of care as both an approach and a context for design practices. As will become evident to the reader, culture in this publication spans many definitions.

According to *Merriam Webster's Collegiate Dictionary* culture can be understood as:

> *a: the customary beliefs, social forms, and material traits of a racial, religious, or social group; also : the characteristic features of everyday*

> *existence (such as diversions or a way of life) shared by people in a place or time*
> *b: the set of shared attitudes, values, goals, and practices that characterizes an institution or organization*
> *c: the set of values or social practices associated with a particular field, activity, or societal characteristic*

It is by understanding culture as dynamic, variant, and practised that we are able to expand our perception of care, and how we design with care or for care. The chapters in this collection present case studies that position the cultural dimensions of care from this breadth of understanding.

In Chapter 2, founded on some of the principles of care ethics, I endeavor to present a case for design as a practice of care. Through a response to the writing of Maurice Hamington, I propose that if it is possible for us to conceive of care as a practice that involves an interplay between imagination, empathy, and action, as he does, we can likewise see that design, with its comparable qualities, may also be conceived of as a practice of care. It is through this conception that our ability to understand the value and contribution of design to facilitating care can be expanded.

In Chapters 3 and 4, authors Cathy Smith, Sue Anne Ware, and Brad Haylock present a range of student-led case studies of design partnerships and interventions with organizations that are focused on the care of citizens outside conventional institutional settings. Smith and Ware present projects by the all-female design collective "out(fit)," initiated by a group of designers and educators frustrated by the seemingly intractable problem of gender inequity in the discipline of architecture. They discuss two projects—The Looking Glass (2016), a temporary gallery for abandoned shopfront windows; and the ongoing Jenny's Place (2016–), a design-build of a children's outdoor playspace and minor repair works for a local women's refuge—as a means to explore how design-led interventions add value for urban citizens. Haylock continues with this citizen-led focus through an account of a series of communication design, graduate-student projects in collaboration with the Sentencing Advice Bureau in Melbourne, Australia. The aim of these projects was to develop ways to communicate to the public data on sentencing implications and profiles of offenders within the judicial system. In this way access to information is a performance of care.

In Chapter 5, Shana Agid proposes that designing with people is, at least in part, a means for learning and articulating what we want so that we might imagine and build our desired outcomes. How we understand the questions from which we begin to frame needs and desires, and the contexts and relationships through which we engage them, is critical to design practice. Agid examines this idea through a conversation with scholars, activists, and writers, many of whom are from outside design fields. Through these conversations, the chapter frames four ideas: problem-posing, multiplicity, imagining, and building, and argues that learning from others' long-term engagement with social and political change is essential to being responsible and accountable in our work.

This focus on the role of designers in projects is continued in Chapter 6. Here Laurene Vaughan, Shanti Sumartojo, and Sarah Pink respond to the considerable bodies of literature that propose care as a design paradigm for the health sector. From the global challenges of aging communities to the particularities of specific health and medical facilities, there has been a growing focus on human-centered design methods and approaches and their potential to provide particular and site-specific ways to design into this domain. The ambition of researchers and practitioners has been to identify ways to align the physical experiences of being in a state of institutional care, with new paradigms of patient-centered care as realized within the medical services that hospitals and other such care facilities provide. This discussion takes place around their research into the design of the psychiatric unit of a regional hospital redevelopment.

Chapters 7 and 8 explore two participatory design interventions into aged-care and aging communities, in two different cultural contexts. In Chapter 7, Rachel Clarke reflects on an exploratory, design-led case study inquiring into potential future technologies for older people's participation in urban planning. While older people's perspectives were collected in the redesign of citywide pathways in Newcastle upon Tyne, UK, their feedback was considered valuable in limited ways, highlighting physical mobility and accessibility rather than broader psychosocial, cultural, and aesthetic interests. Through experimental design workshops and urban walks with researchers, alternative futures were imagined for how communication might be improved between city planners and elders. This provided opportunities for reimagining technology to engender temporal communities of care that nurture appreciation of future visions, interdependent processes, cultures of mobility, and layers of expertise rather than focusing on collecting "Smart City" data.

This is followed by Yanki C Lee, Niels Hendriks, and Albert S Y Tsang's discussion of their development of the dementia experience tool. In Chinese society, as in many cultures, people with dementia suffer some level of stigmatization. A dementia research and care center commissioned a social design research lab team (including two of the authors) to design empathic tools.

One of the main challenges was to find a way to empathize with a complicated condition such as dementia, as traditional empathic tools mostly focus on simulation of a specific physical or mental impairment.

Chapter 9 explores interdisciplinary art- and design-led approaches to addressing the affordable housing crisis. Neal Haslem, Keely Macarow, Margie MacKay, Per-Anders Hillgren, Marcus Knutagård, and Mim Whiting introduce their project Homefullness as a response to the crisis. The design principles and philosophy underlying Homefulless as a codesign project are discussed through a description of the current housing conditions in two cities on opposite sides of the world, Melbourne and Malmö. Homefullness is a multidisciplinary inquiry into the ongoing, seemingly intractable issue of homelessness and housing stress. It investigates how art and design processes and artifacts, applied through co-design methods, can work with manifold stakeholders to produce innovation in response to and conceptualization of social issues.

Child welfare and institutionalized models of care for young people have been topics of much public scrutiny. In Chapter 10 Lily Hibberd examines how emergent practices of strategic design are transforming public and private power relations to create cultures of care. This is done through an analysis of Parramatta Female Factory Precinct Memory Project, through which past residents of Parramatta Girls Home—a former state-run child welfare institution in Sydney, Australia—collaborate across disciplinary boundaries with artists, activists, historians, architects, and urban designers to transform this traumatic institutional place into a space of care. It highlights the significance of expanded paradigms of design as the means to transform the entire system: design as a human-centered practice of collaborative, responsive, and adaptive approaches that are able to develop better social outcomes in the production of cultures of care.

Small arctic towns in Norway are under considerable pressure because of changes in fishing rights and livelihoods. Alternative futures, often based on the extraction of oil and gas, have been proposed, but not always realized. At the same time, climate change has become more visceral in the daily lives of arctic communities, wedged between large state and commercial geopolitical actors. In Chapter 11, Andrew Morrison, Maria Bertheussen Skrydstrup, Angeliki Dimaki-Adolfsen, and Janike Kampevold Larsen discuss the development of a former hotel into a "cultural hub" for a local community in the town of Vardø. Drawing on ethnographic and other methods, the research involved a delicate process of negotiation and gradual development of an approach to cultural innovation in which care was needed at many levels to protect local needs and interests while introducing new spaces of both cultural and commercial possibility.

Chapters 12 and 13 show how cultural production in the form of artworks can contribute to community and public experience of care in place. In Chapter 12 Jordan Lacey, Ross McLeod, Charles Anderson, and Chuan Khoo discuss their collaboration with the City of Casey to create a public artwork in the North Clyde Community Centre plaza. The collaboration is a unique example of two interdisciplinary teams coming together to create a work that promotes community engagement. The first phase of the project saw the development of a robust conceptual framework that puts community needs at the center of the creative process. The result of this design process was an amorphous and abstract "other" that can inhabit any civic space with the goal of weaving community into place. The relationship of memory and place, so considered, gave rise to the concept of an "other" that remembers. The memory-place connective is manifested by an embedded interactive systems design that uses technology to interweave community interaction with spatial and temporal expressions.

In Chapter 13 Claire Mc Andrew and Itai Palti revisit the idea of the Conscious City, arguing that the vision of the conscious city has entered the radar. It takes as its heartland the idea of a "conversation" between inhabitants, digitally imbued objects, and responsive architectural fabrics on a city scale. They wonder whether advances in the internet of everything, neuroscience, AI, and big data can enable social opportunities in a more sentient city. This chapter considers the ethics of an architectural dialogic—bringing questions of computational neutrality and democratic participation to the fore in the design and curation of "intelligent architecture."

Cameron Tonkinwise proposes in Chapter 14 that to be human is to be concerned about things, but too many concerns can be overwhelming. Humans can alleviate some of their concerns by designing things, but this can lead to an accumulation of too many things. Humans can also alleviate each other's concerns, especially when they dwell in proximity to each other, in cities. Commercial services involve people being paid to take care of people they do not otherwise know. Sharing Economies are adding new peer-to-peer dimensions to these transactions. To preserve the ways in which these peer-to-peer services re-embed economic exchanges in social relations, designers must be careful not to reduce the social friction involved too much.

In Chapter 15 the narrative collection shifts from an understanding of a culture of care as being an interplay between people and their physical well-being. Here Noel Waite reflects on four examples of co-design that took place in Dunedin, New Zealand, between 2014 and 2016. Waite explores the possibilities of UNESCO Creative Cities as sites of locally specific narrative layers of care that might combine cultural and ecological knowledge and practices to strengthen the relationship between people and their environment. Waite identifies four layers of care that can underpin a Creative City and its relationship to the international UNESCO Network and 2016 UN Sustainable Development Goals in order to ensure a strong foundation of care and dependence between the natural environment and the people and cultures it sustains.

In Chapter 16 the collection comes to a close through a conversation between Laurene Vaughan and Mick Douglas, who explore what it means to perform practices of care. The authors meander through the proposition, unpacking ideas on the basis of their concerns and preoccupations around design, art, and the poetics and pragmatics of practices performed.

2

Design as a Practice of Care

Laurene Vaughan

Design. Care.

Designing. Care(ing).

This mixture of nouns and verbs, of things and actions, of dispositions and propositions—in the singular and/or the collective—is the focus of this discussion. On first encounter it seems simple or straightforward. We shall design with care. It is in or through care that we will design outcomes of meaning and connectivity. But as one explores more deeply, and considers each of the elements, alone and together, the complexity becomes apparent and you realize this combination of words is both an invitation and a declaration for how we might design, why we will design, and the value of this designing for the present and for the future. In this chapter, I will explore what care might offer for how we practise design.

As many readers will know, over the past ten to fifteen years there has been a shift in how we understand and articulate design and its capacity to contribute to the world that we manifest or destroy. Through contemporary discourses and movements in sustainable design, human-centered design, participatory methods, codesign, and the possibilities of connectivity through digital technologies, definitions of design as a problem-solving, materials-oriented suite of professions have been, and continue to be, challenged. With this some have argued that design is a socio-technical domain of practice (Kimbell 2015), which leads us in the right direction for expanding our thinking about design. Such critiques capture the links between social and cultural aspects of design, while retaining a focus on the material practices that are for the most part the basis for design practice. At the same time we have also seen the rise of design thinking as a particular articulation of design and its application to organizational or business contexts in particular.

Fundamental to this transformation in how we define design has been the evolution of new domains or contexts for design practice. These have been realized in areas such as service design, social innovation, and urban planning. Digital technologies and the rapid increase in the usage of digital things in everyday lives have, through their proximity to our bodies and pervasiveness in our private lives, the capacity to make the most intimate aspects of us public with the click of a button. This is coupled with the capacity to print things, make things, from all kinds of materials from the comfort of home, our office, or the back garden shed. We no longer have to rely on the manufacturing sector in the way we did in the past. All these new phenomena have called for us to transition our understanding of design, the materials that we design with, and the contexts for design practice and production. Increasingly, people and their communities are the "material" of our design practices.

Relationships

With the evolution of human-centered design and the systemic uptake of its principles across different domains of design practice, we have seen a transformation in how designers relate to, and engage with, the people that they design for. Whereas people were once understood through demographic classifications or as generic users, audiences, or customers of "design," there is now a recognition that it is real people, with all their complexities and differences, who are at the heart of our design acts. This recognition demands that we re-humanize our approaches to designing—from our methods to the design outcomes.

Re-humanizing keeps our focus on the humans, and as such this is a speciest frame for understanding care. Care needs to embrace the entire living ecosystem that we inhabit and practise within. This perspective is supported by Bates, Imrie, and Kullman (2017:1) who declare that "now more than ever, a rethinking and reappraisal is required about the connection between design and care." We must understand the relationality between what we design and the impact that it has on all life- forms and systems.

From this perspective it can be argued that design as a practice of care would be a relational practice—that is, founded on the relationship between a designer and the contexts, within a range of proximities, of their practice. If this is the case, how much connection must there be between a designer and the contexts of practice and those that they design for? What are drivers for such care? For example, what is the relationship between love and care? Do we have to love or have a relationship with the subject of our practice to care?

Bernard Weicht (2015) asks us to question the intersubjectivity of care. He poses that care is something that happens in and through relationship. Care is gendered, cultural, and temporal. It involves our physical, emotional, mental, and spiritual selves, and if this is the case, then what does it mean for professional practices of care? What does this mean for teachers, nurses, doctors, clergy, or police—those that have traditionally performed what we might think are the professions of care?

How we perceive a practice of care will vary depending on whether it is a professional practice or a personal disposition. This is something that happens across various situations in our lives: care can be a responsibility, a duty, an expectation, or a gift.

How we participate in a care exchange will be informed by the many aspects of ourselves; it may be formal or informal, professional or private. It may also be a representation of our morals, morality, values, and humanity (Weicht 2015, p.24). And it is essential that we understand that care is a social construction and how we relate to it or participate in it may be personal, institutional, and, at times, "forced." By "forced" I am referring to the social expectations that we *will* or *do* care. We are expected to care for family members, children, our pets, our neighbors or colleagues, the environment, and those that are less fortunate. Although it may be uncomfortable to acknowledge and even more so to act upon, to not care is as feasible as to care. For some, there is what we can only call the *burden of care*, a burden that may be enforced upon them because of their position in a family, their participation in a relationship with the subject of care. More broadly it may be because of public expectations—it is your duty to care. As adult humans we have the capacity to choose to care, but that choice can be as fragile or dynamic as any choice that we make that involves another.

The closer we are to the subject of care, the greater the social and cultural expectation that care will take place. This of course includes self-care. As we move through this discussion I propose that there are practices and cultures or contexts of care that are framed by the following dimensions:

- the dynamic and relational context of care;
- the proximity of the subject of care to the carer;

- the motivation for care and the levels of free choice and other driving forces that catalyze the care;
- the sense of burden or ease that the carer feels about expectations of care—both from others and from their conscience.

Care as a practice

In 2010 Maurice Hamington published an article for Hypatia, Inc. titled "The Will to Care: Performance, Expectation, and Imagination." Preparing this chapter I came across this article that I think poses some interesting frameworks for the consideration of care as a disposition for the practice of design. In 2017, Hamington built on this initial work in an article for the *Journal of Business Ethics* entitled "Integrating Care Ethics and Design Thinking." Later in this chapter I will respond to the 2017 publication, but first I wish to discuss and position the key points that he makes, as I see them, in the 2010 article.

Hamington (2010:676) states that "caring actions or performances are the result of the workings of a moral imagination that both empathizes and favorably anticipates making a difference. Empathy participates in the moral imagination and is a catalyst for action, but it is not the sufficient condition of it." How we create the conditions that lead us to want to respond to others in a caring manner is the challenge of establishing a practice of care. What are the catalysts for such responses or, as he calls them, imaginings? Imagination in the sense of this article is best understood as the link between who I am, and what I know of the other, but more importantly *how I relate to the other* so that I can care about their situation in such a manner that I am driven to act.

As Hamington unpacks his core argument he is clear about the need to "distinguish caring actions from empathy." At a time when empathy and developing empathy are foundations for human-centered design, this differentiation is essential. It would be easy to conclude from discourses in design literature (e.g., Carmel-Gilfilen 2016; Kolko 2014; Koskinen, Battarbee & Mattelmäki 2003) that increasing designer empathy will result in caring designers and designers who design outcomes that care. I find Hamington's proposition that there is a difference between care and empathy enticing, and possibly essential if we are to realize the ambitions of the design and empathy discourse.

Hamington bases his definition of care on Victor Vroom's (1964) *expectancy theory*, which, put simply, claims that our expectation of the outcomes from our efforts will influence our commitment to action. In relation to care it can be said that our expectations about the capacity of our care to have an impact will affect our level of care and any caring response we may have. And this is the fundamental difference between empathy and care within this discussion. Empathy can be passive; it is an emotive and/or affective response to another. Care, by contrast, is active. Care may be based on empathy, but empathy may or may not result in acts of care.

It is this active and actionable nature of care that care ethicists have used as the basis to propose "practices of care" (Hamington 2010:677). Hamington (2010:678) cites Evelyn Nanako Glenn's (2000) three defining aspects of a practice of care: first, caring practice is something that everyone needs; second, care is always practiced in relationship; third, caring practices can occur in diverse ways. Although care can be used in everyday vernacular as a means to articulate emotional connection to a person, place, or thing, it is the actions of care—the things that we do—that are the true articulation of care in practice. A practice of care is an external or public articulation of a moral position; and this is the precarious aspect of care in the world. To say that we care but to act otherwise opens us to criticism and judgment from others. This could be argued to be the precarity of care in, or as, a practice—or in fact any proposition or call for a greater practice of care as a collective moral position for the betterment of society.

Whether we conceive of culture through a national, ethnic, organizational, or subcultural categorization, there are culturally based caring norms and associated expectations of behavior. These norms will inform a person's care actions and how that person is perceived and measured by those around them. When actions are aligned to the norm they will be perceived positively; when they are too much or too little, or completely different, they will be subject to criticism and challenge. We see this manifest in different cultural norms for child-rearing or caring for the aged. What may be acceptable to one group maybe an outrage to another. Our caring norms reflect and evolve with our societies and our ways of living. For example, there is an expectation that I, as a first-world, middle-class, white woman, will care for the less fortunate. That I will care for those who are victims of poverty or climate/political atrocities and that I will evidence this care through my actions, predominantly by the giving of money, goods, and, on occasion, time to various causes. This is a broad social expectation but not one of overt judgment. In contrast my approach to caring for my aging parents is a local and personal issue that has more potential for critique by those around me as it has more exposure within a greater social care ecology. There are spectrums of care that are evidenced through a scale of actions—a weekly phone call, a weekly visit, a daily meal service, or co-housing. Each of these is an act of care, realized as caring through communication, services, and presence. They are actions and can therefore contribute to a practice of parental care, but the scale of each of these can draw external comment as well as subjective personal evaluations.

Practicing care is complex and value-laden. Developing norms of care takes time and must be understood not just through the relationship between the carer and the subject of care, but also through greater sociocultural contexts and expectations.

> *Caring, in an ethically meaningful sense, is not merely a sentiment, but describes a collection of actions tied to disposition and linked to identity. Caring is actualized through performance. Caregivers must "do" something for others. . . . Caring integrates a disposition of openness and positive intentions with a performance of actions that leads to the flourishing of the one cared for. Positive iterations of care, although making further caring actions easier, do not make them automatic. Expectations of our effectively being able to care still play a role in our decision.* (Hamingtonn, 2010, p. 679)

It might therefore be possible to think that an empathetic disposition plus any action grounded in good intention will be an adequate basis for a practice of care; but this is not enough. Just any old action undertaken with good intention will not do. Performing a practice of care must also be grounded in skill, expertise, and a capacity to realize the desired outcome of care.

From the discussion so far I propose that a practice of care would be grounded in the following:

- Connection to the subject of care—either through relationship or empathy.
- Expectation that the actions of care will have an impact or meaning for those being cared for.
- Capacity to perform the actions of care in a skillful and useful manner.

Establishing a practice of care

Establishing a practice of care is as challenging as establishing any practice. It involves commitment and repetition. We must see value from our actions—we must have a sense of impact or improvement, or value for those that we care for. Caring practices are not rote repetitions of the same actions to every site of care, but are open-ended systems of responses to those encountered. Iterations of care, or multiple experiences of care, help us develop a suite of expertise that can be applied in new circumstances (Hamington 2010, p. 690).

However in light of Hamington's (2010 p. 682) observation that "caring is like other human actions: we generally do not undertake those actions that we perceive to be futile," what do we do when there is no certainty of an outcome from our care? Hamington argues that there must be a leap of faith, a level of trust or belief in the value of the care that goes beyond the certainty of impact. This proposition seems to be at odds with what Hamington and other care ethicists argue is essential to a practice of care—evidence of outcome from action. In reality we can never be sure, but we must be committed enough to the integrity or relevance of our actions to see them through. This is the moral dimension of the practice of care.

"Caring for unknown others is so challenging because the farther we move from the familiar, the less control we have and the more risk of failure there is" (Hamington 2010, p.684).

It is in this way that the role of imagination becomes pivotal—not only to facilitate empathy to drive care, but also empathy with those we know little about so that we can enact care. The greater our distance from the context of care, the greater the gap between imagination and impact. As I discuss further in the next section, Hamington (2017) poses that humility, ambiguity, imagination, and a disregard for the rules are fundamental for a practice of care, one that can be better served through a link to design. These, he proposes, are what many would see as the foundations of design practice, and human-centered design in particular.

"Caring involves an imaginative leap of faith. . . . One must believe that one's efforts can lead to caring actions that make a difference. The existence of the will to care can bring about the fact of caring" (Hamington 2010. p. 868).

Establishing a practice of care requires that we work at and evolve the practice. At times the impact and value of the practice will be evident; at other times it will be less so. And like the development of any form of practice we must persist, be patient with ourselves as we evolve, and know that benefits (for ourselves and others) may take time and leaps of imagination in the process.

Practices of care and design

In this final section I wish to explore what design as a practice of care may involve. To do this I return to my earlier proposition that human-centered care is an effective means through which to consider and explore the value of care and empathy within design practice. And I also reiterate that the focus on humans can be limiting. We must remember that the use of humans as the focus for a practice must be done with an awareness that they are the place-holder for all life-forms and systems.

I wish to draw on Hamington's 2017 article "Integrating Care Ethics and Design Thinking" as a means for exploring what design as a practice of care may be.

Care ethics and Care theory are the theoretical frame for Hamington's (2017) argument. As he states: "The definition employed in this article describes care as consisting of performed acts that promote wellbeing and flourishing of others and ourselves based on knowledge and responsiveness to the one cared for." This definition emphasizes the epistemic, responsive, and action-orientated character of care ethics, crucial to the relationship with design thinking being argued in the article.

It is important to note that the article is published in a business journal and Hamington is particularly focused on design as design thinking. His particular interest in exploring the intersections between care ethics and design thinking, results in his proposition that it is through the integration of these two practice areas into business that we may see a transformation in the ethics of business practices. He states: "The relational and responsive dimensions of design thinking is analogous in some important ways, namely empathy and inquiry, to the relational and responsive approach of care ethics." The basis for this proposition is the relatively successful uptake or interest in design thinking by a range of business and organizational contexts. Hamington argues that design thinking's "relational and empathetic approaches" grounded in values can be the link between the two. "I propose that care ethics can be the moral corollary to design thinking and integrating the two is not only possible but desirable and beneficial."

Care is often perceived as a responsive act—when we care, we respond to the needs of another. Harington (2017) proposes that design as a proactive form of practice has the capacity to overcome this constraint and can "enliven" care within other domains of care.

But what does he mean by design thinking? Hamington builds on the work of Schweitzer, Groeger and Sobel (2016) who argue for the value of mind-sets for design thinking as a means for understanding what underpins the design thinking process:

- Empathy with people's needs and context
- Collaboration and embracing diversity
- Being inquisitive and open to new perspectives and learning

- Being mindful of process and thinking modes
- Experiential intelligence
- Deliberate and overt action
- Conscious creativity
- Accepting uncertainty and being open to risk
- Modeling behavior
- Having the desire and determination to make a difference
- Critically questioning

I propose that any designer reading this list would see it as being to varying extents accurate, if not desirable. There is an element of idealism here, for unfortunately we cannot claim that all design thinking in practice embraces diversity or models behavior or is open to risk. But this is the rhetoric and the ambition of design thinking and, I would argue, design practice as well. And this is the point of difference from Hamington's proposition, that I wish to make.

I reiterate a recognition that Hamington's arguments are made within the context of business and organizations, but to call for a practice that he calls "caring design" based on an understanding of design as design thinking limits the potential of design to be a practice of care and to contribute to the evolution of the other practice domains that it engages with.

Hamington (2010, p. 690) states that "caring requires engaging with diverse peoples to understand their specific circumstances and thus moving beyond distress over the unfamiliar to honouring difference and finding the commonalities that can give birth to connection."

In 2017 he goes on to provide the following definition for the practice he calls Caring Design.

> *Caring Design is a human-centred innovation and problem solving methodology/ process as well as a moral and epistemological ideal grounded in a commitment to inquiry, empathy, and care of constituent stakeholders.*

However, if we embrace design as a material and propositional practice that is grounded in sociocultural contexts, that is far more than problem-solving in the service of others, but rather exists in relation to others, then I think that the real potential for design to be a practice of care becomes evident. For if we understand that design is more than a form of professionalized cognitive logic, that it is not only in service of others, but makes problems as well as resolving them part of its innovation and creative processes, we are able to understand the intersections between the practices of care and the practices of design in new and exciting ways.

By framing the relationship between care and design as an intersection of practices and dispositions, we are able to move beyond the limited yet also valuable understanding that the design of care is about the design of things and systems that care or provide care. This is not to say that these systems and artifacts of care are not important, they are. Significant work is being undertaken through interdisciplinary collaborations with the sciences, health services, organizations, and designers to design better and more caring outcomes. These include healthcare systems, aged-care facilities, and artifacts to support the disabled or unwell. Sometimes this is through participatory or co-design methodologies, at others it is through material innovations with end users in mind. As has been discussed in this chapter, these are all aspects of care and design. I am proposing that design as a practice of care is practiced in *all* design contexts, not just explicit "care" contexts. It is a disposition of practice that utilizes a design mind-set within a framework of care ethics. When a sustainability axis is part of design process, the environment itself may be the subject of care. This would be present alongside a concern for all the readers of a book on the practice of publication design; in wayfinding systems for all those who use a particular space; for users seeking comfort and access in chairs, kitchen appliances, pens, or any digital device. Such a design practice founded in care is more than human- or user-centric; it is situated in an ecology of care where all living elements are considered and designed for in the practice of design.

Conceiving of design as a practice of care is a conscious means of articulating an approach to design that is considered as sustainable and sustaining. This not a call for design practice that is dull, unimaginative, or situated only in the realms of what is already known. Rather, it is far from it. Design as a practice of care understands that there is much for design to contribute in collaboration with other disciplines and practice domains.

References

Bates, C., Imrie, R. and Kullman, K. (2017), *Care and Design: Bodies, Building and Cities*, Sussex, UK: Wiley Blackwell.

Carmel-Gilfilen, C. (2016), "Designing with Empathy: Humanizing Narratives for Inspired Healthcare Experiences," *Health Environments Research & Design Journal*, 9 (2): 130–46.

Glenn, E. N. (2000), "Creating a Caring Society," *Contemporary Sociology*, 29 (1): 84–89.

Hamington, M. (2010), "The Will to Care: Performance, Expectation, and Imagination," *Hypatia*, 25: 675–95.

Hamington, M. J. (2017), "Integrating Care Ethics and Design Thinking," *Journal of Business Ethics,* doi:10.1007/s10551-017-3522-6 (accessed November 11, 2017).

Kimbell, S. (2015), *The Service Innovation Handbook: Action-Oriented Creative Thinking Toolkit for Service Organizations*, Netherlands: BIS Publishers.

Kolko, J. (2014), *Well Design: How to Use Empathy to Create Products People Love*, Cambridge, MA: Harvard Business Review Press.

Koskinen, I., Battarbee, K. and Mattelmäki, T., eds (2003), *Empathic Design*, Helsinki: IT Press.

Schweitzer, J., Groeger, L. and Sobel, L. (2016), "The Design Thinking Mindset: An Assessment of What We Know and What We See in Practice," *Journal of Design, Business and Society*, 2 (1): 71–94.

Vroom, Victor H. (1964), *Work and Motivation*, New York: Wiley.

Weicht, B. (2015), *The Meaning of Care: The Social Construction of Care for Elderly People*, London: Palgrave Macmillan.

3

Out(fit)ting the City: Care and Contribution in Post-Industrial Newcastle, Australia

Cathy Smith and SueAnne Ware

Care, gender, and the construction of the city

This chapter explores the notion and practices of care as it relates to a very specific design entity called out(fit): a collective of built environment professionals and volunteers (including ourselves) based in Newcastle, Australia. Through its twin focus on gender and socioeconomic inclusivity, the out(fit) group was self-initiated by a group of female designers, landscape architects, construction managers, and architects loosely affiliated with the School of Architecture and Built Environment at the University of Newcastle (UON) in regional Australia. out(fit)'s mandate is twofold: first, to increase the visibility of successful female architectural graduates and the allied building professions through showcasing the work in public settings and second, to provide pro bono consultancy to deserving local communities lacking the financial and/or cultural acumen to otherwise access professional design and building services. An additional ambition is the promotion of the often-radical and thought-provoking work of both female and male university students in order to strengthen the university's ties to local communities (Figure 3.1). Now composed of both university-affiliated members and independent practitioners, out(fit) remains simultaneously independent of, and interdependent with, UON's institutional structures.[1] Charities, volunteer work, and unpaid labor are dominated by female workers: although unpaid labor and caring can be equalized in terms of their economic contributions (Gibson-Graham 2006: 263), our own adoption of these activities may initially appear to reinforce a gender stereotype, but this is not the case. out(fit)'s remit was always contingent upon project opportunities, membership capacities, and, fiscal circumstances and as such, could be affiliated with the

Figure 3.1 out(fit) launch and Looking Glass gallery with Lord Mayor Nuatali Nelmes and the eight original members of out(fit). Photo Credit: Ramsey Awad.

broader "care ecosystem" (Thackara 2015: 132) already extant in communities. Yet because of its links with a higher-educational provider, out(fit) is neither a straightforward charity nor commercial design entity; it resists straightforward operational categorization.

The intention of the present chapter is neither to generalize the broader applicability of the out(fit) project beyond its specific circumstances nor to measure and evaluate its success per se (particularly given both its emergent nature and the complexities of the influencing factors). We wish instead to invoke the project as one practice methodology that is specific to our post-industrial milieu while being potentially relevant to other urban settings. While the projects and experimental processes examined in the present chapter are still relatively emergent, our concurrent reflection on them produces a situated knowledge that is itself available for further productive transformation. Both the out(fit) entity and the work it enables resonate with what Italian-American feminist Teresa de Lauretis calls the "politics of experience of everyday life" (1986: 10). The posthumanist feminists Donna Haraway (1990) and Rosi Braidotti (2013) similarly question the foundational myths of traditional objectivity and the attendant essential readings of gender as the biological determinant of identity. Haraway writes: "There is nothing about being female that naturally binds women together into a unified category. There is not even such a state as *being* female, itself a highly complex category constructed in contested sexual scientific discourses and other social practices" (1990: 152). She argues that feminists should consider creating coalitions based on affinity rather than identity (1990: 153). Framed in this way, the out(fit) collective produces specific coalescences of like-minded individuals producing their city in subtle and frequently ephemeral ways.

For the purposes of the present chapter, we would like to focus on the operational challenges involved in initiating a voluntary interdisciplinary practice with caregiving and gender equity as its self-determined goals. What concerns us here is care as a motivational focus and driver of practice, rather than the "ethics of care" and the attendant historical construction of the sexualized subject synonymous with French cultural theorist Michel Foucault's later writings (Foucault et al. 1987). As such, reference will be made to contemporary discourses on design and urbanism that prioritize social and cultural impacts over economic gain alone, including select writings by Bernard Stiegler (2013) and the collaborating feminists Julie Graham and Katherine Gibson (Gibson-Graham 2006). Stiegler's nuanced notion of care is of particular interest because it is posited as a phenomenon constitutive of human life itself—an expression of our sense of attachment to people, places and things. In the first instance, Stiegler symbolically ascribes care to the maternal space: "something that holds between the mother and child" (Stiegler 2013: 1), and, as such, could invoke the biological reductionism associated with the idealized figure of the woman-as-caregiver. This association of caregiving with women and placemaking should not diminish its efficacy, particularly when these practices are: "contributing to changes in the livability of urban space for women" (Gibson-Graham 2006: 81). Even caregiving itself can be monetized by assigning its constituent activities an equivalent economic value (Gibson-Graham 2006: 261). That said, and as noted by Graham-Gibson, a larger question relates to whether these practices should be considered beyond the parameters of capitalism itself and: "Capital as the 'identities' which define women/space [. . .] and the subordinate role that economic urban script confers" (2006: 81). Stiegler himself connects the construction of the twenty-first-century city to the aforementioned culture of care (Stiegler and Rue89 2013) as evidenced in community-focused cooperative economic models of production and consumption often referred to as "cooperative capitalism" (Stiegler in Lemmens 2011: 39) or the "sharing economy." In turn, these connections between capitalism and urbanism begin to shift the notion of care from a peripheral, secondary, and somewhat gendered phenomenon to the core of the capitalist apparatus.

out(fit): Gender diversity in the architectural profession

The out(fit) project initially emerged from a collective sense of frustration with gender discrimination within the architectural academy, and a desire to contribute more meaningfully to the construction of built environment, particularly (though not exclusively) in relation to the discipline of architecture. Despite the numerous architecture-specific publications confronting the notion and topic of gender equity (Colomina 1996: Hughes 1996; Agrest, Conway and Kanes Weisman 1996; Coleman, Danze, Henderson 1997; Rendell, Penner and Borden 1999; Petrescu 2007; Burns 2001; Stratigakos 2016), several recent surveys suggest that gender-based discrimination continues (Braidwood 2017; Thether 2016). Given the extent of discriminatory behaviors within the discipline, it is somewhat unsurprising that much of these discriminatory behaviors are first experienced in university settings—the effective birthplace of the architectural profession (Corroto 2005; Smith 2015). We also noted limited local opportunities and forums in which students and practitioners alike could encounter both gender diversity and gender-specific issues. To borrow from the words of North American architectural academic Despina Stratigakos:

> Privileging male voices in this way sense a strong message about who a school consider and authority and deems worthy of an audience. It also discourages female students. As one student-respondent to the 2014 Architects' Journal survey stated, "Women architects are never discussed or celebrated in school. It is almost perceived as a negative to be a woman in architecture." (Stratigakos 2016: 25)

Indeed, it would seem that an individual's caregiver status is itself anathema to female career development. The recent survey results conducted by the North American group "Equity By Design (EQxD)" indicates that while male architects who are "caregivers" are the highest remunerated staff within practice, female architects who are caregivers are, by contrast, the most poorly remunerated (2016). As such, and for women, it appears as if architectural practice and caregiving are mutually exclusive endeavors. The differences in salary may be partially explained by the already-known connection between career progression in architecture and the long working-week hours known to disadvantage employed mothers and others with external life responsibilities (Parlour 2014). Notwithstanding this known workplace expectation, one might also wonder if the *very notion of universal care and nurture* is itself a problematic construct within a discipline that continues to be associated with gender discrimination, and socioeconomic exclusivity more broadly.

The all-female design group out(fit) is another kind of experiment focused on disrupting the practice cultures that support discriminatory behaviors, both within and without the architectural academy.[2] The university's philanthropic arm generally deals with donations to the institution for student scholarships, endowed chairs, and capital works programs, and as such, out(fit) appears to be an institutional anomaly. Accordingly, an outreach program which seeks to improve the lives of women and children in need requires a parallel educational and promotional strategy highlighting the inherit value of student work and female practitioners. Such a university-affiliated initiative is not without its reputational risks but, thus far, it has been a mutually enriching experience. The emergent nature of out(fit) and our loose fit with UON Philanthropy has sparked early synergies compared to traditional research centers or school-based research laboratories. UON Philanthropy has matched the out(fit) group with potential donors and, in return, we have provided them with an active community platform for building its reputation.

Window dressing: The Looking Glass gallery project (2016)

In direct contrast to the negative association of female characters with some of the city's colonial foundations (University of Newcastle 2013), the out(fit) team—and the Looking Glass shopfront gallery project more specifically—sought to affirm the positive influence and contributions of women in constructing the twenty-first-century Newcastle. Inspired by Lewis Carroll's *Through the Looking-Glass* and *What Alice Found There* (2009), where Alice ponders what the world is like on the other side of a mirror's reflection, out(fit)'s Looking Glass gallery featured the contributions of women and students: two groups that are often overlooked, but that offer limitless potential in architecture and design. Throughout 2016, a rotating series of exhibitions, the gallery re-activated an abandoned corner of a prominent site in Newcastle's CBD. Our temporary occupation of the windows was facilitated *au gratis* by its then-landowners, the GPT group.

In late February 2016, the first exhibition "A Newcastle Taxonomy" featured lighting contraptions and various other student explorations of luminosity

Figure 3.2 The Looking Glass gallery's first exhibition "A Newcastle Taxonomy" featured UON Masters of Architecture students' work, which examined Newcastle's history both dark and light. University of Newcastle.

(Figures 3.1 and 3.2). The launch of the gallery project also served as out(fit)'s launch. Lord Mayor Nuatali Nelmes, Newcastle's second female mayor in its over 150-year history, significantly opened the event (Figure 3.1). Poignantly the first exhibition and launch embodied both the hope and the motivations behind out(fit). The illuminated installation for an inner-city community site, an iconic ex-department store building, reconciled divergent qualities of the site: the past and the future; the dark and the light (Figure 3.2). The students' projects emphasized, using inexpensive, upcycled materials, a theme which continues across all of out(fit)'s design-build work. Throughout the 2016 occupancy period, the Looking Glass gallery rotated exhibits and featured a diversity of practices.

The Looking Glass project became an important armature for extending our reach beyond traditional social and print media. Perhaps more importantly, it also provoked conversations about the potential for design to assist in the Hunter's regional transformation. Much like the moment when Alice scales the fireplace mantle and pokes at the mirror above, and finds to her surprise, that she is able to step through it to an alternative world; the gallery exhibits revealed another view of architectural practice through alternative visions of, and for, our city. The Looking Glass gallery's location, the windows of the once-vibrant David Jones department store building, was also highly significant. The windows have become the locus of their host city's shared cultural memory. Many Novocastrians[3] remember the expertly crafted window dressing and the highly anticipated animatronic Christmas scenes viewed by local families in

Figure 3.3 Exhibition of Newcastle's Women in Building Associated Services (WIBAS) organization, a professional group that provides events and services where women can network with their colleagues, exchange ideas and experiences that will support and mentor the other women, while obtaining relevant, specialist industry-specific information. Photo Credit: Bobbie Bayley.

the evenings. These collisions of nostalgia and aspiration imbue notions of care and concern for the city, past and present. By re-investing in both the dormant window facades of buildings and those often overlooked in the highlights of architectural practice, the Looking Glass provided dual caretaker roles. While the project was quite small, its significance is an on-the-ground thoughtfulness on how we might tend to a neglected city in combination with those whose work is often shuttered behind the scenes (Figure 3.3).

The Looking Glass exemplifies what Manuel de Sola Morales, and more recently Finnish architect Marco Casagrande, describes as "urban acupuncture" (2013: 304). In the same way that the medicinal practice of acupuncture alleviates stress in the human body, the goal of urban acupuncture is to similarly relieve stress, in this case within the built environment. This form of city re-invigoration favors a localized, grounded community approach over large-scale urban renewal projects that are financially and environmentally unsustainable. Casagrande argues that in an era of constrained budgets and limited resources, urban "acupunctions" could democratically and cheaply offer a respite to urban dwellers, using small-scale interventions to transform the larger urban context. For Casagrande, the regimes of care endemic to acupuncture treat the points of blockage and let relief ripple throughout the body, to the city (2013: 306). In a similar vein, the Looking

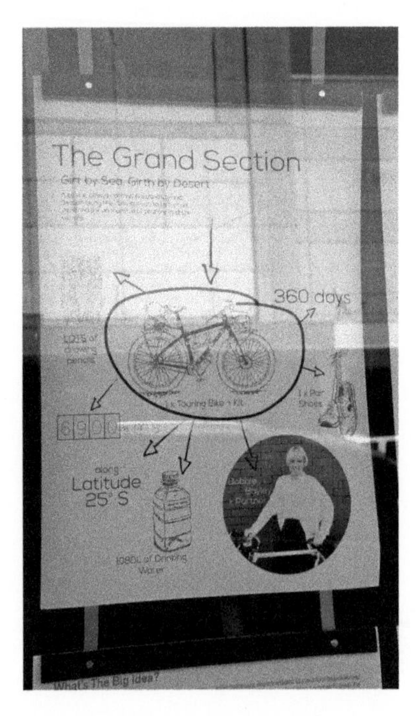

Figure 3.4 Close-up of out(fit)'s Looking Glass gallery where the outside and the inside are reflected back on one another. University of Newcastle.

Glass project attempted to respond to a localized need for street activation as part of a wider urban assemblage converging at the David Jones Department Store redevelopment site. By examining diverse, often lateral, visions of Newcastle's future from other and less empowered practice regimes in situ the project sought to release pressure at a strategic point, with the aim of opening up the whole city's dialogue about design procurement process (Figures 3.4 and 3.5). Although the property's current redevelopment precipitated the removal of the Looking Glass installation in December 2016, its ephemeral presence nonetheless stimulated the publics' imagination, thus functioning as an early, important catalyst for subsequent out(fit) endeavors. While larger economic forces ultimately precluded out(fit)'s long-term occupation of the shopfront, those same forces (during a period of economic downturn) also provided a unique opportunity for the out(fit) participants to compose and announce their own identities during Newcastle's ongoing transformation. The Looking Glass project reinforces that intentionally "noncapitalist" (Gibson-Graham 2006: 263) forms of production and care can coexist with mainstream urbanism and property development, however temporary this coexistence may be.

Figure 3.5 Close-up of exhibition featuring 2017 Byera Hadley Travelling Scholarship recipient, UON architecture recent graduate Bobbie Bayley. Photo credit: Emma Guthrey.

Jenny's Place (2016–): Creating place for the displaced

In parallel with the Looking Glass gallery project, out(fit) initiated a collaboration with a local women's shelter, Jenny's Place. Established in 1977, Jenny's Place is a nonprofit community organization which

> provides a safe and supportive environment to empower women to make informed decisions in their lives. Jenny's Place provides crisis accommodation and support through information, referral and advocacy for women and children escaping domestic violence and/or who are homeless or at risk of being homeless. (Jenny's Place Women's and Children's Refuge 2017)

Jenny's Place, and the service it provides are essential within an urban setting significantly impacted by the broader phenomenon of domestic abuse. On a national scale, one in every three women experiences physical or sexual violence in their lifetime (Australian Bureau of Statistics 2013); one in four children are exposed to domestic violence in Australia (Australian Institute of Health and Welfare 2014). Further, domestic and family violence is the principal cause of homelessness for women and their children (Australian Domestic and Family Violence Clearinghouse 2001). Local statistics include 2974 reported incidents of domestic violence in the Hunter region alone in 2013 (Rigney 2013); and in 2016, the Bureau of Crime Statistics and Research reported a domestic violence rate in Newcastle almost twice that of the NSW average (Swinton 2016).

Moreover, the above statistics are the recorded cases of domestic violence: countless more go unreported. The Victorian Royal Commission into Family Violence recently acknowledged that children witnessing domestic violence are also "silent victims" (O'Brien and Fitz-Gibbon 2016) in their own right who are frequently excluded from current statistics. Given the extent of this worrying phenomenon in Australian society—and the Hunter Valley and Newcastle more specifically—it is hardly surprising that the crisis accommodation available for women and mothers seeking refuge is severely limited in both quantum and environmental quality.

out(fit)'s social imperative—to work with community organizations positively impacting on the everyday lives of women and children—strongly resonated with both the needs and mission of Jenny's Place. Their facilities needed immediate improvement to make it a better, safer, and healthier environment. With this in mind, out(fit) members embarked on a program of remedial works that were broad in scope and enacted through a design-build methodology: from smaller initial maintenance activities, through to larger-scale interior and landscape works. Built interventions reflected both client need and best practice. For example, while research has shown that outdoor settings, including exposure to sunshine and access to views of trees, and so on, can provide healing effects on those recovering from trauma (Kaplan and Kaplan 1989: Ulrich 1986; Ulrich et al. 1991), many children staying at Jenny's Place cannot play in public parks because their anonymity and whereabouts must be protected. out(fit) focused their initial attention on an under-utilized courtyard area, an important space for the mental and physical well-being of women and their children. This required an intensive strategy of local, grassroots fundraising efforts, the recruitment of volunteer labor, and intensive design preparation. The design proposal itself included places for exploratory, imaginative, interactive, and physical play: vital environments for children who are recovering from trauma (Wood and Martin 2010). Importantly, the courtyard space also catered for the needs of mothers. Clear sightlines between the patio and decking areas enabled mothers to oversee their children without being in the same physical space. This separation allows the mothers to prepare barbeque meals, learn, talk to an advocate, and so on, while their children play, read, or study. The courtyard space therefore enhances opportunities for reflection, connection with children, privacy, and physical activity.

The collective acumen of the out(fit) team and the diversity of their interests and expertise, meant that each of the eight founding members initially played a pivotal role in the care and development of the courtyard. In September

2016, some out(fit) members and thirty-eight volunteers devoted a weekend to repurposing existing elements on the site: updating the courtyard with donated materials and completing the first stage of the project. The working bee process itself became pivotal in the culture of care enacted by all the participants. In order to understand out(fit)'s still-evolving operative mode, we might borrow from an indigenous notion invoking the blurring of gender boundaries during collective work. Our collaborative labor grouping for the Jenny's Place design-build evolved much like the pre-colonial Native American Cherokee *Gadugi* (Cherokee Nation 2017). In the same way that the men and women of the *gadugi* tended the fields and garden lots of elderly or infirm members of the village (Cherokee Nation 2017); the mixed gender group refurbished the refuge's existing outdoor playground and garden area through hands-on participation, irrespective of gender. This design-build work included laying concrete and paving, moving a fence, sprucing up the cubby house, installing a chalk-board, and painting a mural and outdoor furniture (Figure 3.6). While some out(fit) members were less involved in the actual design and construction works, they played an active role in fundraising, recording, supporting, and providing sustenance both in the form of food for thought as well as literal catering in food. Consistent with out(fit)'s spirit of collectivity and a mutuality of social purpose,

Figure 3.6 out(fit) members and volunteers working on refurbishing a children's cubby house for Jenny's Place. Please note that images 3.6, 3.7, and 3.8 have been edited to ensure confidentiality and protection of location for Jenny's Place clients and staff. Photo credit: Raichel Le Goff.

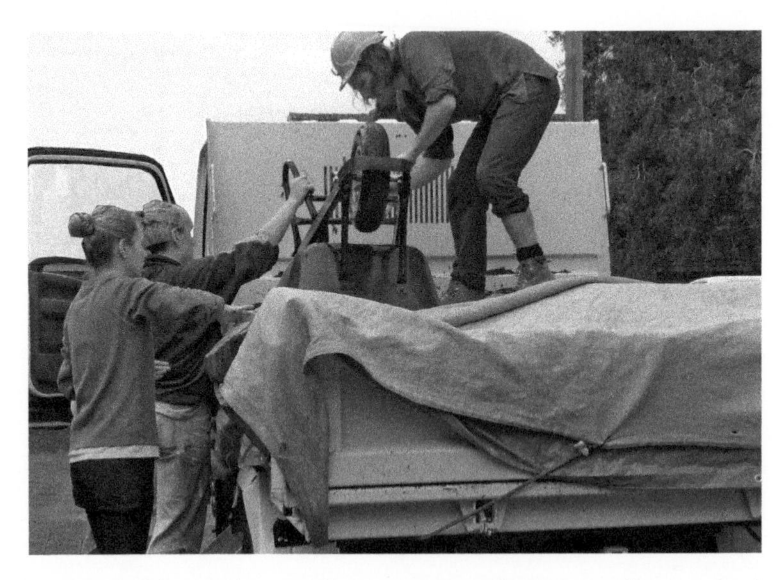

Figure 3.7 out(fit) members and community volunteers tending to landscape improvements much like a Cherokee gadugi. Photo credit: Raichel Le Goff.

those who worked "behind the scenes" were of equal importance to those who were more visible: this continues to be acknowledged (Figure 3.7).

Social media outlets such as Facebook, Instagram, and Twitter, along with out(fit)'s own website, only reach a particular demographic. By contrast, publicity within the mainstream local media extends the reach of the organization to other like-minded community groups (potentially seeking further collaborations), while simultaneously raising general awareness about the need for caretaking in the built environment. Importantly, the efforts of out(fit) have not gone unnoticed by local conventional media outlets including the *Newcastle Herald* (Gregory 2016) and ABC Radio (Marchant 2016). The launch and call for volunteers for the first phase of the Jenny's Place project occurred across multiple media platforms and produced a diverse volunteer cohort comprising not only of out(fit) team members, but students and representatives from the broader local community. out(fit)'s focus on social inclusion was rewarded: nearly 40 percent of our volunteers were outside of our immediate circles of students, staff, and friends.[4] As such, the caretaking practices of the Jenny's Place project breached conventional social divisions based upon ethnicity, age, and gender (Figures 3.8 and 3.9), not dissimilar to the phenomenon of domestic violence itself which also operates across multiple sociodemographic contexts and scales. Somewhat paradoxically, it is also the same capacity to bridge stereotypical social constructs that enabled diverse members of the broader Newcastle area

Figure 3.8 Volunteers came from outside of our immediate circles prompting us to learn that care in Newcastle extends well beyond our own limited reach. Photo credit: Raichel Le Goff.

Figure 3.9 Participation in Jenny's Place project took various forms of kindness, both apparent and hidden. Photo credit: Raichel Le Goff.

to exercise mutual caregiving for a vulnerable community in need, producing a temporary "social ensemble" (DeLanda 2016: 4)—a multiplicity.

The willingness of friends, family, colleagues, and strangers to engage in unpaid after-hours labor reinforces that our work represents only a small fraction of the Novacastrian regimes of care involved in rebuilding our post-industrial city.[5] This is particularly evident in the recent success of our grassroots fundraising efforts for the next phase of upgrades in the Jenny's Place courtyard: by mid-2017, our donations have increased in value from just over $5,000 to $50,000.[6] Despite the limited number of images available for project promotion (due to the need for client confidentiality and security), the press coverage of our Jenny's Place's work to date has harnessed Newcastle's wider network of compassion. While larger cities in Australia certainly have philanthropic and charitable entities, post-industrial economies and regional centers such as Newcastle have faced difficult social and economic challenges which continue to test its resilience and adaptability (Figures 3.8 and 3.9). Almost all of the members of out(fit) team knew someone who has been affected by domestic violence: one member was herself a former "silent victim" within a childhood setting; as such, many of us sensed we were just one person away from knowing their world ourselves.

Care, community, and city

While both of out(fit)'s aforementioned projects have positively contributed to participants and communities alike, they are not immune to difficulty and criticism. Project realization has been largely dependent upon voluntary, unpaid labor, which in turn may restrict who and how individuals may contribute. While this noncapitalist production is directed toward social good (specifically in the case of Jenny's Place), volunteers inevitably sustain other forms of capital production to self-fund their own voluntary contributions. out(fit) necessarily exists alongside mainstream design practices: a small and local response to a larger practice problematic and polemic related not only to the presence and representation of women in city-making, but the often-invisible caregiving practices that sustain and maintain our urban milieus. From the temporary activation of an abandoned shopfront, through to the promotion of work by student and female practitioners, and more recently to the ongoing repair and revitalization of a women's shelter; work by out(fit) unsettles conventional conceptions of university-affiliated activism, community outreach, and research. We are particularly mindful that the mandate for social inclusion and appreciation of "otherness" intrinsic to out(fit)'s caregiving is interwoven with, and sustained by, interdisciplinary feminist thinking. Simply stated, out(fit) requires engagement with the work that women do in the world, with knowledge they create in the course of that work and therefore, with women as knowers.

It may be difficult to evaluate the success and efficacy of the out(fit) efforts according to standardized university performance metrics or economic modeling, but such metrics mean little to the communities we serve, and to the small joys shared afforded by our collective practice. It is perhaps better therefore to engage with out(fit) according to its aspirational capacity, its social processes, and its evident built outcomes, however transitory or subtle: transforming frustration and adversity into hope and productivity, in and through the remaking of the built environment. To conclude with the words of the feminist Elizabeth Grosz, speaking of generosity and architecture: "The gift of architecture is always in excess of function, practicality, mere housing or shelter. It is also always about the celebration of an above-subsistence sociality, a cultural excess that needs elevation, not diminution" (2001: 165). out(fit) welcomes the notion that caregiving is interdependent with, and indeed essential to, the construction of any built environment—and the architectural academy as a whole.

Notes

1 As an entity, out(fit) has been affiliated with the University's overall nonprofit and charitable endeavors. While there is an incredibly pragmatic rationale for this decision in terms of infrastructural support, public liability coverage, and access to creative as well as other expertise, this is also a deeply ethical one.
2 Our caregiving activities were initially difficult to accommodate within preexisting institutional structures for research-related endeavors. Our efforts were instead welcomed by the University's philanthropic arm. We also wanted to escape university overheads for research projects (upward of 25%) in order to ensure our fundraising efforts could be fully dedicated to the design/build projects themselves—a paramount concern, given the limited funds available.
3 A self-description term and adjective colloquially used by residents of Newcastle, Australia.
4 Based on an out(fit)'s internal documentation of participant volunteers primarily kept for insurance purposes.
5 Most notably the work of Marcus Westbury and Christopher Saunders for the Renew Newcastle not-for-profit scheme involving the grassroots urban regeneration of abandoned CBD buildings, see http://renewnewcastle.org/ (Accessed March 04, 2017).
6 For general ongoing project information and Jenny's Place more specifically, see http://www.outfit.org.au/projects.

References

Agrest, D., Conway, P. and Kanes Weisman, L., eds. (1996), *The Sex of Architecture*, New York: Harry N. Abrams.

Australian Bureau of Statistics (2013), *4906.0-Personal Safety, Australia, 2012.* Available online: http://www.abs.gov.au/ausstats/abs@.nsf/mf/4906.0 (accessed March 6, 2017).

Australian Domestic and Family Violence Clearinghouse (2001), *The Impact of Domestic Violence on Children: A Literature Review*, Sydney: The University of New South Wales.

Australian Institute of Health and Welfare (2014), *Specialist Homelessness Services: 2013–2014*, cat. no. HOU 276, Canberra: AIHW. Available online: http://www.aihw.gov.au/publication-detail/?id=60129550000 (accessed March 6, 2017).

Braidotti, R. (2013), *The Posthuman*, Cambridge: Polity Press.

Braidwood, E. (2017), "AJ Student Survey: Nearly Half of Female Students Experience Sexism," *Architects Journal* (July 18). Available online: https://www.architectsjournal.co.uk/news/aj-student-survey-nearly-half-of-female-students-experience-sexism/10021695.article (accessed August 15, 2017).

Burns, K. (2001), "Women in Architecture," *Architecture Australia*, 100 (4) (3 October). Available online: http://architectureau.com/articles/women-in-architecture/ (accessed November 18, 2016).

Carroll, L. (2009 [1871]), *Alice's Adventures in Wonderland; and, Through the Looking-Glass and What Alice Found There*, New York: Penguin Classics.

Casagrande, M. (2013), "Ruin Academy – Casagrande Lab," in Ariane Lourie Harrison (ed.), *Architectural Theories of the Environment: Posthuman Territory*, Abingdon: Routledge, 304–10.

Cherokee Nation (2017), "The Origin of Gadugi," *www.cherokee.org*. Available online: http://www.cherokee.org/AboutTheNation/History/Facts/TheOriginofGadugi.aspx (accessed March 5, 2017).

Coleman, D., Danze, E. and Hendersen, C., eds. (1997), *Architecture and Feminism*, New York: Princeton Architectural Press.

Colomina, B., ed. (1996), *Sexuality and Space*, New York: Princeton Architectural Press.

Corroto, C. (2005), "The Architecture of Sexual Harassment," in J. E. Gruber and P. Morgan (eds.), *In the Company of Men: Male Dominance and Sexual Harassment*, Boston: Northeastern University Press.

DeLanda, M. (2016), *Assemblage Theory*, Edinburgh: Edinburgh University Press, 2016.

de Lauretis, T., ed. (1986), *Feminist Studies/Critical Studies*, Bloomington, IN: Indiana University Press.

Equity by Design (EQxD) (2016), "Equity in Architecture Survey 2016: Salary by Caregiver Status," *eqxdesign.com*. Available online: http://eqxdesign.com/survey-2016 (accessed January 1, 2016).

Foucault, M. with Fornet-Betancourt, R., Becker, H., and Gomez-Müller, A. (1987), "The Ethic of Care for the Self as a Practice of Freedom: An Interview with Michel Foucault on January 20, 1984," *Philosophy Social Criticism*, trans. J. D. Gauthier, 112–31, doi:10.1177/019145378701200202.

Gibson-Graham, J. K. (2006), *The End of Capitalism (As We Knew It): A Feminist Critique of Political Economy*, Minneapolis: University of Minnesota Press.

Gregory, H. (2016), "Hunter Women's Group Out (fit) Improve Refuge Jenny's Place," *Newcastle Herald*, News: Local News (21 November). Available online: http://www.theherald.com.au/story/4306614/hard-work-for-victims/ (accessed February 28, 2017).

Grosz, E. (2001), "Architectures of Excess," in *Architecture From the Outside: Essays on Virtual and Real Space*, Elizabeth Grosz, Writing Architecture series, Cambridge: The MIT Press.

Haraway, D. (1990), "A Cyborg Manifesto: Science, Technology, and Socialist-Feminism in the Late Twentieth Century," in *Simians, Cyborgs and Women: The Reinvention of Nature*, Abingdon-On-Thames: Routledge, 149–82.

Hughes, F., ed. (1996), *The Architect: Reconstructing Her Practice*, Cambridge: The MIT Press.

Jenny's Place Women's and Children's Refuge (2017), "Jenny's Place," *Domestic Violence Newcastle*. Available online: http://www.domesticviolencenewcastle.com.au/jennysPlace.html (accessed March 03, 2017).

Kaplan, R. and Kaplan, S. (1989), *The Experience of Nature: A Psychological Perspective*, New York: Cambridge University Press.

Lemmens, Pieter (2011), "This System Does Not Produce Pleasure Anymore: An Interview with Bernard Stiegler," *Krisis, Journal for Contemporary Philosophy*, no. 1.

Marchant, Jenny (2016), @jen_marchant [Twitter feed]. Twitter image available online: https://twitter.com/jen_marchant/status/712774872686923776 (accessed September 3, 2017).

O'Brien, W. and Fitz-Gibbon, K. (2016), "Silent Victims': Royal Commission Recommends Better Protections for Child Victims of Familyviolence," *The Conversation, Politics & Society* (1 April). Available online: https://theconversation.com/silent-victims-royal-commission-recommends-better-protections-for-child-victims-of-family-violence-56801 (accessed March 5, 2017).

out(fit), "Projects-(out)fit," in *outfit.org.au*. Available online: http://www.outfit.org.au/projects (accessed August 3, 2017).

Parlour, "02: Long Hours Culture," *Archiparlour* (2014), Melbourne and Brisbane: Parlour, The University of Melbourne and the University of Queensland. Available online: http://www.archiparlour.org/wp-content/uploads/2014/05/Guide2-LongHours.pdf (accessed November 21, 2016).

Petrescu, D., ed. (2007), *Altering Practices: Feminist Politics and Poetics of Space*, London: Routledge.

Rendell, J., Penner, B. and Borden, I., eds. (1999), *Gender, Space, Architecture: An Interdisciplinary Introduction*, Abingdon: Routledge.

Renew Newcastle (2017), *Renew Newcastle*. Available online: http://renewnewcastle.org/ (accessed March 4, 2017).

Rigney, Sam (2013), "Domestic Violence Up in the Hunter," *The Herald*, News: Local News (September 13). Available online: http://www.theherald.com.au/story/1773196/domestic-violence-up-in-hunter/ (accessed March 03, 2017).

Smith, C. (2015), "Hidden Hegemonies," in *Archiparlour: Women, Equity, Architecture*, "At Work: Mentoring" section (November 23). Available online: http://archiparlour.org/hidden-hegemonies/ (accessed September 3, 2017).

Stiegler, B. (2013), *What Makes Life Worth Living: On Pharmacology*, trans. Daniel Ross, Cambridge: Polity Press.

Stiegler, B. and Rue 89 (2013), "Bernard Stiegler: 'We Are Entering an Era of Contributory Work'", in *Spatial Machinations* (website), trans. Sam Kingsley (6 February). Available online: http://www.samkinsley.com/2013/02/06/bernard-stiegler-we-are-entering-an-era-of-contributory-work/ (accessed August 15, 2017).

Stratigakos, D. (2016), *Where are the Women Architects?* Princeton and London: Princeton University Press.

Swinton, S. (2016), "Central Hunter Detective Inspector Mitch Dubojski Reveals Officers Visit 20 Domestic Violence Incidents in Lower Hunter Every Day," *Newcastle Herald*, News: End of News Cycle (24 November). Available online: http://www.theherald.com.au/story/4315566/shocking-rates-of-domestic-violence-in-newcastle/?cs=171 (accessed March 3, 2017).

Tether, B. (2016), "Results of the 2016 Women in Architecture Survey revealed," *The Architectural Review*. Available online: https://www.architectural-review.com/archive/results-of-the-2016-women-in-architecture-survey-revealed/10003314.article (accessed November 18, 2016).

Thackara, J. (2015), *How to Thrive in The Next Economy: Designing Tomorrow's World Today*, London: Thames & Hudson.

Ulrich, R. S. (1986), "Human Responses to Vegetation and Landscapes," *Landscape and Urban Planning*, 13: 29–44.

Ulrich, R. S., Simons, R. F., Losito, B. D., Fiorito, E., Miles, M. A. and Zelson, M. (1991), "Stress Recovery During Exposure to Natural and Urban Environments," *Journal of Environmental Psychology*, 11 (3): 201–30.

University of Newcastle (2013), "Corporal Wixtead and The Fate of Newcastle's First Settlement in 1801," in *Hunter (Living) Histories – Coal River Working Party* [online blog], Newcastle: The University of Newcastle. Available online: https://hunterlivinghistories.com/2013/01/15/corporal-wixtead-and-the-fate-of-newcastles-first-settlement-in-1801/ (accessed January 6, 2017).

Window dressing: The Looking Glass gallery project, rotating Exhibitions (2016) Former David Jones Department Store Windows, Hunter Street, Newcastle, NSW.

Wood, L. and Martin, K. (2010), *What Makes a Good Play Area for Children?*, unpublished report, Perth: Centre for the Built Environment and Health, The University of Western Australia. Available online: http://www.web.uwa.edu.au/__data/assets/pdf_file/0011/1857467/What-makes-a-good-play-area-literature-summaryfeb2011.pdf (accessed March 30, 2016).

4

Picture Education Today: Data Visualization as a Practice of Critique and Care

Brad Haylock

Data visualization has a rich history as a type of communication design practice that renders visible social realities and bodies of knowledge that might otherwise remain imperceptible. In the second quarter of the twentieth century, Otto and Marie Neurath led a team that developed the Vienna Method of Pictorial Statistics (Wiener Methode der Bildstatistik), a system that became better known as "Isotype," an acronym derived from the initial letters and syllables of its later descriptor, the "International System Of Typographic Picture Education" (Neurath 1936: 12). From its inception, this work was intended to meet educational needs: the Vienna Method was intended to inform the Viennese public about their city (Burke et al. 2013: 38), and later Isotype sought to take that program to an international audience (Neurath 1936: 22–32). While Isotype has received some sustained scholarly attention (Neurath 1936; Vossoughian 2008; Neurath and Kinross 2009; Neurath et al. 2010; Burke et al. 2013), and some scholars, notably Edward Tufte (1983; 1990; 1997; 2006), have examined the history and practice of information graphics and data visualization more generally, few writers have considered the significance of these graphic practices from the viewpoints of political theory or moral philosophy. For this reason, I sketch here a typology and a theory of data visualization as a practice of critique and of care.

Against the background of a post-Marxist, agonistic political framework, I seek to unpack the ways in which the visualization of data can be understood as a counter-hegemonic practice—a process of unmasking and of promoting pluralism—within a broader democratic project. I propose a (non-exhaustive) typology of critical data visualization: projects that are manifestly counter-hegemonic; those that unmask the workings of structures of government or other forms of subjugation, notably juridical systems; and those that foster epistemic pluralism, for example, by making public knowledge more public. These types represent points on a spectrum, from more explicitly critical to more nuanced.

My broad approach here is critical theoretical (Horkheimer 2002), but within this I employ a collective case study (Stake 1995: 3–4): I examine three sets of related examples in an instrumental fashion to understand the types of knowledge and social practice that data visualization might render visible. Since these operations of unmasking and of making knowledge more public have historical and practical overlaps with education, I draw upon writings on critical pedagogy. And I look to discourses on care ethics to begin to conceive of an ethical framework that would complement theories of agonism, and to argue that critical data visualization can be understood as an act of care.

Mapping networks of power

In this and in each of the two case discussion sections that follow, I begin with a description of the projects and practices in question, before moving on to an analysis of their significance. The first examples of critical data visualization that I discuss are expressly counter-hegemonic in their intent, that is, they are markedly anti-capitalistic and generally concerned to unmask relations of power. The cases discussed here are the web-based mapping tools They Rule and Oligrapher.

They Rule

They Rule (www.theyrule.net), launched in 2001, "aims to provide a glimpse of some of the relationships of the US ruling class" by mapping networks of power, exposing connections between boards of directors of the top 1,000 US companies (They Rule n.d.). The site allows users to navigate corporate boards to find companies with directors in common. Users can search for persons or companies, as well as certain other institutions such as think tanks, research institutes, and universities. The critical motivation behind this project is unambiguous:

> A few companies control much of the economy and oligopolies exert control in nearly every sector of the economy. The people who head up these companies swap on and off the boards from one company to another, and in and out of

> government committees and positions. These people run the most powerful institutions on the planet, and we have almost no say in who they are. This is not a conspiracy, they are proud to rule, yet these connections of power are not always visible to the public eye. (They Rule n.d.)

The site offers a "Find Connection" functionality, to expedite the visualization of the link(s) between two companies. Rarely does this function return no connection, and a surprising number of companies are separated by only one or two degrees of remove. Users can also create and save maps for others to view, based on current relevance or topics of interest, which I discuss below.

Oligrapher

Oligrapher is a mapping tool that is a part of LittleSis, a website launched in 2009 by a collective of activists, lawyers, and academics concerned with social change. LittleSis—a play upon the "Big Brother" of George Orwell's *Nineteen Eighty-Four*—is an open-source database that aims to "bring transparency to influential social networks by tracking the key relationships of politicians, business leaders, lobbyists, financiers, and their affiliated institutions" (LittleSis n.d.).[1] The LittleSis database draws upon a variety of publicly accessible data sources, including news articles and government filings (such as Securities and Exchange Commission filings[2]) and is updated through a combination of data scraping and user community input, in a wiki-style arrangement (but with stricter-than-usual referencing requirements).[3] The mapping tool Oligrapher was added in 2014, "designed to help advanced users create storytelling aides that represent particular slices of power network information in the database" (Connor 2014).

Social networks of the US elite

They Rule and Oligrapher are tools for social network diagramming. Like other projects of this type, such as the website Muckety (www.muckety.com) and Mark Lombardi's "narrative structures" artworks, They Rule and Oligrapher render visible relationships of power and influence that may otherwise go unseen. To appreciate the types of relationships that might be unmasked, and then to appreciate the significance of this unmasking, let us look at two specific examples.

In the lower left quadrant of the They Rule map "Big Banks USA," created by user "foxbai" on May 11, 2017, we see that two directors of the Bank of America Corporation, Charles K Gifford and Gary L Countryman, sit on the board of CBS Corporation, and that Countryman and fellow Bank of America director Thomas J May also sit on the board of Liberty Mutual Insurance Group. Maps like this reveal to audiences that individual relationships might lie behind networks of corporate power. But while They Rule is limited to the visualization of connections via shared directors, Oligrapher permits a more nuanced mapping by visualizing the other types of relationship that are documented in the LittleSis database. The Oligrapher map "MoMA and Finance," created by user "Matthew" on September 5, 2014, visualizes connections between The Museum of Modern Art (MoMA) and the finance sector. In the lower left quadrant of this map, we see that MoMA trustee Jill Kraus is the spouse of Peter Kraus, co-head of investment management at Goldman Sachs; that MoMA trustee Glenn Fuhrman is also a Goldman Sachs managing partner; and that MoMA chairman emeritus, Robert B. Menschel, is a limited partner of Goldman Sachs. We also see that there are two more documented relationships between MoMA and Goldman Sachs, and numerous relationships between the museum and other finance giants.

Both of these maps expose the interpersonal relationships that connect powerful organizations, thus allowing audiences to appreciate the human foundations and therefore the contingency of power structures that might otherwise seem abstract and universal. By revealing that cultural and economic systems are *not* "presuppositions about which one can do nothing" (Horkheimer 2002: 207), these data visualizations work to reverse the tendency of ideological apparatuses to "transform history into nature" (Barthes 1973: 129).

The question of accuracy and "truth" in data

The veracity of the data underpinning such visualization practices is surely important, yet the challenges to the accuracy of that data are many and various. As noted on They Rule,

> We do not claim that this data is 100% accurate at all times. Corporate directors have a habit of dying, quitting boards, joining new ones and most frustratingly passing on their names to their children who not entirely coincidently are also found to be members of US corporate boards. There is no single easily parsed single [*sic*] authoritative public record containing these shifting datasets. (They Rule n.d.)

The sheer complexity and the ever-changing nature of the social networks in question, and the various sources that need to be combed and aggregated by way of qualitatively dissimilar tools and methods, mean that there is a possibility of inaccuracies in the data at any given moment, and a risk of imminent obsolescence whenever a subset of the data is published.

However, not only do practical barriers to accuracy challenge the truthfulness of such datasets, but so too do ontological questions. As critics of digital positivism point out, citing unavoidable biases and value-laden selection processes, as well as the inevitable flattening or reductiveness that characterizes data, there are fundamental dangers in mistaking big data for the social reality it may be purported to represent (Boehnert 2016: 2–4). To use a Borgesian analogy, the map should not be mistaken for the territory (Borges 1999).

Although the LittleSis dataset and others like it face both practical and ontological challenges, I must argue that data visualization does not necessarily succeed or fail as a critical practice on the basis of the accuracy of its underlying data. While the nuances of the processes of subjugation may be open to debate, in line with questions around the accuracy of a specific dataset or around the truthfulness of data per se, such data visualizations enable their audiences to situate themselves within these networks of power, and so, irrespective of the margin of error in a given dataset, the visualization of networks of power affords—or perhaps even compels—a re-articulation of political subjecthood. This can be understood to hold true for the other types of data visualization discussed below.

Unmasking juridical systems: Visualizing sentencing in Victoria

In this section, I discuss a series of works completed by students in the Master of Communication Design program at RMIT University, Melbourne, in 2016 and 2017, undertaken in collaboration with the Sentencing Advisory Council (SAC). The SAC is an independent statutory body in the state of Victoria, Australia, established in 2004. The SAC's mission is to bridge the gap between the community, the courts and government by informing, educating, and advising on sentencing issues (Sentencing Advisory Council n.d.). Students were asked to visualize data from the SAC in order to help the organization better communicate to existing and new audiences and stakeholders, in order to advance community knowledge of sentencing in Victoria, and to increase awareness of the Council's activities.[4]

Students were invited to take a self-directed approach, navigating all available SAC data through SACStat, the Council's publicly available online tool for accessing data on sentences imposed in the Victorian higher courts and the Magistrates' Court of Victoria, or they could choose to visualize one of a number of prescribed sets of data. The students prepared images for social media campaigns across Twitter and Pinterest, targeting one or more of the SAC's key social media audiences.

Histories of sentencing in Victoria

A comparative look at the work of two students—Aimee Phillips and Jennifer Lea—allows us to consider the ways in which complex data can be differently navigated to meet the challenging task of concise communication through social media channels. Phillips and Lea visualized Victoria's imprisonment rate from 1871 to 2015 in different ways. Using graphic charts, bold numerals, and short explanatory texts, Phillips's work for the Pinterest platform (see Figure 4.1) allows insights to be drawn from the data, including details of imprisonment rate by gender, noting that the female imprisonment rate grew more than the male imprisonment rate during the decade 2006–16, and details of the imprisonment of Aboriginal and Torres Strait Islander persons in Victoria, from

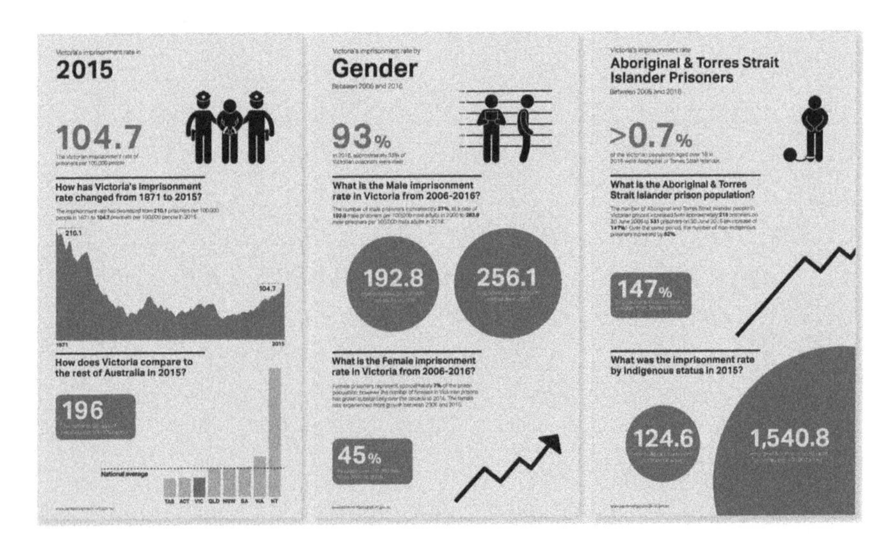

Figure 4.1 Visualization of Victoria's imprisonment rate, for Sentencing Advisory Council Pinterest feed. Data sources: Sentencing Advisory Council and Australian Bureau of Statistics / ©2017 Aimee Phillips.

which we can see that the imprisonment rate of Indigenous persons, as of June 30, 2016, was more than twelvefold that of the non-Indigenous population. Lea's work, by comparison, emphasizes snippets of compelling information for dissemination via Twitter, with each post in her campaign comprising a simple chart graphic, a corresponding Tweet text, written to capture attention with few words, and relevant hashtags. For example, Lea writes: "Between 2012–2014 the imprisonment rate went up by 20%. That's the biggest increase seen in the last decade! #data #prison."

Targeting at-risk audiences

Two other students, Dennis Grauel and Brendan Coghlan, navigated SACStat to articulate narratives from the data relevant to a specific demographic that faces a higher-than-average likelihood of involvement in the justice system for particular offenses—namely young persons who are statistically likely to be sentenced for crimes on public transport or for graffiti-related offenses. Employing an appropriately contemporary visual language, Grauel's images for Pinterest reveal that eighteen- to twenty-four-year-olds are the age group most commonly sentenced for prohibited language, for placing feet on seats, and for littering on public transport (see Figure 4.2). Stacked column charts communicate sentence types in a format suitable for mobile devices, and snippets of text clearly communicate key messages or data, such as "Under 25s receive the most sentences

Figure 4.2 Visualization of sentences related to littering on public transport, for Sentencing Advisory Council Pinterest feed. Data source: Sentencing Advisory Council. / © 2016 Dennis Grauel.

for littering" and "71% of cases result in a court-ordered fine."[5] In Coghlan's work, also designed for Pinterest, we see a concise visualization of key data relating to the Graffiti Prevention Act 2007. Presented in a vernacular, visual language appropriate for the audience, evoking 1980s and 1990s transit authority graphics, Coghlan's social media images visualize the number of cases brought to the Victorian Magistrates' Court for the offences of "Marking graffiti" and "Possession of a prescribed graffiti implement on the property of a transport company" during the period July 2011 through June 2014. For each offense, pie charts communicate the proportions of sentence types, as well as sentence quantum data for fines, community correction orders, and imprisonment in each dataset. For the offence of "Marking graffiti" during this period, we can quickly read that, for men aged 18–34, 165 cases were brought to the Magistrates' Court, of which approximately one-third received fines and one-third community correction orders, that fines of $500–1000 were most common (approximately twenty-five cases), and that 71.9 percent of the community correction orders were 12–18 months in duration.

Communicating anti-subordination knowledge

In the examples of Phillips's and Lea's work, we see data visualizations that offer the public an easily digestible and historically informed snapshot of sentencing in Victoria. In the examples of Grauel's and Coghlan's work, highly pertinent information about the justice system is communicated—through a relevant channel and in an appropriate voice—to a demographic at risk of being sentenced for the offenses in question. Whether speaking to general or specific audiences, these visualizations reveal to Victorian citizens new perspectives of the justice system to which they are subject. Such data visualizations represent important, critical work because legal and justice systems hold great power over citizens' lives, but are generally not well understood. As Francisco Valdes has noted, legal education can "teach antisubordination knowledge and foster the ability of students to decolonize themselves and others" (2003: 65)—Valdes is here discussing formal legal studies, however popular legal knowledge is also a type of anti-subordination knowledge that allows citizens to decolonize themselves. Indeed, practices that foster popular legal knowledge, such as the visualization of sentencing data, are particularly important, since legal discourse "typically analyzes legal problems based on the implicit assumption that individuals know the law and adjust their behavior accordingly," despite empirical work that has "documented high levels of ignorance of the most basic legal principles among lay people" (Kim 1999: 448).

Making public knowledge more public

In this third case discussion, I again look to data visualization projects by RMIT Master of Communication Design students, here undertaken in 2017 in collaboration with the Australian Centre for the Moving Image (ACMI).[6] In 2016, contemporaneous with metadata releases by Europeana, Cooper Hewitt Smithsonian Design Museum, Tate, MoMA, and the Digital Public Library of America, ACMI made their film archive metadata publicly available (Chan 2016). This dataset contains approximately 40,000 records, representing the museum's collection of films, which spans many genres and formats. Students were tasked with an open brief to interpret and visualize the dataset in novel ways. The outcomes are variously humorous, sober or sobering, and range from richly multidimensional data visualization through to playfully illustrative infographics, but all reveal new perspectives on Victoria's public film collection.[7]

The shape of the collection: Japan and monsters

Lorenzo Villar's series of proportional area charts gives us an insight into the international character of the ACMI collection. We read that 386 of the 38,750 items in the collection are from or about Japan; that, of these, 64.3 percent are in English, 33 percent are in Japanese, 2.33 percent have no spoken words, 0.25 percent are in Polish, and 0.25 percent are silent; and that more of these films were created in 1965 than in any other year. Charlotte Scales's playfully lo-fi "photoviz" images (Felton 2016) tell us about the prevalence in the collection of films featuring monsters and other strange creatures, such as vampires, werewolves, aliens, Godzilla, and King Kong. These "monster" films, we read, represent only 0.4 percent of the collection: garishly contrasted against a light blue background, a bright yellow rubber ball (representing all non-monster films) towers over a cheap plastic gorilla figurine (see Figure 4.3).

Gender representation and the politics of educational films

Decidedly less whimsical are Jacqueline Rossetti's visualizations of the disproportionate representation of women in films about the visual arts and crafts. Rossetti's dot matrix and proportional area charts show us that 850 films in the collection feature male creatives, while only 53 feature female creatives (see Figure 4.4). Not only are female creatives less well-represented overall, but so too

Figure 4.3 Visualization of Australian Centre for the Moving Image collections data. Data source: Australian Centre for the Moving Image. / ©2017 Charlotte Scales.

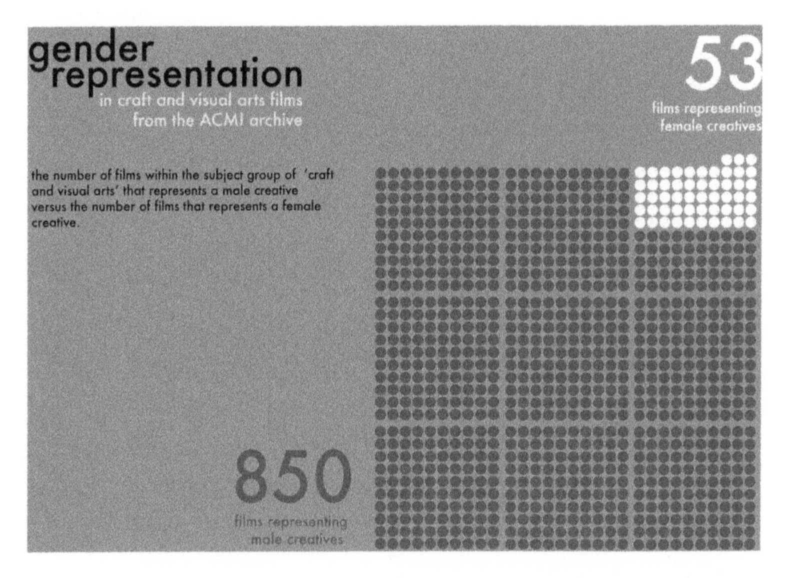

Figure 4.4 Visualization of Australian Centre for the Moving Image collections data. Data source: Australian Centre for the Moving Image. / ©2017 Jacqueline Rossetti.

does each female practitioner receive less individual exposure in the collection: there are, on average, 3.5 films featuring each male creative, but only 1.8 films, on average, per female creative. Similarly interrogative are Jacob l'Huillier Lunt's visualizations of the history of educational filmmaking in Australia under different political regimes. For the period 1949–2016, l'Huillier Lunt maps

Australian federal election results against the production date of educational films held in the ACMI collection, with a focus on three themes: agriculture and business, the environment, and the military. We see that during this period 290 films with military themes were produced under centre-left Labor governments, as compared with 273 under centre-right Liberal governments;[8] however, more agriculture and business films and more environment films were produced under Liberal rule (808 and 717, respectively) than under Labor (690 and 671, respectively).

Keeping democracy alert and well informed

Rossetti's and l'Huillier Lunt's works have an expressly critical dimension insofar as they reveal historical imbalances in gender representation in film and something of the relationship between party politics and cultural production. Yet, irrespective of how overtly they may or may not interrogate balances of power, all of the visualizations discussed here have a critical dimension, since, for some audiences, they would draw attention not only to the composition of the state film collection but indeed to its very existence. In this way, these visualizations of cultural collection data reveal this public good: they make public knowledge more public. While not wanting to take an idealistic or culturally deterministic view of the matter, an awareness of such repositories of public knowledge in all of their diversity is surely an important force in "political hygiene":[9] as the headline of a 1960 newspaper article about the State Film Centre states, this collection was at that time already "keeping democracy alert and well informed through film" (Swift 1960).

Toward a politics and an ethics of data visualization

This analysis of data visualization is conducted against a backdrop of Ernesto Laclau and Chantal Mouffe's theory of hegemony (Laclau and Mouffe 2001), and Mouffe's later writings on agonism (Mouffe 2005).[10] Drawing upon but extending what Mouffe (2008) has written on artistic practices vis-à-vis agonism, I have argued elsewhere that design, notably "critical design," can be understood as a counter-hegemonic practice that reveals the historically contingent character of various stati quo (Haylock 2018). This counter-hegemonic tendency is clear in the examples of They Rule and Oligrapher, which unmask relationships across traditional domains of power, such as economic and party political spheres. But can the visualization of datasets from the Sentencing Advisory Council or the Australian Centre for the Moving Image also be understood as political work? And according to what ethical framework might we understand the moral imperative behind such work?

Data visualization as critical education

I intimated in my introduction that the data visualization work discussed here extends a tradition of information graphics designed for the public good, which is interwoven with pedagogical matters. The Isotype system was conceived to improve the teaching and learning of difficult material, particularly the introduction of complex matters such as social organization and history. "Our experience is that the effect of pictures is frequently greater than the effect of words, specially at the first stage of getting knowledge" (Neurath 1936: 24). A system of "teaching-pictures," Neurath argued,

> gives the learner the guide to deeper knowledge and to science, without the danger which is so frequent in education by words: that of taking note only of the details and seeing nothing of the general view. If the general view is given by teaching-pictures, it will be kept in mind. (Neurath 1936: 24–26)

Notably, Neurath's goal was not an education system concerned with bettering the best, but rather with improving the situation of the majority.[11] This social agenda for the betterment of education systems has parallels with Paulo Freire's later writings on critical pedagogy, which entails meeting learners on their own terms, and which holds the emancipatory potential of education in clear view. Education can produce a "critical consciousness," holds Freire, that allows one to "go a step beyond the deception of palliative solutions," and to "engage in authentic transformation of reality in order, by humanizing that reality, to humanize women and men" (Freire 2000: 183). The process of subject formation of which Friere writes cannot be prescribed but must always be dialogical. The unmasking of systems and processes of subjugation, as exemplified by the visualization of data describing the history of sentencing decisions in Victoria, and the greater accessibility of public repositories of knowledge, as exemplified by the visualization of data describing the composition of the state film collection, equip citizens with the insights and resources—the "anti-subordination knowledge"—necessary to begin to embark upon the transformation of their own realities.

Data visualization as a care ethical practice

While we might aspire to rise to the Freirean challenge to "confront, to listen, to see the world unveiled" (Freire 2000: 39), how might we prepare ourselves for the enormity of this task, and what is our moral obligation to act upon what we may find? In other words, as Mouffe (2000) has asked, "which ethics for democracy?" Suggesting, if not an answer, then at least a path toward addressing this question, she posits,

> Abandoning the very idea of a complete reabsorption of alterity into oneness and harmony such an ethics would strive to create among us a new form of bond, a bond that recognizes us as divided subjects and does not dream of an impossible reconciliation. (Mouffe 2000: 94)

Here we might look to the ethics of care, aka care ethics, a strand of moral philosophy with its roots in psychological theory and feminist discourse (Gilligan 1982; Noddings 1984). Care ethics mobilizes a series of critiques of the sovereign individual at the center of contractualist and deontological ethical theories, and emphasizes instead the interconnectedness of persons, replete with dependencies and needs.

One of the key thinkers in this field, Nel Noddings, distinguishes between "caring for" and "caring about." The former is direct care, an interpersonal care for those with whom one has a close relationship—such as one's children or family—while the latter is a care directed toward persons at degrees of remove. While in her early work Noddings is dismissive of caring-about (1984: 112), she later revisits its importance:

> Caring-about moves us from the face-to-face world into the wider public realm. If we have been well cared for and have learned to care for a few intimate others, we move into the public world with fellow-feeling for others. We are moved by compassion for their suffering, we regret it when they do not experience the fruits of care, and we feel outrage when they are exploited. Often we wish that we could care directly, but because that is impossible, we express our care in charitable gifts, in the social groups we support, and in our voting. (Noddings 2002: 22)

A later thinker in this lineage, Michael Slote has described Noddings's categories of caring-for and caring-about as, respectively, "personal caring" and "humanitarian caring" (2007: 11), or as a concern for "near and dear" as compared to a concern for "distant and unknown others" (2007: 31). Slote draws upon the psychology of empathy to extend the discourse on care ethics, arguing that "empathy and differences of empathy can plausibly function as criteria for moral evaluation and moral distinction-making" (2007: 28). Slote's thinking about "a care ethics that makes criterial use of the idea of empathy" (2007: 19) is significant to the present discussion because a criterial use of empathy both permits and constructively challenges an understanding of the ethics of critical data visualization. He argues that caring-about

> can be understood broadly enough to take in not merely animals, foetuses, and people, but also ideas and ideals. It is not at all clear, though, that the latter are appropriate objects of moral concern, and certainly it is difficult to make sense of empathy with abstract objects. (2007: 19)

Slote concludes that the question of empathy vis-à-vis ideas and ideals is too difficult, and limits his project to "discussing care and empathy directed at, or responsive to, people or groups of people" (2007: 19). Does this mean that the question of caring-about democracy or justice is beyond the scope of an ethics of care? While such abstract objects may be beyond the scope of Slote's work, I would argue that they are certainly within the remit of an ethics of care, precisely because of their implications for others, however far removed across time and space those people might be. If one cares about the ideals of democracy and justice, surely this is because one cares about all of those people who might benefit from the actualization of these ideals.[12] Here Noddings is illuminating: while she holds that there is "no adequate substitute for caring-for (direct caring)," she acknowledges that "intelligent, conscientious caring-about can suggest ways to extend caring-for to many more recipients" (2002: 23).

Care ethics emphasizes relationality and interdependency by foregrounding the importance of care for others, near and far, in moral decision making. Between the poles of, on the one hand, a universal moral subject—the impossible "reabsorption of alterity into oneness"—and, on the other, subjects atomized beyond any possibility of reconciliation, an ethics of care allows us to imagine, after Mouffe, a bond between divided subjects without entailing a reduction of differences.

Caring about transparency, decolonization, and pluralism

Thus we have points of reference that allow us to better understand both the politics and the ethics of data visualization practices that would seek to unmask not only networks of power, but also systems of subjugation and bodies of knowledge. These are acts of informal education undertaken in the public interest. While the first and second types of data visualization discussed here are clearly emancipatory, and may even be seen as contestational, as the expression of a clash of ideologies, or as a symptom of antagonism, the third is not adequately parsed at the level of the political. How do we explain the act of making public knowledge public, a manifest commitment to epistemic pluralism?

Not only the unmasking of networks of power and of systems of subjugation but also the publicizing of public knowledge can be viewed as acts of caring-about: caring-about the struggles of others who may not yet have recognized that established relationships among the already powerful create glass ceilings that contradict capitalism's promise of upward mobility; caring-about those who may be at increased risk of involvement in the criminal justice system; or caring-about those whose taxes contribute to the development and maintenance of public cultural collections, but who may not yet have sought out the joys of knowledge that these collections contain. While admittedly not unique in any of these capacities, data visualizations of these types are powerful examples of design practices through which we might care for others by seeking to reveal a world less veiled and in all of its diversity.

Notes

1 The two cases under discussion here, They Rule and LittleSis's Oligrapher, are related not merely by their similarity: while the first two iterations of They Rule used static datasets gathered from company websites to map the top 100 US companies (from 2001) and then the top 500 US companies (from 2004), in 2011 the site was updated to connect to LittleSis, in order to draw upon the latter's larger and more regularly updated dataset. See: http://www.theyrule.net/about.

2 For more details regarding LittleSis data sources, see: http://www.littlesis.org/features.

3 At the time of writing, the LittleSis database comprised 3,582,814 citations documenting 1,187,534 relationships between 187,093 people, 69,927 organizations, 63,339 business people, 23,625 businesses, 16,258 political fundraising committees, 12,060 academics, 11,940 lobbyists, 8,678 political candidates, 7,432 lawyers, 6,440 public officials, 5,529 private companies, 4,204 elected representatives, 3,543 media personalities, and the list goes on. See LittleSis (n.d.) "About LittleSis." Webpage. Retrieved August 28, 2017, from http://www.littlesis.org/about.

4 I would like to acknowledge the contribution to this section by the RMIT Master of Communication Design students whose work is discussed here, and by SAC staff, most notably Chris Gill, senior education and engagement officer, who has been the SAC lead on this collaborative project.

5 Notably, Grauel also proposes a context-specific extension to the campaign: stickers that could be placed around train stations or in carriages, featuring the summary verbal messages and QR codes that would link to the full infographics.

6 ACMI is Australia's national museum of film, television, video games, and digital culture. It is a facility for the preservation, exhibition, and promotion of Victorian, Australian, and international screen content.

7 I would like to acknowledge the contribution to this section by the RMIT Master of Communication Design students whose work is discussed here, and by ACMI staff, especially Seb Chan, Nick Richardson, and Andy Serong, who facilitated and supported this work.

8 While the term "liberal" typically refers to the political left, the Liberal Party in Australia is the major centre-right party, where it is the leading power in the conservative coalition within the nation's predominantly two-party system.

9 I borrow the term "political hygiene" from Slack and Semati (1997).

10 Laclau and Mouffe follow a Lacanian trajectory to posit the ineradicability of a fundamental antagonism that pervades the social—an anti-universalist move that entails the impossibility of any enduring political consensus. This marks a decisive break from the Marxist tradition from which they depart, while retaining many of the salient features and critical apparatuses of that tradition. For example, Marxist conceptions of ideological apparatuses and ideological critique are, on an agonistic view, terminologically supplanted but practically survived by understandings of hegemonic structures and counter-hegemonic practices that, respectively, work to either crystallize or destabilize various aspects of a social formation.

11 Neurath (1936: 26) wrote: "The teaching system which has the greatest value is not the one which in the hands of good teachers gets the learners the furthest, but that which makes it possible for the least able teachers to do good work."

12 Here an ethics of care may come to closely resemble a utilitarian or consequentialist ethics. Yet, as Slote (2007: 11) has noted, "as compared with consequentialism, an ethics or morality of caring is partialistic," and a discussion of the implications of this partialism in relation to an agonistic political framework is beyond the scope of the present chapter.

References

Barthes, R. (1973), *Mythologies*, St Albans, Herts: Granada.

Boehnert, J. (2016), "Data Visualisation Does Political Things," *DRS2016: Design + Research + Society: Future-Focused Thinking*, University of Brighton: Design Research Society.

Borges, J. L. (1999), "On Exactitude in Science," London: Penguin Books, 325.

Burke, C., Kindel, E., Walker, S., eds. (2013), *Isotype: Design and Contexts, 1925–1971*, London: Hyphen Press.

Chan, S. (2016), "First Batch—Open Collection Data from ACMI," *ACMI Labs*, Melbourne: ACMI, Avalilable online: https://labs.acmi.net.au/first-batch-open-collection-data-from-acmi-ef0a6720d716 (accessed August 28, 2017).

Connor, K. (July 22, 2014), "Introducing Oligrapher: Power Mapping on LittleSis," Webpage. Retrieved August 28, 2017, from https://news.littlesis.org/2014/07/22/introducing-oligrapher-power-mapping-on-littlesis/

Felton, N., ed. (2016), *PhotoViz: Visualizing Information Through Photography*, Berlin: Gestalten.

Freire, P. (2000), *Pedagogy of the Oppressed*, New York and London: Continuum.

Gilligan, C. (1982), *In a Different Voice: Psychological Theory and Women's Development*, Cambridge, MA, and London: Harvard University Press.

Haylock, B. (2018), "What Is Critical Design?" in G. Coombs, G. J. Sade and A. E. McNamara (eds.), *Undesign: Critical Practices at the Intersection of Art and Design*, London and New York, Routledge, forthcoming.

Horkheimer, M. (2002), *Critical Theory: Selected Essays*, New York: Continuum.

Kim, Pauline T. (1999), "Norms, Learning, and Law: Exploring the Influences on Workers' Legal Knowledge," *University of Illinois Law Review*, 1999: 447–516.

Laclau, E. and Mouffe, C. (2001), *Hegemony and Socialist Strategy: Towards a Radical Democratic Politics*, London and New York: Verso.

LittleSis (n.d.), "About LittleSis," Webpage. Retrieved August 28, 2017, from http://www.littlesis.org/about

Mouffe, C. (2000), "Which Ethics for Democracy?," in M. B. Garber, B. Hanssen and R. L. Walkowitz (eds.), *The Turn to Ethics*, London and New York: Routledge, 85–94

Mouffe, C. (2005), "On the Political," London and New York: Routledge.

Mouffe, C. (2008), "Art and Democracy: Art as an Agnostic Intervention in Public Space," *Open* 14: 6–15.

Neurath, M. and Kinross, R. (2009), *The Transformer: Principles of Making Isotype Charts*, London: Hyphen Press.

Neurath, O. (1936), *International Picture Language: The First Rules of Isotype*, London: Kegan Paul.

Neurath, O., Eve, M., et al. (2010), *From Hieroglyphics to Isotype: A Visual Autobiography*, London: Hyphen Press.

Noddings, N. (1984), *Caring: A Feminine Approach to Ethics and Moral Education*, Berkeley: University of California Press.

Noddings, N. (2002), *Starting at Home: Caring and Social Policy*, Berkeley and Los Angeles: University of California Press.

Sentencing Advisory Council (n.d.), "Establishment and Functions," Webpage. Retrieved August 28, 2017, from https://http://www.sentencingcouncil.vic.gov.au/about-us/establishment-functions

Slack, J. D. and Mehdi Semati, M. (1997), "Intellectual and Political Hygiene: The 'Sokal Affair,'" *Critical Studies in Mass Communication*, 14 (3): 201–27.

Slote, Michael A. (2007), *The Ethics of Care and Empathy*, London and New York: Routledge.

Stake, Robert E. (1995), *The Art of Case Study Research*, Thousand Oaks: Sage.

Swift, D. (1960), "Keeping Democracy Alert and Well Informed Through Film," *The Age*, Melbourne: David Syme and Co., 18.

They Rule (n.d.), "They Rule: About," Webpage. Retrieved August 28, 2017, from http://theyrule.net/about

Tufte, Edward R. (1983), *The Visual Display of Quantitative Information*, Cheshire, CT: Graphics Press.

Tufte, Edward R. (1990), *Envisioning Information*, Cheshire, CT: Graphics Press.

Tufte, Edward R. (1997), *Visual Explanations: Images and Quantities, Evidence and Narrative*, Cheshire, CT: Graphics Press.

Tufte, Edward R. (2006) *Beautiful Evidence*, Cheshire, CT: Graphics Press.

Valdes, F. (2003), "Outsider Jurisprudence, Critical Pedagogy and Social Justice Activism: Marking the Stirrings of Critical Legal Education," *Asian Law Journal*, 10 (1): 65–96.

Vossoughian, N. (2008), *Otto Neurath: The Language of the Global Polis*, Rotterdam: NAi Publishers.

5

What Do We Want?: Designing Cultures of Care in Conditions of Precarity

Shana Agid

> *How to ask and answer questions and hear the world in our asking and answering is the task before us.*
>
> Ruth Wilson Gilmore, "What Is to Be Done?"

I am writing this chapter at a time when I long to be in conversation with others. I am writing at a specific moment in US and global political history, marked by a specific, if not unfamiliar, precarity for people whose bodies are subject to racialized, gendered, and economic power, as well as to the guarding of borders and to state and interpersonal violence often beyond their immediate control. This precarity and its violence is shaped, as well, by some people's fears of lost power—also racialized, gendered, economic, national. For some, the fear is that this power appears to be already lost, for others, it is perceived as at-risk and in need of defense. In this specific, if not unfamiliar, moment, I long to be in conversation with others because these are times in which I need help making sense of things.

If design with people is, at least in part, a means for learning and articulating what we want so that we might imagine and build it, then how we understand the questions from which we begin to frame those needs and desires, and the contexts and relationships through which we engage them, is critical. Here, I work through four interrelated ideas that shape design with people: problem-posing, multiplicity, imagining, and building, as these offer capacities for making collective, actionable knowledge toward designing cultures of care. The conversation to follow, with the words, ideas, and work of scholars, poets, and scholar-activists mostly outside design fields, is an attempt to ask a critically important question for this (specific, yet familiar) moment: how do we design capacities for care and well-being as resistance to (designed) infrastructures of harm?

Puig de la Bellacasa (2011) reminds us that "care" in this larger sense is not a relationship of one person or entity "caring for" another in a position of power or dependency, but is, instead, an always-already state of relationality and being, what she calls caring as "relationality into the doings of thinking and knowing." De la Bellacasa (2011: 199) argues that care "articulates a notion of *thinking-with* that resists the individualization of thinking." In this sense, then, "care" is both an engagement—the doings of thinking and knowing—and a manifestation of this dynamic set of practices and relationships, formed and reformed in the interpersonal and systemic interactions through which thinking and knowing take place. This is an orientation to care that presumes that it is in asking questions and imagining together that we also recognize the real stakes of everyday work.

Working with "care" in this sense is a move away from contested, but still quite present, ideas of design as an instrument for "helping" (or "caring for") others through, for example, community-engaged design projects (Center for Urban Pedagogy 2015). Rather, working toward building cultures of care changes the focus of design toward a willingness to engage with, and reimagine, shifting (infra) structures, which are themselves relational in nature (Star and Ruhleder 1996), and people's experiences of them as a means for making knowledge and action together. In participatory design practice, "infrastructuring" is the work of designing, revealing, and/or intervening on infrastructures (Neumann and Star 1996; Karasti 2014), imagined both as large-scale systems and as sites in which new possibilities for local or smaller-scale organization and resources might be made, often in relationship to the larger-scale infrastructures which surround them (Agid 2016; Björgvinsson, Ehn, and Hillgren 2012; Karasti and Baker 2004; Karasti and Syrjänen 2004). At any scale, these infrastructures are rarely neutral. What counts as "care," and how it manifests through these social, political, technological, and historically shaped structures, is defined differently by different people, of course, but it is also often defined differently *for* different people, without them. This happens as often through "non-inclusive" top-down processes as it can in nominally "engaged" ones, from NGO- and government-led projects to so-called social design ones.

But how can we account for what Avery Gordon (2008: 5) calls "complex personhood," for "conferring the respect on others that comes from presuming that life and people's lives are simultaneously straightforward and full of enormously subtle meaning" in design with people? In this chapter, I propose that one way of manifesting "care" in relationship to the design of spaces, infrastructures, and systems, is to work toward design processes and outcomes that do not preclude anyone's ability to survive, and at the same time seek to assure that people are not subjected to what Ruth Wilson Gilmore (2007: 28) calls "group differentiated vulnerability to premature death," one localized manifestation of structural forces. Through an engagement with a range of voices in and outside design, and their layered articulations of power, precarity, and resistance, I argue for a way of designing and making that grapples with "care." Beginning with Ruth Wilson Gilmore's invitation above to ask, answer, and hear, this chapter asks what is at stake in our questions and in the way we ask them, in the answers we imagine we might hear, and in what we make with what we learn along the way?[1]

Problem-posing

> *The prison has become a key ingredient of our common sense. It is there, all around us. We do not question whether it should exist. It has become so much a part of our lives that it requires a great feat of the imagination to envision life beyond the prison.*
>
> Angela Y. Davis, *Are Prisons Obsolete?*, 2003, p. 18–19

> *The proliferation of antiprison groups during this decade [1997–2007] indicates how many kinds of people understand that prison is not a building "over there" but a set of relationships that undermine rather than stabilize everyday lives everywhere.*
>
> Ruth Wilson Gilmore, *Golden Gulag*, 2007, p. 241

> *Patricia Monture-Angus and Mishuana Goeman noted that the logics of settler colonialism are based on the continual commodification of land, such that we must always be competing among each other for who gets to control and operate a particular piece of land or territory. So indigenous sovereignty gets structured in a very exclusivist way, right? When there's encroachment on indigenous land, the only response you can say in the US legal system is: It's not your land, it's our land. But we don't get to say: "Why should this be anybody's land?"*
>
> Andrea Smith, *Race in 21st Century America*, Baltimore, Maryland, 2010

The philosopher Donald Schön (1983) argued that designers and others who do their work *through practice* do not begin with a known issue for which they create a "solution," but rather "set" the problem through exploration, observation, and prior experience. But this process—determining both what the "problem" might be, how it might be examined, and, finally, what acceptable parameters of a "solution" look like—is itself shaped by power, histories, and context (Greenbaum 1991; Suchman 2002). Critical pedagogy activist and scholar Paulo Freire ([1970] 2010: 83) argued for "problem-posing" as the active collective process of "people to develop their power to perceive critically *the way they exist* in the world *with which* and *in which* they find themselves," so they might take action together to change it.[2]

Angela Y. Davis, Ruth Wilson Gilmore, and Andrea Smith similarly (re)frame possibilities for both *knowing* and *asking* questions. As scholars in African American and feminist studies, geography, and indigenous studies, respectively, and long-time organizers and activists, they suggest that even as we might begin to know intimately the limitations of systems with which we live and the ideas of what can be known and asked, we still struggle—perhaps in different ways, from different locations—to imagine differently. These authors offer propositions for asking about specific contexts' histories, conditions, and foreclosures by asking new kinds of questions. Rather than seeking to "fix" prisons, Davis asks us what might happen if we engage the "great feat of the imagination" that would allow, or require, envisioning life beyond it. Rather than presuming that prisons are distant, doing the work of producing "safety" "over there," Gilmore asks us to consider what it means that so many understand it as "a set of relationships that undermine rather than stabilize the lives of people everywhere." Rather than presume the only question to be asked—and the only "rights" to be asserted—regarding the lands on which people live and make communities is, "Who owns this land?," Smith proposes, we ask the following (unimagined, disallowed) question instead: "Why should this be anybody's land?" These scholar-activists propose that reframing the question is a critical component of the practice of reimagining both the conditions of a given "problem" and the work that might be done in relationship to it.

Multiplicity

> *Reality is as much about configurations of disarrangements, failures and fixes, pressures, forces, and possibilities as it is about vision and success. . . . This commitment to complexity, then, also embodies a fundamental political commitment: namely that change is never well served by reducing complexity to simplicity.*
>
> Lawrence Grossberg, *Cultural Studies in the Future Tense*, 2010, p. 17

> *It's requiring a radical epistemological shift in how we even understand ourselves as selves. If under Western philosophy we see the self as radically separate from other peoples, that we understand ourselves as being different from somebody else, then the nations we create become exclusive. We know we have a nation because it's not another nation. But if we understand ourselves as radically connected to all people*

> *and all creation, then the nations we create will also be radically connected, will also share a larger responsibility for the world.*
>
> Andrea Smith, *Race in 21st Century America*, Baltimore, Maryland, 2010

> *Ethics is acting in the "between-ness" among entities that are coming together to discover and reflect upon who "we" are, and question, converse about, and propose how "we become" with one another.*
>
> Ann Light and Yoko Akama, "Structuring Future Social Relations: Politics of Care in Participatory Practice," *Participatory Design Conference*, 2014, p. 159

Grossberg, Smith, and Light and Akama, writing from cultural studies, indigenous studies, and participatory design, impress upon us as actors in the world, and as designers working to imagine and build it, that we have the option and opportunity not only to imagine differently, but to imagine *knowing* itself as inherently complex, multiple, and connected. Grossberg reminds us that what we know and experience as "real" is shaped as much by what goes wrong or remains only in the realm of the possible as it is by what succeeds or can be readily envisioned and done. This "commitment to complexity," he argues, binds us to an understanding that "change is never well served by reducing complexity to simplicity," no matter how tempting, or how well it appears to serve the project at hand. As we enter into the work of making knowledge with people toward making action, systems, structures, and infrastructures, Andrea Smith's call for a "radical epistemological shift" away from Western colonial individualism toward seeing ourselves as deeply connected means understanding that what we make has different implications for the lives, histories, and possibilities of variously situated people and lands. If, then, we presume that there is always a multiplicity of ideas, experiences, people, histories, positions, boundaries, and connections across them, the "between-ness" to which Light and Akama refer allows a means for imagining and planning for ways in which people might "reflect . . . question, converse, and propose how 'we become' with one another."

Here, we are pushed to consider whether and how processes of problem-posing allow for "radical connection" and "between-ness," by asking if we've prioritized multiplicities of experience(s) and shared responsibility as a condition of any outcome. These authors bring into relationship the need to take complexity seriously in the work of infrastructuring, to not allow a desire for solutions or simple endings to obscure the importance of maintaining space for multiple and conflicting desires. They propose that building capacity for "becoming with" is a means for navigating and negotiating multiplicity, in large and small ways.

Imagining

Critical work, at its best, works—analytically, theoretically, and imaginatively—in the gap between the failed present and the impossible future, but there is no guarantee, no dialectical logic, which connects the two. When critical work overemphasizes the negativity of the present, reinscribing its pessimism, it leaves the positive as the imagination of a different future—free-floating, dissociated from any sense of the way it can be actualized. . . . That is to say, critical work has to articulate the negativity of the present to the positivity of the future . . . it is only because the present did not have to be the way it is that the future can be some other way than where it appears to be heading.

Lawrence Grossberg, *Cultural Studies in the Future Tense*, 2010, p. 94

If the abolition of slave-manacles / began as a vision of hands without manacles, / then this is the year; / if the shutdown of extermination camps / began as imagination of a land / without barbed wire or the crematorium, / then this is the year; / if every rebellion begins with the idea / that conquerors on horseback / are not many-legged gods, that they too drown / if plunged in the river, / then this is the year.

From Martín Espada, "*Imagine the Angels of Bread*," 1996

We need to know where we live in order to imagine living elsewhere. We need to imagine living elsewhere before we can live there.

Avery Gordon, *Ghostly Matters: Haunting and the Sociological Imagination*, [1997] 2008, p. 5

If the act of posing a "problem" in designing starts in designers' and/or participants' ideas of the situation at hand and the knowledge and experience we bring to it, this in turn shapes our understandings and our imagination of what else might be possible or desirable. Grossberg, Espada, and Gordon propose imagination as a site of power, recognition, and transformation. In each, imagination is a precondition for being able to move, for seeing through what Friere ([1970] 2010: 83) called the "static" sense of reality, and beginning the concrete work that enables "living elsewhere." These authors, a cultural theorist, a poet, and a sociologist, set out the possibilities for imagining otherwise as a site of production, not only for generating vision, but for articulating and framing action.

Grossberg argues that it is in the very act of rooting our sense of the future in a rejection of the idea that the present is inevitable and common sense that we become able to envision a future that "can be some other way than where it appears to be heading." His insistence on keeping the past, present, and future in meaningful relation to each other is reflected in the reminders Martín Espada offers in his poem "Imagine the Angels of Bread" in which things that have happened, things known to us from experience or stories, are proposed as precedents for future possibilities. These become models of imagination, connecting the past to a future that begins in the here and now ("this is the year"). To this, Gordon adds the critical instruction to study our context—to "know where we live"—in order to imagine differently. Here, Gordon offers a process clearly grounded in what is before us. First, find out where you are. Then, imagine what else might be. Finally, make that new place so that you might live there.

Building

> *If we take to heart the fact that we make places, things, and selves, but not under conditions of our own choosing, then it is easier to take the risk of conceiving change as something both short of and longer than a single cataclysmic event. Indeed, the chronicles of revolutions all show how persistent small changes, and altogether unexpected consolidations, added up to enough weight, over time and space, to cause a break with the old order.*
>
> Ruth Wilson Gilmore, *Golden Gulag*, 2007, p. 242

> *The agenda in the case of design becomes working for the presence of multiple voices not only in knowledge production, but in the production of technologies as knowledge objectified in a particular way.*
>
> Lucy Suchman, "Located Accountabilities in Technology Production," 2002, p. 93.

> *Our job is to think the unthinkable, imagine the unimaginable, and make the impossible a reality.*
>
> Andrea Smith, *Race in the 21st Century*, quoting Dylan Rodriguez

What might it mean to build cultures of care? What are services, systems, or infrastructures that contribute to people's lived experiences of the present, build on or differentiate their operations from people's understandings of the past, and contribute to how we imagine and work to make a future world? If we understand design through the lens design anthropologist Lucy Suchman offers in the quote above—as a relational process that produces "knowledge objectified in a particular way"—then we can begin to articulate designing as a political process with things at stake, in which people are making claims to knowledge through objects, systems, spaces, and services that enact those claims. Simultaneously, when arguments for the change-making capacities of design are everywhere, Gilmore's reminders that change is often a process of accumulation and action, circumstance and organization, coalition-building and chance, bring those arguments into perspective. Design is just one of many forces and strategies and designers are not alone in both seeking to understand and to affect what can be made in the world and how the world is made. Gilmore argues critically that we can learn about making change through understanding its relationship to larger socioeconomic and historical processes, processes of which design is always a part.

We can find, if we look, the multiple sites of crossover and difference between the long histories of political and social organizing and those of design. These are represented in Smith's invocation of ethnic studies scholar-activist Dylan Rodriguez's claim that "our job is to think the unthinkable, imagine the unimaginable, and make the impossible a reality." Both Rodriguez and Smith are speaking not to designers, but to activists, organizers, scholars, and people working toward the abolition of systems and infrastructures of racism, sexism, settler colonialism, policing, imprisonment, heteronormativity, capital, border enforcement, and more. What could it mean for designers to also imagine positioning ourselves here, critically aware of and engaging with the many already working from multiple locations to render the unimaginable and the impossible both visible and real?

What is at stake?: Self-determined design

What are the possibilities of nonreformist reform—of changes that, at the end of the day, unravel rather than widen the net of social control through criminalization?

Ruth Wilson Gilmore, *Golden Gulag*, p.242

What is our role as designers in learning to differentiate between systems and infrastructures of harm versus those that might develop and sustain cultures of care? Harm and care are defined differently by different people, in both brutal and nuanced ways. Given this, what are the ethics of our engagement with designing for "care"? How might we begin to imagine designing for the present as a means of bringing imagined futures into view while also working mindfully to keep from foreclosing possibilities through reform-oriented change in relation to infrastructures of harm? How do we become or remain open to undoing common-sense notions of, for example, punishment or borders, in our design work, in order to imagine differently? This raises critical questions about how we position ourselves as part of people's larger and ongoing efforts toward self-determination, toward ending historical and contemporary conditions of precarity, some of which will also already be our struggles. This includes taking seriously questions about where and with whom we do this work, and how we address its critical presents and future orientations. How do we learn through designing with people what best supports capacities and needs for caring across a range of structures, spaces, and times? In our collaborations, how do we respond to Lucy Suchman's (2002: 95) critical question about designing the things with which we live and work: "Who is doing what to whom here?"

To imagine these proposals in action, I conclude with an example from Critical Resistance (CR), an organization that works toward ending the prison industrial complex (PIC),[3] "the overlapping interests of government and industry that designate surveillance, policing and imprisonment as solutions to economic, social and political problems" (Critical Resistance 2004: 59). I worked as an embedded design-researcher with CR organizers in Oakland, California, focused on making policing obsolete by finding other ways to address the harms that policing is theoretically meant to address and ameliorating the harms it causes (for instance, through surveillance, stop and frisk tactics, and violence).[4]

The project we made, called The Oakland Power Projects (OPP), built on CR's previous organization[5] while also opening new conversations with Oaklanders through interviews about the city, experiences with police, and their ideas, knowledge, and visions for creating well-being in Oakland. We designed an "interview notepad" to track themes and key concerns in interviews using categories developed by listening together (Figure 5.1), then designed a large wall-chart to map this information, allowing organizers to identify a first project: organizing to decouple medical and mental health care from policing. Members of CR gathered interviewees and healthcare workers to learn more about overlaps of health care and policing, to design capacities to shift or interrupt them, and organize the means to begin that work. Beginning with the politically radical premise that policing does not produce safety or well-being, the long-term goal of OPP is to build a range of projects using this process (Figure 5.2) which,

Figure 5.1 CR organizers working with the interview notepad, Credit: Shana Agid and Critical Resistance.

together, over time, seeds capacities to imagine well-being without police, and to build self-determined structures and resources.

The members of CR and I designed the parameters of the new campaign first by engaging in the "between-ness" of our ways of working together to negotiate meaning and process, and then used an epistemological framework that prioritized collective knowledge and reflected different perceptions and experiences. As we worked, we created new tools and processes internally to facilitate knowledge production. This engendered an imagination of a campaign that both built upon and exceeded CR members' expectations of possible next steps to create well-being and make policing obsolete in Oakland. The idea behind OPP is that people can and do care for each other in ways that surpass, ameliorate, and help to navigate what state and other systems do to, and/or for, them. It is one example of what it might mean to use design processes to highlight, question, refuse, or fight to change the very conditions in which design work is taking place. Through shifting the sense of the "problem" by first reframing "safety" defined in limited ways to "well-being" defined more broadly, CR members imagined other ways to value and build "care," both interpersonally and systemically.

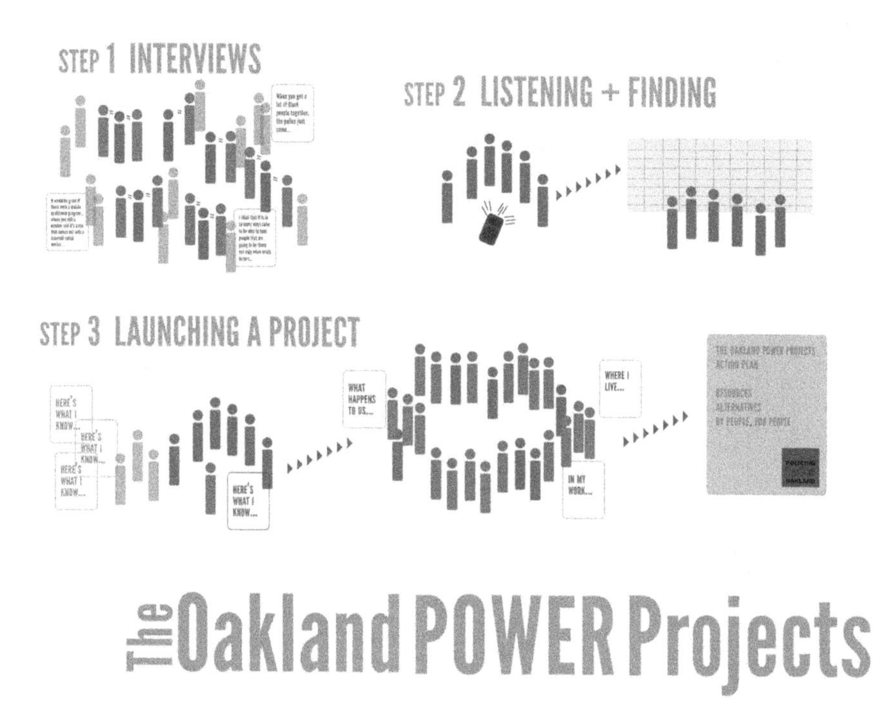

Figure 5.2 Oakland Power Projects—How We Do It poster. Credit: Shana Agid and Critical Resistance.

How we work with the notion of "care" in design, as a way of working or a thing to be made through those processes, or both, requires attention to and respect for contradiction and nuance. Care can be what we might call looking out for others, or being aware of ourselves and others (including nonhuman others). It is also shaped by what we know and are open to learning, for example, knowing about histories that shape the present moment, and taking care to learn them when we don't, so that we might see the legacies of racism, colonialism, sexism, or state-building in design decisions and contexts (Wilson 2016). Care can manifest in our abilities to see and be open to seeing whole landscapes of possibility, especially those that challenge our positions and privileges (Gordon [1997] 2008). Working with care might also be framed as being open to and present for the work, in its emergent forms (Agid 2016; Akama 2015). In other words, this approach to design means knowing that, as a designer and researcher, I need the words, insights, knowledge, and thinking of other people to fully understand anything at all, so that I might act responsibly and thoughtfully, with respect for what has shaped this present moment, and what is shaping it *right now*.

Notes

1 This approach of starting a conversation to find a way forward is one I learned from Sekou Sunditata's project, *the 51st (dream) State*, which began as a series of community conversations and "community sings" undertaken following the 9/11 attacks and in the midst of the US response, domestic and international, that followed. Through these conversations, he set out to better understand "America" as an African American man in the early twenty-first century as fraught ideas of "America" past, present, and future proliferated around him. For more, see: *finding the 51st (dream) state: Sekou Sundiata's America Project* (2007).

2 For a close engagement with problem-setting and tacit knowing in design that explores the role of designers' tacit beliefs and their role in problem-setting, and an exploration of Paulo Friere's arguments for the collective process of "problem-posing," see Agid 2011 and forthcoming.

3 I am a long-time member of CR. I brought with me an understanding of organizational processes and norms, and an understanding of and shared belief in the group's political mission. This does not mean that we did not disagree or debate meanings, tactics, and what was necessary for the work we undertook. It does mean I was invested in the political possibilities of the design research, and in my relationships with CR organizers. I would argue, though, that this possibility is not limited to someone who is already a part of a given organization or movement.

4 See, for example, the 2016 American Public Health Association policy statement, "Law Enforcement Violence as a Public Health Issue."

5 Members were key members of the Stop the Injunctions Coalition (STIC) which fought to end the use of gang injunctions, a civil law enforcement policy that heavily impacted former prisoners and people of color in the city by imposing curfews and limiting both movement and associations. For more on gang injunctions, see Greene and Pranis, 2007. For more on STIC, see https://stoptheinjunction.wordpress.com/.

References

Agid, S. (2011), "'How Can We Design Something to Transition People from a System that Doesn't Want to Let them Go?': Social Design and Its Political Contexts," *Design Philosophy Papers*, 3: 1–11.

Agid, S. (2016), "'. . . It's Your Project, but It's Not Necessarily Your Work . . .': Infrastructuring, Situatedness, and Designing Relational Practice," *Proceedings of the 14th Participatory Design Conference*. Aarhus, Denmark, 15–19 August, 81–90.

Agid, S. (Forthcoming), "Making 'Safety', Making Freedom: Problem-Setting, Collaborative Design, and Contested Futures," in T. Fisher and L. Gamman (eds.), *Tricky Design: The Ethics of Things*, London: Bloomsbury.

Akama, Y. (2015), "Being Awake to *Ma*: Designing in between-ness as a Way of Becoming With," *CoDesign*, 11 (34): 262–74.

American Public Health Association (2016), *Law Enforcement Violence as a Public Health Issue, Policy Number: LB-16-02.* Available online: https://apha.org/policies-and-advocacy/public-health-policy-statements/policy-database/2016/12/09/law-enforcement-violence-as-a-public-health-issue (accessed April 15, 2017).

Bjögvinsson, E., Ehn, P., and Hillgren, P.-A. (2012), "Agonistic Participatory Design: Working with Marginalized Social Movements," *CoDesign*, 8 (2–3): 127–44.

Center for Urban Pedagogy (2015), *Dick and Rick*. New York: Center for Urban Pedagogy. Available online: http://welcometocup.org/Projects/TechnicalAssistance/DickRick (accessed February 1, 2017).

Critical Resistance Abolition Toolkit Workgroup (2004), *The CR Abolition Organizing Toolkit*. Available online: http://criticalresistance.org/resources/the-abolitionist-toolkit/ (accessed April 1, 2017).

Davis, A. Y. (2003), *Are Prisons Obsolete?* New York: Seven Stories Press.

De la Bellacasa, P. (2011), "Matters of Care in Technoscience: Assembling Neglected Things," *Social Studies of Science*, 41 (85). Originally published online December 7, 2010.

Espada, M. (1996), *Imagine the Angels of Bread: Poems*, New York: W.W. Norton.

Finding the 51st (dream) State: Sekou Sundiata's America Project (2007), [DVD] Dir. Stanley Nelson, New York: Firelight Media.

Friere, P. ([1970] 2010), *Pedagogy of the Oppressed*, trans. M. Bergman Ramos, New York: Continuum.

Gilmore, R. W. (2007), *Golden Gulag: Prisons, Surplus, Crisis and Opposition in Globalizing California*, Berkeley: University of California Press.

Gilmore, R. W. (2011), "What is to Be Done?" *American Quarterly*, 63 (2): 245–65.

Gordon, A. ([1997] 2008), *Ghostly Matters: Haunting and the Sociological Imagination*, Minneapolis: University of Minnesota Press.

Greenbaum, J. (December 1991), "A Design of One's Own: Towards Participatory Design in the US," DAIMI Report Series, [S.l.], n. 375. ISSN 2245-9316. Available at: http://ojs.statsbiblioteket.dk/index.php/daimipb/article/view/6607 (accessed April 15, 2017).

Greene, J. and Pranis, K. (2007), *Gang Wars: The Failure of Enforcement Tactics and the Need for Effective Public Safety Strategies* [online]. Washington DC: Justice Policy Institute. Available at: http://www.justicepolicy.org/uploads/justicepolicy/documents/07-07_rep_gangwars_gc-ps-ac-jj.pdf (accessed April 15, 2017).

Grossberg, L. (2010), *Cultural Studies in the Future Tense*, Durham: Duke University Press.

Karasti, H. (2014), “Infrastructuring in Participatory Design,” *Proceedings of the 13th Conference on Participatory Design*, Windhoek, Namibia, 6–10 October, 141–50.

Karasti, H. and Baker, K. S. (2004), “Infrastructuring for the Long-Term: Ecological Information Management,” *Proceedings of the 37th Hawaii International Conference on System Sciences*, Big Island, Hawai'i, 5–8 January, 1–10.

Karasti, H. and Syrjänen, A.-L. (2004), ‘Artful Infrastructuring in Two Cases of Community PD,” *Proceedings of the 8th Conference on Participatory Design*, Toronto, Canada, 27–31 July, 20–30.

Light, A. and Akama, Y. (2014), “Structuring Future Social Relations: The Politics of Care in Participatory Practice,” *Proceedings of the 13th Participatory Design Conference*, Windhoek, Namibia, 6–10 October, 151–60.

Neumann, L. J. and Star, S. L. (1996), “Making Infrastructure: The Dream of a Common Language,” *Proceedings of the 4th Conference on Participatory Design*, Cambridge, MA, 13–19 November, 231–40.

Schön, D. A. (1983), *The Reflective Practitioner: How Professionals Think in Action*, New York: Basic Books.

Smith, A. (2010), *Race in 21st Century America* [Lecture at Red Emma's], Baltimore, Maryland, 20 October.

Star, S. L. and Ruhleder, K. (1996), “Steps Toward an Ecology of Infrastructure: Borderlands of Design and Access for Large Information Spaces,” *Information Systems Research*, 7 (1): 111–34.

Suchman, L. (2002), “Located Accountabilities in Technology Production,” *Scandinavian Journal of Information Systems*, 14 (2): 91–105.

Wilson, M. (2016), “Carceral Architectures,” *E-flux Architecture*. Available online: http://www.e-flux.com/architecture/superhumanity/68676/carceral-architectures/ (accessed April 15, 2017).

6

Patient-Centered Care and the Design of a Psychiatric Care Facility

Laurene Vaughan, Shanti Sumartojo, and Sarah Pink

This shift to a patient-centered care paradigm has implications not only for how hospitals provide care but also for how they are experienced and perceived by patients and communities more broadly. It confronts the traditional and outdated perceptions of hospitals as sites of authority and manifestations of power relations, a phenomenon prevalent in psychiatric facilities in particular (Foucault 1982, p. 790). In the past power has been realized through structures of authority, hierarchy and expertise, the allocation of treatment modalities, and inclusion or exclusion of patient families and carers from the care process through simple things such as visitation access or participating in treatment decisions. Contemporary models of health care have begun to challenge this perception and enactment of power that has been prevalent in the past. The evolution to new models of care within medical contexts, and particularly nursing (Curtis et al. 2013, and Wagner 2010), marks a shift from power realized through a "treatment" relationship, to one of patient care and the provision of health services. In this chapter we reflect on what this transition from treatment to care means for designers and their approaches to the design of contemporary psychiatric care facilities through a focus on the design approaches to one facility in particular.

The project context: Bendigo Hospital

The site of the research (Design for Wellbeing Project) is the Bendigo Hospital located in regional Victoria, Australia (Figure 6.1), and the design and development of new psychiatric facilities in the hospital during a major

Figure 6.1 Bendigo Hospital. Photo credit: Laurene Vaughan.

redevelopment. The methodology for the research is design ethnography and the research is being undertaken over a three-year time span (2016–2018) by an interdisciplinary team of researchers. This discussion focuses on insights from interviews with the architects and landscape designers of the new facility that were undertaken in Year One of the study.

The new hospital development has resulted in the psychiatric care unit being moved from three discrete locations that focused on different needs, to one integrated psychiatric facility within the new hospital complex. This transition has resulted in the establishment of new contexts for care in the new facilities; the upgrade of facilities; the integration of current discoveries from research on the relationship between environments and health and well-being through spatial design; and the integration of digital technologies for care and safety. The aim of the chapter is to begin to draw insights about the relationship between the design of the aesthetic qualities of environments and alignment to the hospital's model of care.

The design and development of a new hospital psychiatric facility has been a complex process involving a range of stakeholders, referred to as user groups by the project team, these include operations and governance structures, as well as staff (medical, administrative, and service), patients, families, and allied community care services. There are also occupational health and safety requirements, and patient safety and therapeutic guidelines that need to be considered in design responses. Guiding all this is the Hospital Model of Care, a document which articulates their patient-centered care approach. This model is the foundation for the development of the project brief and all day-to-day actions of hospital staff.

Within the literature on the design of hospital spaces, and psychiatric units in particular, there are consistent themes of concern. These include evaluations of space and volume, serviceability to patient numbers, materials, and their associated qualities, and spatial configurations that support care, safety (patients and staff), and external (family and community) participation in day-to-day care (Curtis 2013, Wood et al. 2013a, 2013b).

Wood et al. (2013a) argue that psychiatric hospitals can be classified as "'spaces of transition,' intended to prepare the 'service user' to return to life in the community, by encouraging a degree of connection between the community setting and the clinical environment" (p. 123). They argue, based on the work of Schweitzer, Gilpin, and Frampton (2004 in Wood 2013a), that there needs to be a degree of "managed permeability" whereby buildings encourage opportunities for "social contact and engagement"'(p. 123). It is in this way that psychiatric hospitals can be considered "therapeutic landscapes, which are not only efficient but also offer physical, social, and symbolic features that are beneficial for one's sense of well-being and therefore help to promote healing in a more holistic sense" (p.123). Addressing the possibility of this was particularly prominent in the design of the external spaces by the landscape designers in the Bendigo Hospital Project.

Typically the term "flexible" or "customizable" would be used to describe designs that are responsive to use or need. Schweitzer, Gilpin, and Frampton (2004) propose permeability as another way to conceive of a fluidity and flexibility through design. Permeability can manifest in the physical environment and the systems of hospital design, while also being a guide for the hospital's practices of care and engagement. In contrast, surveillance is a theme that is raised in the literature and refers to the ways that medical staff engage with patients throughout the day. The classification of the nursing station as a surveillance hub is a common reference in discussions of sight lines and observation methods by clinical staff with patients in the literature

(May 1992, Salzmann-Erikson and Eriksson 2012). Salzmann-Erikson et al. observe that "the patient spaces in the mental health institution are subtly linked to different mechanisms of control and surveillance" (p. 501). They propose that designing spaces that allow for patient privacy while ensuring safety and care is one of the core challenges of hospital design. Developing systems and processes of observation that ensure patient well-being, while also honoring the desire and need for privacy, is equally challenging. Too much observation can be interpreted as an invasion of personal space while ensuring high levels of care; too little observation can be interpreted as the reverse, whereby high levels of personal space may also be interpreted as a low level of care (Salzmann-Erikson and Eriksson 2012).

The links between the design of physical spaces and the quality of an experience is noted in the literature through a thematic concern for the material nature of therapeutic spaces and the impact this has on both the physical and psychological well-being of patients. Wood et al. (2013b), in a study of a new psychiatric hospital in the UK, report that hospital staff need to "match material security standards to provide containment as well as refuge" (p. 205). They go on to report that in this case "'safe' spaces on the wards had predominantly 'smooth' surfaces. Protruding features were considered hazardous, such as free-standing metal poles . . . or sharp surfaces" (p. 205). Concerns within their hospital case study were particularly focused on opportunities for self-harm or suicide. To address the issue of any metal building materials being left after construction, such as screws, the entire building was swept with metal detectors. This level of care, about what might be seen as minor oversights at the end of construction, is a real and lived concern for those working in psychiatric care.

From a design perspective these concerns about the material qualities of therapeutic spaces can be seen as a recognition of the material/physical aspect of care and the design of experiences and processes that enable care. Tonkinwise (2006) argues that it is possible for us to see the things of the material world as empathetic agents of care. It is through our designed world that care happens. What for Wood et al. (2013a) are the material qualities of surfaces and things that realize care are, for Tonkinwise, building on the work of Latour (1992) and Scarry (1985)—supportive environments that perform acts of care in conjunction with the human actors (carers) in a synchronized environment. The challenge for those charged with the design and development of new institutional care facilities is to design the material realization of a proposition of care that will be experienced through a range of lived contexts.

The brief: The model of care

The guide for the design and development is the hospital's Model of Care. This comprehensive document outlines every aspect of the hospital, the different units, and services including the new psychiatric precinct. The document was consistently referred to by the architects and design team throughout their interviews (N&B architects 2016 and Occulus Landscape Design 2016). It formed the backbone of the project brief and expectations for all aspects that were being delivered.

The Bendigo Hospital Model of Care states:

> *The Model of Care outlines specific areas required for the management of acutely behaviourally disturbed, acute adult psychiatric patients, acute aged psychiatric patients, secure extended psychiatric patients and mother and baby psychiatric patients within the ED (Emergency Department) and the New Facility Psychiatric IPUs.*
>
> *BH (Bendigo Hospital) is committed to providing culturally sensitive care to the people in its catchment. Ensuring cultural sensitivity in the Psychiatric IPUs is of particular importance.* (p. 248)

A 120-page detailed specification outlines the needs of the hospital. Notable are the key and consistent spatial and service requirements for the mix of patients that the unit will service, including: "The patient centred approach to psychiatric care will mean that, as far as possible, patients and carers are informed and involved in the decision making process in relation to all aspects of care" (17.2 p. 252).

On the nature of facilities to address patient safety: "ensure new and refurbished mental health inpatient units meet new safety guidelines, including removing ligature points, installing air locks and facilitating gender separation" (p. 252). This includes nine guiding principles spanning sight lines, lockable bedrooms, levels of security appropriate to patient population, separation by gender for some units (17.5.4. pp. 257-258).

The level of detail and the specifics of care within a psychiatric context are consistent with the guidelines and principles proposed in the literature from other such hospital developments. The accommodation requirements include

- all services must be tamper proof;
- there must be no ligature points;
- no sharp corners, ledges, protrusions, and so on;

- special consideration of the load bearing of potential ligature points such as curtain rails, towel rails, and hung in a manner that will collapse when 15kg or more is applied;
- maximize opportunities for controlled privacy and recreation of patients;
- provide a domestic rather than institutional-style setting.

During the interviews the architects and designers referred to this document as the guiding framework for their design process while also being engaged in extensive consultation processes with the relevant stakeholders (user groups) who would be using the spaces and environments. Although they were engaged in the design of the greater hospital development project, our discussions focused on the psychiatric facilities in particular. The following are some of the insights that emerged through the interviews, and which illustrate the rich dimensions that designing into a patient-centered care model demands and enables.

Architect—designing care environments

The architects' design outcome was their response to the project tender brief, in conjunction with their prior research and experience in hospital design and best practice models. They are experienced in working in this domain, and are committed to being leaders in healthcare design and planning. In the course of the interviews, they emphasized that there is an increased demand for mental health facilities within a range of contexts, and that there were new kinds of clients in need of them. This phenomenon is driven by increasing numbers of dementia patients due to the aging population, and increases in the number of psychosis patients as a result of drug use, crystal methamphetamine in particular. The stigma around the treatment and care of mental health is changing, resulting in new expectations around the design of healthcare facilities. In particular there is a demand or preference for less institutional-style facilities that have dominated the design and service models since the Victorian Era. The evolving model is one of integrated care.

The architects' design involved the integration of the hospital's Model of Care with greater social expectations and research in space and facility design. They referred to this as a "spectrum of care." In the old hospital the facilities were spread across three discrete locations, two of which were on the main hospital campus. In the new hospital the psychiatric wards are on the second floor, and are accessed via the main entrance to the building although acute admittance occurs either through a discrete and secure entrance or via the Emergency department (with transfer to the precinct through staff and patient-only corridors and lifts). This decision to place psychiatry within the public thoroughfare of the hospital should be seen as an act by the hospital to normalize mental health care as one aspect of healthcare services for the community.

Throughout the interview conversations the key terms that were used by the architects when speaking about the project were risk, robustness, mental health recognition, integration with external life, integration across the mental health units, and flexibility in the use of spaces. It became clear that these were the elements that they had had to focus on throughout the design process. They were aligned to the experience of the patients and the practices of the carers (both professional staff and family and friends), and articulated what they felt was the need for the space to "care for the carers." This is an additional dimension to the prominent discourse on patient-centered care, and was their response to other review data that the hospital provided and the feedback from the various stakeholder groups in the design and consultation process. For the architects it was essential to incorporate the means for the carers to feel safe. They were careful to articulate that the carers' feeling nurtured by the space was as important as providing a caring environment for the patients. It would be easy to keep all the design focus on the needs of patients, but the staff in all their different roles are also part of the everyday ecology of care in the facility and their needs had to be catered for.

Consistent with the literature and the views articulated by the patients and carers in this study, the architects also reflected on issues of scale, comfort, and domesticity as being important characteristics of a care environment. This was often articulated as "homeliness," and is a direct response to or rejection of old models of institutional care. To achieve this experience of the space, the architects endeavored to design the environment to function on a domestic scale despite the fact that the facility is large. This was an aesthetic approach that aimed to support patient transition between hospital care and home or post-hospital care. Balancing the need for staff and patient safety while designing spaces that support well-being and long-term health is an ongoing dimension of our discussions. As Wood et al. (2013) recount, ensuring the physical safety of patients and staff had to be designed into every aspect of the unit. Risk is an ever-present dimension of the design of public spaces and even more so in a psychiatric facility. Ensuring that patients cannot harm themselves is essential, most typically removing all ligature points in the space. During our first site visit to the new hospital we were shown all the points where design interventions

Figure 6.2 Interior details. Photo credit: Laurene Vaughan.

have been made to minimize ligature points, and they are also clearly included in the list of possible vulnerable points in the Model of Care document.

One of the challenges for the architects was to ensure that they were addressing the literal points of risk and safety in the unit, while also using aesthetics and the material qualities of the space to support the experience of care. On walking through the space the various design elements that perform this care become apparent. Curved finishes, walls, and floor patterns, a color palette that is deemed to be uplifting, a furniture selection that references the domestic environment rather than an institution, all contribute to a sense of homeliness which is sought after (Figures 6.2 and 6.3). The abundant use of natural light and large windows revealing the outside world is another aspect of this use of the material and aesthetic qualities of the designed environment to support well-being (Figure 6.4).

In the old hospital the nurses' stations functioned in the classic panopticon model of observation. They were sealed glass rooms in central locations for maximum viewing and observation of patients, carers, and visitors. In the new hospital these stations are opened up, and the glass removed; there is a sense of accessibility. At the same time, the counters are deep, creating space between the two sides. The new stations are still at junctures of corridors and activity spaces, often with a social or open workspace beside them (Figure 6.5). The viewing station is no longer about observation and evaluation; it appears to be a hub in the social, cultural, and clinical care activities of the unit, continuing to provide safety and respite for the caring staff. This is just one example of how features of

Figure 6.3 Interior details. Photo credit: Laurene Vaughan.

Figure 6.4 View from lounge area, Bendigo Hospital. Photo credit: Laurene Vaughan.

Figure 6.5 Psychiatry reception area, Bendigo Hospital. Photo credit: Laurene Vaughan.

safety and concealment have been subtly built into the environment. There are discrete rooms for staff to retreat to should they feel threatened.

Patient-to-patient communication is an essential aspect of the care approach of the psychiatric precinct, though not all patients are interested or able to participate. In the old facilities, patients had the option of "wishing trees," pictures of trees or a tree painted onto a wall, where patients were encouraged to leave messages of hope, healing, and community for each other. Acknowledging that communication is an essential element of care it was necessary for the architects to design a range of means that support and enable interpersonal communication and community, as well as self-expression, each patient's door has a white board where messages and drawings can be left, there are also whiteboards in the rooms (Figure 6.6). Sealed cabinets for artworks are located throughout the hallways. These initiatives are the main forms of interpersonal communication that have been designed into the space, although the staff have expressed a desire for wishing trees in the common areas.

A key concern for the architects was that they were designing "future-looking care contexts." This is how they articulated their design approach to working with the expertise of others—internally from the hospital client—through best practice examples. At times this required them to challenge stakeholder values of what is or was in the old hospital, and try to lead people into future opportunities of care in the new hospital.

Figure 6.6 Section of patient room. Photo credit: Laurene Vaughan.

Landscape—therapeutic spaces for healing

The scope and location of the outside spaces were initially designed by the architects, and the landscape designers then had the challenge of interpreting and translating this into a living spatial design. They describe their design approach as being user-centered design, where their focus is on integrating client/user needs with issues of scale, security, and risk mitigation. Their underlying design approach to landscape and external environments is "therapeutic landscape design" (Wood et al. 2015). Through this approach they aim to harness the positive effects of direct and indirect experiences of nature, a biophilic design approach that is realized through the following principles and constraints:

- the use of color to support health, with no use of red or black;
- plants that would flourish, and were also unlikely to be allergens;
- no plants that produced berries;
- no plants that can be fashioned into weapons for self-harm;
- views to enable patients and staff have a strong sense of place, within the local community and landscape;
- time outdoors is part of the therapeutic regime;

- outdoor furniture needed to be fixed so that it cannot be thrown;
- spaces for walking and for rest;
- moments of delight;
- no trees or vertical planting that can be climbed or used as ligature points;
- plants with healing qualities in their material and aesthetic features, such as pattern, color, scent, and seasonal changes.

Again there was a strong desire by the designers to ensure that the environment had a domestic feel rather than institutional orientation, and it needed to allow for a variety of needs and expectations of the natural environment. The design of the space was undertaken with a range of user groups and evolved quickly in response to timelines and consultation opportunities. The designers wanted to provide opportunities for exercise within the outdoor environment, and the possibility that any equipment may be used for self-harm had to be taken into account (Figure 6.7). There was a desire to include a basketball hoop and stationary bicycles. Both of these were identified as ligature risks for patients,

Figure 6.7 Exterior recreation space, Bendigo Hospital. Photo credit: Laurene Vaughan.

and so the designers, in conjunction with the hospital, needed to identify ways to facilitate exercise while avoiding risk.

It was at this stage that smoking became part of the conversation with the designers. Throughout the project design phase there were a range of responses to address patient preferences to smoke, despite the hospital and legal rulings on smoking in public spaces. At one stage it was thought that a smoking area would be catered for, but this was later removed. Patients who are able to come and go from the facility are able to go out of the hospital grounds to smoke, but those without such freedoms will have to be supported through nicotine withdrawal.

There was a clear commitment to place-based design, with maximum opportunity for people to have a sense of being in the landscape and the local community, through a range of vistas (long and short) and the selection of plants from the region (Figure 6.6). It was proposed that this would support emotional well-being, it is also essential that the plantings can survive and flourish. Providing opportunities for patients to be able to create their own gardens and to care for the garden was also part of this vision (Figure 6.8).

The landscape designers felt that practitioners outside the field of mental health are unable to comprehend fully the need to balance risk and self-harm against other principles of care and healing through landscape. In response to this, they had a commitment to kindness as a design principle that informed their entire design process and outcomes.

Figure 6.8 Ground floor entrance, Bendigo Hospital. Photo credit: Laurene Vaughan.

Humanizing care and the practices of design

In this research three discrete yet interconnected approaches to care have been discussed within the context of the design of a psychiatric precinct of a regional Australian hospital: patient-centered care, human-centered design, and therapeutic landscapes. What has been revealed through this discussion is that there is a greater link between these than might perhaps seem apparent. Through the discussions with the architects and landscape designers in conjunction with the hospital's Model of Care, it has become apparent that there are synergies across these domains in their practices and their intent.

Paul Jones (2013) boldly states in his opening sentence to *Design for Care* that "Care, and healthcare, is about taking care of humanity" (p. XV). Through focusing on humans, people, and our humanity, whether it be individually or in relation to others, the key connection between contemporary design methodologies such as human-centered design, and the evolution of patient-centered care in the medical fields can be realized. It is the people, not the infrastructure, that is the binding element.

Patient-centered care has evolved over twenty years, and as Kitson et al. (2012) argue, there is no one agreed definition of what this means in practice across the various aspects of the healthcare sector. What is consistent is that the patient is transitioned from being the passive subject of health services to being an active and engaged participant in their own care and wellness regime. This focus on action and participation is the vital and perhaps unexpected link to design and the design practitioners in this research. Richard Buchanan (2001) proposed design approaches, which recognize that "human dignity and human rights deserved careful consideration" (p.37). It was this proposition that helped to move the discourse away from user-centered design toward human-centered design, which in turn expanded our understanding of the role of people in projects as being more than end users. Since then a substantial body of literature and projects have gone on to explore how this can be done with increasing depths of humanity to ensure that the people we design for and with are not seen as the passive consumers of design labor, but rather active participants in the design process and the ongoing inhabitation of our design outcomes.

The introduction of therapeutic landscape design by the landscape designers in the project opens up a broader perception of humans as patients in these design approaches and contexts. Therapeutic landscapes are deeply connected to emotional well-being (Wood et al. 2015). Environments and landscapes (both natural and in the built environment) are the sites of our lives. They often provoke or build on past memories, and through encounter become the basis for future memories. This may be a positive or negative experience (p. 84). Like all aspects of design undertaken in conjunction with people and their lived experiences it is essential that designers and the people they design with are cognizant of the potential impacts of our design actions on people's lives.

In this chapter "care" has been used as a way to position awareness of the potential impact of and connection to the lived experiences of design. It has been framed within a psychiatric hospital setting that has particular demands and dimensions. Over recent years we have seen an increase in publications exploring empathy as a way of framing design that responds to and works with the people that we design with. In this research, the landscape designers proposed designing from a perspective of kindness as another way of approaching a careful and responsive design methodology and design outcomes. Whether we are designing environments, systems, or things, and the material or affective experience of them, to design with kindness, or design as kindness, is a provocation from one designer to their peers that is worth our consideration.

Acknowledgments

The Design for Wellbeing project was funded by an industry partnership between RMIT, Exemplar Health, and Bendigo Health.

References

Buchanan, R. (2001), "Human Dignity and Human Rights: Thoughts on the Principles of Human-Centred Design," *Design Issues*, 17 (3): 35–39.

Foucault, M. (1982), "The Subject and Power," *Critical Inquiry*, 8 (4): 777–95.

Jones, P. H. (2013), *Design and Care: Innovating Health Care Experience*, Brooklyn, New York: Rosenfeld Media.

Kitson, A., Marshall, A., Bassett, K., and Zeitz, K. (2012), "What Are the Core Elements of Patient-Centred Care? A Narrative Review and Synthesis of the Literature from Health Policy, Medicine and Nursing," *Journal of Advanced Nursing*, 69 (1): 4–15.

Latour, B. (1992), "'Where Are the Missing Masses' The Sociology of a Few Mundane Artefacts," in W. Bijker and J. Law (eds.), *Shaping Technology/Building Society*, Cambridge, MA: MIT Press.

May, C. (1992), "Individual Care: Power and Subjectivity in Therapeutic Relationships," *Sociology*, 26 (4): 589–602.

N & B Architects. Interviewed by: Vaughan, L. & Sumartojo, S. (August 26, 2016).

Oculus Landscape Design. Interviewed by: Vaughan, L. & Sumartojo, S. (September 26, 2016).

Salzmann-Erikson, M., and Eriksson, H. (2012), "Panoptic Power and Mental Health Nursing—Space and Surveillance in Relation to Staff, Patients, and Neutral Places," Issues in *Mental Health Nursing*, 33 (8): 500–04.

Scarry, E. (1985), *The Body in Pain: The Making and Unmaking of the World*, New York: Oxford University Bendigo Hospital Functional Brief, April 2012.

Tonkinwise, C. (2006), "Thingly Cosmopolitanism: Caring for the Other by Design," *The Radical Designist*, Issue 0. July 2006 | 10/10 | http://unidcom.iade.pt/radicaldesignist/thingly-cosmopolitanism-caring-for-the-other-by-design/ (accessed April 5, 2017).

Wagner, A. L. (2010), "Care and Concepts of Jean Watson's Theory of Human Caring/Caring Science," Watson Caring Science Institute, https://www.watsoncaringscience.org/ (accessed April 5, 2017).

Wood, V. J., Curtis, S., Gesler, W., Spencer, I. H., Close, H. J., Mason, J., and Reilly, J. G. (2013a), "Creating 'Therapeutic Landscapes' for Mental Health Carers in Inpatient Settings: A Dynamic Perspective on Permeability and Inclusivity," *Social Science & Medicine*, 91: 122–29.

Wood, V. J., Curtis, S., Gesler, W., Spencer, I. H., Close, H. J., Mason, J., and Reilly, J. G. (2013b), "Compassionate Containment? Balancing Technical Safety and Therapy in the Design of Psychiatric Wards," *Social Science & Medicine*, 97: 201–09.

Wood, V. J., Curtis, S., Gesler, W., Spencer, I. H., Close, H. J., Mason, J., and Reilly, J. G. (2015), "'Therapeutic Landscapes' and the Importance of Nostalgia, Solastalgia, Salvage and Abandonment for Psychiatric Hospital Design," *Health and Place*, 33: 83–89.

7

Tinkering in Cities: Aging and Careful Technology Design for Participation in Urban Infrastructures

Rachel Clarke

Introduction

The number of people living in urban areas globally is increasing, and there are many more older people inhabiting, working in, and enjoying those same spaces than there were half a century ago (Buffel and Philipson 2016, Ormerod et al. 2015). Within the UK, this urban aging population has further drawn attention to the need for changes to sustainable infrastructure and the potential of "Smart City" technology to help deliver efficient use of resources and accessibility of space (Greenfield 2013, Kukka et al. 2014, Mulgan 2014, Saunders and Baeck 2015). Policy agendas from local and national governments and international NGOs have articulated what needs to be done to make our cities more inhabitable for the future (Urry et al. 2014, WHO 2007). While these agendas are noble they also raise significant questions about how these initiatives are put into practice as older citizens engage with local government to make change.

The following chapter is a reflection on an experimental design-led inquiry exploring the potential use of technology to facilitate the participation of older citizens in urban planning. The communication and participation processes involved in developing new urban pathways in Newcastle upon Tyne, UK, highlight careful negotiation between different actors. Notions of care as practical and attentive (Mol et al. 2010), engendering a "persistent tinkering" (Mol 2008: 61) toward neglected things (Puig de la Bellacasa 2011) is adopted to highlight what care might mean for two actors who participated in these design interventions: Valerie, a concerned and motivated member of the Elders' Council, and Abi, a City Council engagement officer. With a commitment from Newcastle City Council to become an "Age Friendly City" (WHO 2007), the chapter focuses on discussions of care; being careful, who and what is and isn't cared for and taken care of; as it structures social relations during the design process (Light and Akama 2014).

Acts of care as "persistent tinkering" were distributed and constrained through differently constituted individuals: community engagement officers, members of Newcastle City Elders' Council, transport managers, engineers, cyclists, researchers, citizens. These individuals aimed for meaningful engagement, while managing ongoing tensions created by decision making happening elsewhere. Significant aspects of care in participation and engagement work occurred across different media, people, and communities of interest, to enable participation, keep plans flexible and have clear endings and opportunities for reflection. Care was taken through the materials that were made available, translated, and incorporated into expert plans so they became socio-material realities. Yet there was little attention paid to the care that each of these actors was involved in. The conclusion speculates on what it might mean for citizens and professionals to come together in temporal communities of care to appreciate and celebrate where and how different kinds of "tinkering" in urban planning is enacted, and further reflect on the potential yet contentious role of more carefully oriented technology.

Working at the intersection of multiple agendas

Citizen participation in urban planning can be fraught with challenges. Many local government practitioners welcome participation to make use of citizen knowledge, while also recognizing how organizing feedback and discussion at scale can be complicated and sometimes result in limited engagement (Davies et al. 2012, March 2012, Legacy 2012, Leino and Laine 2012). Increasing urban aging populations (Buffel and Philipson 2016) and proliferating use of technology to facilitate participation (Le Dantec et al. 2015, Taylor et al. 2015) further complicates the landscape of citizens' engagement with the redesign of urban infrastructure (Nassauer 2015, Wilson 2011).

The Age-Friendly City agenda, initially developed by the World Health Organization (WHO 2007) has been adopted by cities around the world to assess how the design of urban areas can be more welcoming for older people to thrive (Buffel, Philipson and Sharf 2012). Yet there has been an emphasis on assessing the physical environment at the cost of recognizing the more psycho-social and cultural issues associated with aging (Buffel and Philipson 2016, Ormerod et al. 2015, Ruza et al. 2015, Steels 2015). This has often resulted in conflating aging with disability, lack of capability, and reduced cognitive capacity, while creating an overwhelming array of requirements that are unrealistic and challenging for organizations to enact (Murray 2015). More provocative strategies have built capacity with older adults to become co-inquirers in documenting and presenting their experiences with policy makers in long-term iterative cycles of knowledge exchange between universities, communities, advocacy, and third-sector organizations such as Age Concern (Buffel 2015). Intergenerational sharing of skills and resources has also enabled a greater capacity for diverse communities to gain insights into the experience of aging across the life course, drawing connections between the needs of elders, young families, and people with disabilities (Facer, Horner and Manchester 2014). Such strategies have moved toward a more critical perspective of aging not associated with diminished abilities, but toward a recognition of the more relational and interdependent nature of aging across the life course and its connection to place and people (Gilroy 2008).

As yet little of the Age-Friendly City agenda has intersected with the proliferation of technology in citizen engagement for urban infrastructure and decision making. Digital systems that connect personal mobile phone data, such as GPS, which can be used to collect data, empowering citizens to feedback and make change in their local environment (Balaam et al. 2015, Kukka et al. 2014, Le Dantec et al. 2015), can also be used to envision a politics of place. This can exclude specific and complex experiences, such as personal and emotional identifications with place, subtleties of tacit routines, and social interactions (Cresswell 2010, 2012, Greenfield 2013, Elliot and Urry 2010). Alternative technologies have been proposed that make use of citizen data to build local knowledge to support decision making to question the use, management, representation, and sharing of data (Le Dantec et al. 2015, Taylor et al. 2015). These initiatives aim to counter visions of "smart cities" that can be considered technologically deterministic, increasing efficiency while reducing agency and control for citizens (Greenfield 2013, Mulgan 2014, Saunders and Baeck 2015). Recent frameworks for the design of technology with and for older people further call for a re-envisioning of data to support concepts of well-being, flourishing, and thriving in aging (Light, Leong and Robertson 2015, Vines et al. 2015).

Designing an approach

Design-led inquiry was chosen as an approach to experiment, raise questions, and draw attention to assumptions about the potential role of technology in the design of urban infrastructure with older citizens (McCarthy and Wright 2015). This approach was purposively provisional, contingent, and situated within the field of design research but also reaching out toward other disciplines, while interpreting and repurposing literature from social gerontology, human geography, and science and technology studies.

Researchers worked for over a year with the local City Council and the Elders' Council trying to understand the many different actors involved in the redesign of a street to improve cycling and walking infrastructure. Researchers involved initially attended public meetings as both interested citizens and committed researchers. They held demonstration days for the Elders' Council and the City Council to critique some of the technologies used to facilitate relationships. Field-notes and photographs were taken and strategy documents reviewed. Through these rich and varied engagements with both organizations, it became clear that the City Council was part of a constant struggle to negotiate technical specifications with existing infrastructure, health and safety regulations, and legal orders while also attempting to fulfill funding requirements and make the process work for people.

More intensive design activity followed, with researchers and members of the Elders' Council using audio, video, and photographic data to collect people's reflections on poetics, politics, and perceptions of place (Figure 7.1). Data collectors walked to encourage embodied and experiential research, drawing on methods developed by Crivellaro et al. (2015) and Pink (2008). Short video interpretations were created and shared with the Elders' Council about individual and collective experiences of place (see Clarke et al. 2016).

A public consultation was also organized by the City Council in the public library for three weeks where a large-scale technical map showing the proposed changes was exhibited. This was accompanied by 3-D animated mock-ups of how the street might look and feel for cyclists. Screenshots were displayed on a large board to show different parts of the route. Postcards asking for feedback on what people liked and didn't like about the scheme

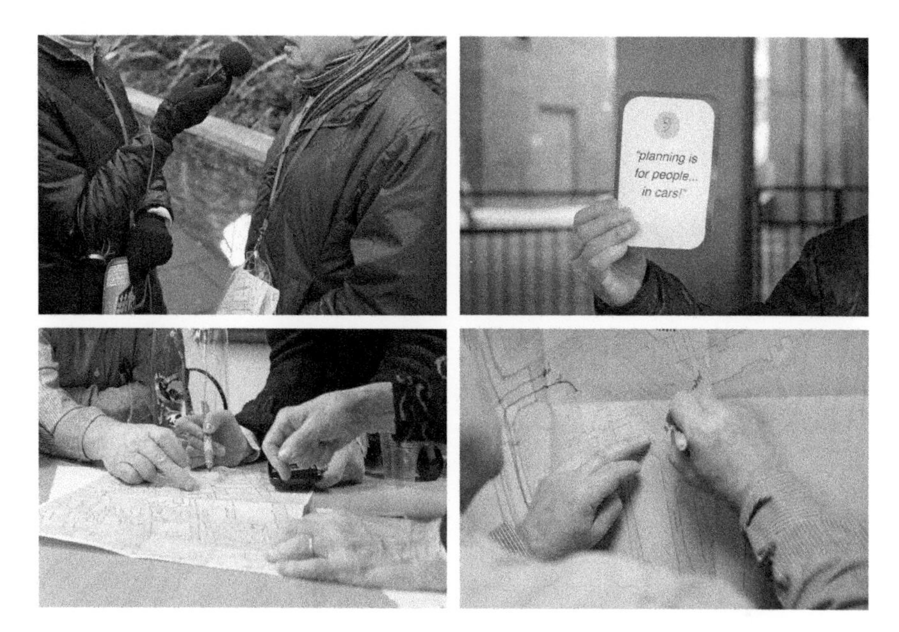

Figure 7.1 Top: Elders engaged in discussion on the street identifying areas that they felt had been poorly designed for people and primarily serviced the needs of drivers rather than pedestrians. Bottom: Elders later evaluated their routes on maps identifying important issues and comments the groups had collected on audio-visual recorded walks. Photo credit: Alexander Wilson, Open Lab, Newcastle University.

were available for people to post in a letterbox. Several members of staff involved in developing the scheme (community engagement officers, transport officers, transport managers, civil engineers) were available to answer questions and an online forum was available for residents to review plans and leave comments.

Members of the Elders' Council attended the consultation and then met to reflect on the experience of collecting data and taking part in the consultation. The group then took part in envisioning and low-fidelity design fiction activities to map alternative communication strategies and tactics for future engagement using technology (see Figure 7.2 also Blythe et al. 2016, Clarke et al. 2016). Researchers also interviewed one of the community engagement officers to gain a clearer perspective on their role.

All activities were audio-recorded and photographed by the research team and shared, selected, and annotated with the Elders' Council members. Transcripts were analyzed using a narrative approach (Clandinin and Connelly 2004, Frank 2010), particularly looking at how people expressed care through material and social interactions.

Figure 7.2 Making cardboard machines and presenting ideas for fantasy tools to improve communication between city planners and older people. Photo credit: Alexander Wilson, Open Lab, Newcastle University.

Valerie: The concerned older citizen

Valerie had been volunteering since the Elders' Council began in the early 2000s. Now in her late 80s, she was particularly proud of the work she had achieved in developing a series of assessments for the city to help older people stay active. Despite national recognition for design work developing better outdoor seating, she felt her recommendations were never followed up by those who could actually make a difference. Valerie felt the Council was trying to shut the Elders' Council out of decision-making processes. She felt the Elders' Council no longer had any direct contact with the City Council, which limited opportunities to discuss their perspectives.

She had recently tried to obtain plans for a local development in the city center. The planning files were too large to access with her limited internet bandwidth at home and so she had to use the library. The document was full of technical language and pages of legislation that she did not understand. Some of the Elders' Council had expressed an interest in using digital technology in their assessments. Valerie expressed more of an interest in direct action, protests, and shaming the Council publicly for not achieving particular goals, and was starting to work more closely with researchers and activists who worked in a similar way.

During our workshops Valerie described how walking and collecting data had enabled her to anticipate the changes.

> *I had more perceptions of what I was looking for in the actual plan. . . . Getting safely across the street, what difference would it make to that? . . . I was also looking to see if there were any indications of how it would be made more attractive. . . . That was completely lacking. There was no vision of making this an attractive street.*

In articulating an alternative future in design workshops she combined concerns for safety, lack of vision, and a feeling that the use of technology was excluding older people.

> *One of the members who is now into her early 90s . . . has a very good motorised scooter, which allows her to get around on level pavements. . . . To help other nonagenarians, who are also IT resistant she has developed a system for marking the best routes through the city using coloured wools.*

But she also proposed adapting the city for older people's scooter use through dedicated pavements and lanes, training facilities and clearer signage. Her vision highlighted the need to consider that there would be a new generation of elderly people living in cities, increasing the need for assistive technology such as scooters, and that urban designers had not considered this shift when developing new pedestrian and cycling pathways.

Abi: The community engagement officer

Abi had been working for the Council for over twenty years on community projects and was increasingly asked to get involved in public consultations, such as transport infrastructure. She felt this had happened because many Council staff lacked the confidence to engage with the community in urban infrastructure planning. Staff were wary of wasting people's time or overwhelming people with information. She felt the involvement of citizens had to be done carefully, where people could have relevant input at appropriate times, recognizing different forms of experience and expertise.

> *My role has been kind of face-to-face and doing people stuff, but its . . . also taking an overview about some of the processes and approaches [transport] were using, trying to make some sense of them, simplify them, make them more accessible . . . because*

> *things were quite confused, different stakeholders had their levels of influence mixed and muddled and so there wasn't much clarity in the process.*

Transport officers had been collecting varying amounts of information on cycle use over the past few years, but for Abi this missed some of the ways in which people could communicate their experiences of places. She proposed more effective communication that involved not only making sense of the process and plans, but also making more accessible the maps and 3-D images for the public, and structuring the feedback to enable teams.

> *There were lots of technical things about where bus stops are and accessibility stuff that came from the Elders' Council and the Disability Forum. People have got intimate knowledge and experience of moving around an area and know things that the engineers just don't know. . . . Having [those things] reconsidered and having them influence the consultation drawing is brilliant. . . . We're [Council] obsessed with ever more inventive ways of getting people to engage with us and talk to us. . . . The resources we put into analysing, interpreting and making sense of it are absolutely minimal by comparison . . . . If you can't use it and it's not going to make a difference, why the hell are you wasting people's time?*

Abi highlighted the value of the Elders' Council's contribution and expressed a belief that people could contribute their local knowledge to make a difference. Despite limited resources for the consultation, she used what she could to enhance the plan with photographs and symbols to show car lanes and landmarks. Nevertheless, she felt the general public would need significant help interpreting the plans to make sense of the abstraction and the changes that were being proposed.

Aging taken care of?

It was difficult for people such as Valerie to link what was discussed with local authorities with their final decisions for the street. Yet Valerie and Abi were engaged in very practical activities to achieve end goals important for them and their organizations. For Abi this involved taking care of meaningful communication across many different actors from citizens to engineers. For Valerie this was communicating experiences of aging in holistic and longer-term ways.

Valerie felt that the Age-Friendly City agenda for older citizens was not taken care of suitably. She had spent time in a group process of walking and collecting "data" about the experience of the street and fed this back, but felt this had not been listened to by engagement officers and engineers. Yet engagement officer Abi felt she had carefully prepared and managed the engagement process through the design of material artifacts, carefully choosing vocabulary, visual prompts, feedback resources, and sessions using a range of different media, and accessing different expertise within the local Council. She expressed care through describing her mediations between public, political, and engineering interests and enacted this through the structured resources and adaptations of technical plans to help communications. She felt that the insights from older people had been invaluable in interpreting technical details into embodied realities, which was important for giving engineers an understanding of the experiences of older citizens and had informed changes to their original plans for the street. This planning was, however, significantly focused on technical and physical accessibility issues and often conflated with disability. Valerie felt that despite the focus on accessibility the plans did not adequately consider the longer-term future mobility needs of an increasingly aging population. Care was therefore expressed by community engagement officers and engineers toward the physical environment and needs of older people, but also limited to accessibility for particular kinds of aged mobility. Despite this limited view of aging, Abi also expressed a more holistic vision to help set the "scene" for wider improvements. This idea, however, was never realized because of a lack of material resources. For Abi, the emphasis on collecting more information rather than communication of vision was the source of significant frustration. Valerie too was concerned about the lack of communication about the look and feel of the city.

Speculating on future care, technology, and aging in place

Design is important for highlighting multiple interests in planning and development (Kempenaar et al. 2016). Reflecting on design as care in the context of this urban redesign case study with citizen elders highlights complex networks and disjuncture between the different actors and agendas involved. Focusing on what care meant for Abi and Valerie through their practical and attentive "tinkering" highlights miscommunication and limitations, but also alignments in recognizing shortcomings and desires for a citywide vision for change. While existing models of citizen engagement in urban development focus on active models of participation, refocusing on acts of care helps to highlight multiple and broader concerns for aging beyond issues of active physical accessibility. While issues of accessibility remain significant, they do not help to engender ideas of flourishing and thriving, aesthetics, memory, and identity also associated with aging (Gilroy 2008) or the significance of social communities (Buffel and Philipson 2016) or social relations (Light and Akama 2014). Paying attention to the practical and material acts of care highlighted the direct and seemingly inclusive engagement of participants with materials, such as technical plans for the street, did not necessarily mean that more holistic perspectives of aging would be considered. Design fiction activities helped expand the timeframe and views of mobility to highlight more aesthetic and political issues around collective experiences of aging.

This final section offers a tentative speculation and framework for nurturing care in future participatory approaches with citizen elders and possible technologies to foster communities centered around particular issues of urban redesign. These insights are mindful of the diverse practices of care discussed with an appreciation for elder citizens as they engage with local government on issues of urban redesign.

Care for future visions

Opportunities for older adults to act as active co-investigators in realizing the Age-Friendly City agenda are already happening in UK cities (Buffel 2015). Yet the case study described here shows how older citizens can be active co-creators of visions and ideas to expand perspectives of what a future city might look and feel like for them. Technology could bring greater attention, and enable an appreciation of multiple visions and points of view to be shared and debated. At the same time care for such future visions requires attention to different modalities of contribution, their potential fragility, and how they might be suitably shared in public (see also Blythe et al. 2016).

Care for interdependent processes

The timescales and complexity of the scheme highlighted the challenges faced in making processes of urban redesign and public engagement visible and palpable. Yet taking care of and making visible some of the key aspects of work and decision making could help to highlight particular narratives of when, where, and how people's involvement really matters. Planning and engagement processes can be fragmented (Legacy 2012), yet caring for how these processes are communicated could offer further ways to draw attention to who is involved at different stages, and situate older citizens' engagement within a wider ecology of redesign. This is, however no small step, and ethnographers have long recognized the complexity and politics of making work visible and the careful navigation of interpretation and voice (Star and Strauss 1999, Suchman 1995). Technology could play a further role here in supporting particular documentation and presentation formats for time-sensitive online distribution or through more public forums such as visualizations and projections; but care also needs to be taken in managing potential conflicts in presentation, particularly because visualizations may distort or support civic participation in creating misleading perceptions of reality (Nassauer 2015).

Care for cultures of mobility

There are many different ways people use the urban environment, and yet an emphasis on transport and accessibility can sometimes limit this view. Care for multiple kinds of movement and mobilities to include aesthetics of place, cultural history, and meanings for older citizens could be further leveraged to broaden the scope of engagement strategies and expand the view of aging in place. This may include combining technology with more material approaches for documenting movement to reflect aesthetic, embodied, and affective expressions and reflections on place (Davies et al. 2012). Collection of data, in this sense may include a wider spectrum of details that repositions the use of technology to avoid narratives of standardization or objectification (Wilson 2011), and replaces them with narratives of speculation, relational connection, and material enactments (Bergmann 2016).

Care for layers of expertise

Many different layers of expertise contribute to public engagements to inform decision making and change to the urban environment (Legacy 2012), yet this is rarely explicitly articulated during the process. Some of this expertise might be considered mundane and everyday, such as embodied, situated, or tacit knowledge of movement by particular people within and around particular locations, while some expertise is associated with professions or modalities of movement such as cycling. Taking care of and caring for these layers of expertise means raising their profile to reflect on who and what expertise is valued at different stages of the engagement processes. Again technology may be more suitably positioned to support local authorities and other organizations to acknowledge, appreciate, and celebrate such expertise more publicly, rather than focusing on the collection of data and information sources. Examples of situated and artful responses to civic engagement in place (such as Caldwell and Foth 2014, Urbanowicz and Nyka 2012) offer further scope for design experimentation with public engagement and urban infrastructure that is potentially more inclusive of older people's concerns.

Conclusion

The role of technology has been purposely played down in this case study in order to bring to the fore qualities of care and reimagine a potential future that avoids tropes of digital efficiency and transparency. Foregrounding the importance of technology can often side-step more subtle negotiations, desires, and fears that potentially undermine older people's abilities to engage. In shifting the emphasis away from active participation more broadly to acts of care as "persistent tinkering," in this exploratory design-led inquiry, opportunities were highlighted to repurpose technology in more holistic ways, to foreground the diverse interests and concerns of older citizens. The use of technology for data collection was of limited value for elders without face-to-face and mediated sense-making, structured organization of information, and discussion with experts. The collection of data in and of itself could not account for the diversity of experiences or the intimate knowledge of embodied experience. Data might be expanded to include different kinds of media presentations on urban infrastructure and processes involved in its evolution, bringing together both the politics of participation and sensory cultural presentation within the built environment in more artful ways. Technology could be configured to provide opportunities for people to gather and appreciate different practices of care and engagement for continuing material deliberation and public reflection. In particular, technology could engender appreciation of the multiple constituencies associated with the complexity of future visions, cultures of mobility, and interdependent processes and layers of expertise. This is a move away from relying on data as evidence to potentially using data to create collective experiences that can navigate diverse ways of being and moving in cities.

Acknowledgments

Thank you to members of the Elders' Council whose passion and enthusiasm made this research possible. Thank you also to Newcastle City Council staff who gave their time and perspectives generously. Also thanks to Clara Crivellaro, Alexander Wilson, Danilo DiMascio, and Pete Wright at Open Lab, Newcastle University, UK; Mark Blythe, School of Design Northumbria University, UK; and Kristina Anderson, STEIM, Amsterdam, Netherlands, for their ongoing contributions to the research. This research was funded by RCUK, EPSRC Grant No: EP/K037366/1. Data supporting this publication is openly available under an "Open Data Commons Open Database License." Additional metadata are available at: 10.17634/123905-1. Please contact Newcastle Research Data Service at rdm@ncl.ac.uk for access instructions.

References

Balaam, M., Comber, R., Jenkins, E., Sutton, S., and Garbett, A. (2015), "FeedFinder: A Location-Mapping Mobile Application for Breastfeeding Women," in *Proceedings of the 33rd Annual ACM Conference on Human Factors in Computing Systems*(CHI '15), New York: ACM, 1709–18.

Bergmann, L. (2016), "Toward Speculative Data: Geographic Information for Situated Knowledges, Vibrant Matter, and Relational Spaces," *Environment and Planning D: Society and Space*, 34 (6): 971–89.

Blythe, M., Andersen, K., Clarke, R., and Wright, P. (2016), "Anti-Solutionist Strategies: Seriously Silly Design Fiction," in *Proceedings of the 2016 CHI Conference on Human Factors in Computing Systems*(CHI '16), New York: ACM, 4968–78.

Buffel, T. (2015), *Researching Age-Friendly Communities: Stories from Older People as Co-Investigators*, Manchester: The University of Manchester Library.

Buffel, T. and Phillipson, C. (2016), "Can Global Cities be 'Age-Friendly Cities'? Urban Development and Ageing Populations," *Cities*, 55: 94–100.

Buffel, T., Phillipson, C., and Scharf, T. (2012), "Ageing in Urban Environments: Developing 'Age-Friendly' Cities," *Critical Social Policy*, 32 (4): 597–617.

Caldwell, G. A. and Foth, M. (2014), "DIY Media Architecture: Open and Participatory Approaches to Community Engagement," in *Proceedings of the 2nd Media Architecture Biennale Conference: World Cities*(MAB '14), New York: ACM, 1–10.

Clandinin, D. J. and Connelly, F. M. (2004), *Narrative Inquiry. Experience and Story in Qualitative Research*, New York: Wiley.

Clarke, R., Crivellaro, C., DiMascio, D., and Wright, P. (2016), "Re-configuring Participatory Media for Citizen Elders in Urban Planning," in *Proceedings of the*

3rd Conference on Media Architecture Biennale(MAB), New York: ACM, Article 12, 10 pages.

Cresswell, T. (2010), "Towards a Politics of Mobility," *Environment and Planning D: Society & Space*, 28: 17–31.

Cresswell, T. (2012), "Mobilities II. Still," *Progress in Human Geography*, 36 (5): 645–53.

Crivellaro, C., Comber, R., Dade-Robertson, M., Bowen, S., Wright, P., and Olivier, P. (2015), "Contesting the City: Enacting the Political Through Digitally Supported Urban Walks," in *Proceedings of the 33rd Annual ACM Conference on Human Factors in Computing Systems*(CHI '15), New York: ACM, 2853–62.

Davies, S. R., Selin, C., Gano, G., and Pereira, A. G. (2012), "Citizen Engagement and Urban Change: Three Case Studies of Material Deliberation," *Cities*, 29: 351–57.

Elliot, A. and Urry, J. (2010), *Mobile Lives*, London: Taylor & Francis.

Facer, K., Horner, L., and Manchester, H. (2014), *Towards the All-Age-Friendly City: Working Paper 1 of the Bristol All-Age-Friendly City Group*, London: Future Cities Catapult.

Frank, A. (2010), *Letting Stories Breathe: A Socio-Narratology*, Chicago: University of Chicago Press.

Greenfield, A. (2013), *Against the Smart City: The City is Here for You to Use.* New York: Kindle edition, Amazon Media.

Gilroy, R. (2008), "Places that Support Human Flourishing: Lessons from Later Life," *Planning, Theory and Practice*, 9 (2): 145–63.

Kempenaar, A., Westerink, J., van Lierop, M., Brinkhuijsen, M., and van der Brink, A. (2016), "'Design Makes You Understand' – Mapping the Contributions of Designing to Regional Planning and Development," *Landscape and Urban Planning*, 149: 20–30.

Kukka, H., Luusua, A., Ylipulli, J., Suopajarvi, T., Kostakos, V., and Ojala, T. (2014), "From Cyberpunk to Calm Urban Computing: Exploring the Role of Technology in the Future Cityscape," *Journal of Technological Forecasting and Social Change*, 84: 29–42.

Le Dantec, C. A., Asad, M., Misra, A., and Watkins, K. E. (2015), "Planning with Crowdsourced Data: Rhetoric and Representation in Transportation Planning," in *Proceedings of the 18th ACM Conference on Computer Supported Cooperative Work & Social Computing*(CSCW '15), New York: ACM, 1717–27.

Legacy, C. (2012), "Achieving Legitimacy Through Deliberative Plan-Making Processes - Lessons for Metropolitan Strategic Planning," *Planning, Theory and Practice*, 13 (1): 71–87.

Leino, H. and Laine, M. (2012), "Do Matters of Concern Matter? Bringing Issues Back to Participation," *Planning Theory*, 11 (1): 89–103.

Light, A., Leong, T. W., and Robertson, T. (2015), "Ageing Well with CSCW," in *ECSCW 2015: Proceedings of the 14th European Conference on Computer Supported Cooperative Work*, 19–23 September 2015, Oslo, Norway: Springer, 295–304.

Light, A. and Akama, Y. (2014), "Structuring Future Social Relations: The Politics of Care in Participatory Practice," in *Proceedings of the 13th Participatory Design Conference: Research Papers - Volume 1* (PDC '14), Vol. 1, New York: ACM, 151–60.

March, A. (2012), *The Democratic Plan: Analysis and Diagnosis.* Oxon & New York: Routledge.

McCarthy, J. and Wright, P. (2015) *Taking [A] part: The Politics and Aesthetics of Participation in Experience-Centered Design*, Cambridge, MA: MIT Press.

Mol, A. (2008), *The Logic of Care: Health and the Problem of Patient Choice*, Oxon & New York: Routledge.

Mol, A., Moser, I., and Pols, J. (2010), *Care in Practice: On Tinkering in Clinics, Homes and Farms*, Bielefield: Verlag.

Mulgan, G. (2014), "Social and Technical Innovation, Future Cities and the Digital Economy," Presentation at *Digital Economy Conference*, Imperial College London, December 2014.

Murray, L. (2015), "Age-Friendly Mobilities: A Transdisciplinary and Intergenerational Perspective," *Journal of Transport & Health*, 2 (2): 302–07.

Nassauer, J. I. (2015), "Commentary: Visualization Verisimilitude and Civic Participation," *Landscape and Urban Planning*, 142: 170–72.

Ormerod, M., Newton, R., Phillips, J., Musselwhite, C., McGee, S., and Russell, R. (2015), *How Can Transport Provision and Associated Built Environment Infrastructure be Enhanced and Developed to Support the Mobility Needs of Individuals as they Age?* London: Government Office for Science.

Pink, S. (2008), "An Urban Tour: The Sensory Sociality of Ethnographic Place-Making," *Journal of Ethnography*, 9 (2): 175–96.

Puig de la Bellacasa, M. (2011), "Matters of Care in Technoscience: Assembling Neglected Things," *Social Studies of Science*, 41 (1): 86–106.

Ruza, J., Kim, J. I., Leung, I., Kam, C., and Yee Man Ng, S. (2015), "Sustainable Age-Friendly Cities: An Evaluation Framework and Case Study Application on Palo Alto, California," *Sustainable Cities and Society*, 14: 390–96.

Saunders, T. and Baeck, P. (2015), *Rethinking Smart Cities from the Ground Up*, London: NESTA.

Star, S. L. and Strauss, A. (1999), "Layers of Silence, Arenas of Voice: The Ecology of Visible and Invisible Work," *Computer Supported Cooperative Work* (CSCW), 8 (1): 9–30.

Steels, S. (2015), "Key Characteristics of Age Friendly Cities and Communities: A Review," *Cities*, 47: 45–57.

Suchman, L. (1995), "Making Work Visible." *Communications of the ACM*, 38 (9): 56–64.

Taylor, A. S., Lindley, S., Regan, T, Sweeney, D., Vlackokyriakos, V., Garinger, L., and Lingel, J. (2015), "Data-in-Place: Thinking Through the Relations Between Data and Community," in *Proceedings of the 33rd Annual ACM Conference on Human Factors in Computing Systems*(CHI '15), New York: ACM, 2863–72.

Urbanowicz, K. and Nyka, L. (2012), "Media Architecture – Participation Through the Senses," in *Proceedings of the 4th Media Architecture Biennale Conference: Participation*(MAB '12), New York: ACM, 51–54.

Urry, J., Birtchnell, T., Caletrio, J., and Pollastri, S. (2014), *Living in the City—Future of Cities: Working Paper*, London: Foresight, Government Office for Science.

Vines J., Pritchard, G., Wright, P., Olivier, P., and Brittain, K. (2015), "An Age Old Problem: Examining the Discourses of Ageing in HCI and Strategies for Future Research," *ACM Transactions on Computer-Human Interaction*, 22: 1, Article 2 (February 2015), 27 pages.

World Health Organisation (WHO) (2007), *Global Age Friendly Cities: A Guide*, Geneva, Switzerland: WHO.

Wilson, M. (2011), "Data Matter(s): Legitimacy, Coding and Qualifications-of-Life," *Environment and Planning D: Society and Space*, 29 (5): 857–72.

8

Magic and Dementia: Designing Culture to Empathize with Dementia

Yanki C. Lee, Niels Hendriks, and Albert S. Y. Tsang

Introduction—the Open Dementia project

The Open Dementia project (2015–17) started with the involvement of experts, the formal caregivers, who are confronted with dementia on a daily basis. We, a group of design researchers, conducted mapping workshops with dementia experts to unfold their tacit knowledge. Collectively we identified the eleven most common symptoms of dementia, which we divided into two stages: "mild" (1–5) and "moderate" (6–11).

1. Memory loss
2. Decline of orientation
3. Decline in problem-solving skills
4. Decline in judgment
5. Visual and spatial problems
6. Decline in motor planning
7. Difficulty in following instructions
8. Difficulty in communicating
9. Misusing objects
10. Decrease in coordination and motor function
11. Decreased ability to focus or concentrate

Dementia is an umbrella term used to describe a variety of psychiatric and cognitive symptoms. Psychiatric symptoms may include personality changes, depression, hallucinations, and delusions. On a cognitive level people with dementia (from mild to moderate) mostly suffer from a deterioration of memory (such as amnesia), difficulties in language and communication (aphasia), the inability to perform purposeful movements (apraxia), and/or orientation in time and place (agnosia). Furthermore, the large majority belong to the group of older persons who might need to deal with physical ailments like impaired eyesight, impaired hearing, or lack of physical coordination. The way dementia affects daily life is different for each person. One may or may not suffer from a diminished capacity to communicate verbally (aphasia) and while one person suffers heavily from hallucinations, another will not. What is common to every person with dementia is that their daily activity and capacity to live a "normal" life is heavily affected and their understanding of and acting in the world might be perceived as strange.

Because of its complexity, dementia is mysterious for many people. While the medical and social care experts are busy developing cures and services to help patients with dementia and their carers, the contribution of design researchers could lie in enabling the public to understand this mystery.

With the risk of exaggeration, in Hong Kong dementia is considered to be part of the natural aging process, and, thus, receives little special attention. Additionally, dementia is being "kept" outside of public life in Chinese society. Dementia suffers from some level of stigmatization, being linked to mental illness and is therefore not openly discussed within the close group of family and friends.

To assist the public understanding of dementia, our partners at a dementia research/care center in Hong Kong asked us to develop a dementia experience toolkit. The toolkit enables those not familiar with dementia to experience dementia directly. Our endeavor to encourage the general public to have an open mind to this stigmatized condition is called the Open Dementia project.

Designing cultural model of aging

Another important role of design research is to experiment with the "Cultural Model of Aging" (Lee 2012). This new model of aging acknowledges both the traditional models, medical and social dimensions of aging, and, in addition, attaches more importance to capturing how older people tackle their own aging issues. Fortunately, like many developed societies, there are a variety of charities and NGOs in Hong Kong who are working hard to provide quality care services to address the physical, psychological, and biological issues of senior citizens. With better health and higher education and less physically demanding jobs available today, more mature persons become active elders who can stay longer in the labor force. Government policy encourages companies to employ more mature workers. Additionally, active elders are keen to contribute more to the community and develop their own interests. They are demanding a new, inclusive service model.

Both models are developing rapidly since the government's blueprint for elderly care of 2014. The policy has two focuses: "aging in place as the core, institutional care as back-up" for those with weaker physical conditions who require support, and "active aging," a social environment for able-bodied senior citizens.

"Ageing in itself is not (just) a policy problem to be solved" (Bazalgette 2011). It is clear that there is room for new ways to address aging. Public policy makers and the social service sector are developing ways to solve the problems of aging in Hong Kong from medical and social perspectives. Design research could bring new contributions to aged culture, as well as link different generations and professions to co-create a better future and come up with innovative and holistic ways to tackle aging-related matters. Our role is to take the concept of aged culture and use the ingenuity of everyday life to inspire design and innovation. One of the first actions to make this a reality is to have the public understand dementia as a culture and not as a loss.

Designing dementia as a culture

How can we articulate the experience of dementia as culture? We do not wish to claim that people with dementia are part of a single culture, for example, the deaf culture (Padden, Humphries & Padden 2009). The person with dementia has his or her own reality, a subjective interpretation and understanding of everyday life, with his or her own ways of behaving that are rooted in the past and his or her relation to and interpretation of the present. The everyday reality of a person with dementia is hard to fathom; their behavior might be perceived as abnormal. We are aware that this project cannot make transparent a person's reality or claim to alter perceptions about dementia. In line with the principles of aged culture, we wish to make visible part of the reality of the person with dementia and show how the life of a person with dementia can be filled with ingenious thinking, moments of joy and surprise. Dementia Culture captures the ingenuity of these patients' everyday lives and can inspire design and innovation (Lee 2012) to reduce stigmatization on the disease.

A character with dementia

We realized at an early stage that to connect with the public about dementia we should tell a "gripping" story. We created a character dealing with dementia. We decided that the character should not have any suggestion of social status, age, gender, or even race. The character has a humanoid physique that can perform daily tasks and has the facial expressions to show psychological states. With reference to the written form of dementia in Chinese, the team chose to highlight the brain as the standout point of the character. The illustrator who created the blue character of 腦人 (Brain-person) (Figure 8.1) added the eraser over the brain to represent the degeneration of the organ.

A large portion of people in Hong Kong define dementia and people with dementia as "strange," "bizarre," outside of the normal, something that is not a person, but more of a body acting strangely (a man, not a person; a static disintegrated someone, not a historic and culturally embedded person). The interplay between what is normal and what is abnormal is at stake when working with persons with dementia. The symptoms lead normal or "neuro-typical" persons to respond with distance, anxiety, or reluctance to get in contact with the person with dementia. Our goal with Brain-person is to reduce this type of negativism and develop the understanding of dementia, letting people with dementia be perceived as fun and not as a dehumanized body.

The Demented City Map

The second step of the disruptive methodology was the development of the Open Dementia City Map (Figure 8.2). It was based on a speculative question, "What if everyone in the city has dementia?" As the Brain-persons form the main population of the "Demented City," the map shows that being perceived as

Figure 8.1 Development of Brain-person. Illustration by Don Mak.

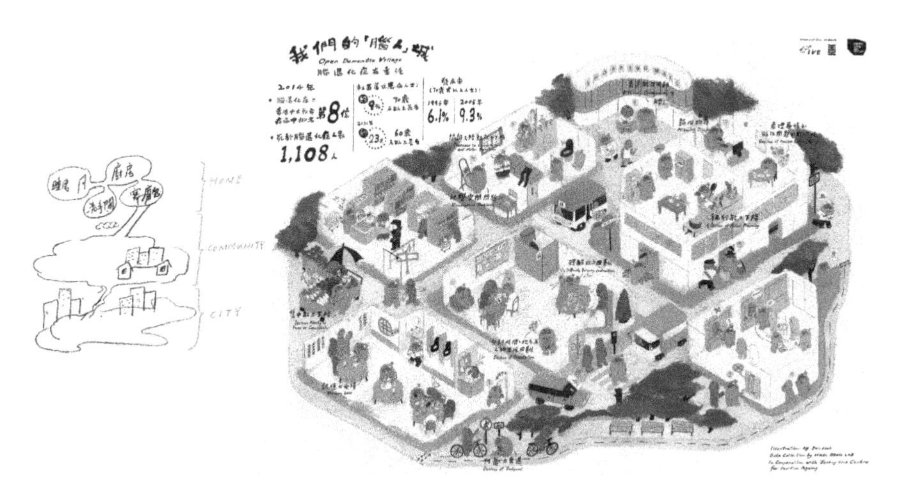

Figure 8.2 Structure of the Dementia map (left) and Open Dementia map (right).

abnormal, irrational, or out-of-the-ordinary is not intrinsic to dementia, but is shaped through the environment and others in the city.

The perception of dementia is highly dependent on the value that is given to the self. Normal and pathological aging (like with dementia) tends to overlap and the demarcation between them is set arbitrarily or as part of a social construction to create order from disorder (Hashmi 2009). Societies in the West, which value individualism, autonomy, and agency, tend to view the person with dementia as "not normal" or "outside of society"; hence the focus on exclusion and segregation, taking the person with dementia to residential care facilities and the stripping of their agency. This perspective is heavily linked to the carer or people surrounding the person with dementia. When a mother with dementia becomes dependent on the support of her child or partner, the agency, individualism, and autonomy of that family member is fundamentally challenged. When we in society are confronted with "the naked truth of the shattered lives" (Longmore, Wilkinson & Rajagopalan 2005), segregation, exclusion, and dehumanization are just around the corner. This relates to the social model of disability, which states that a person is disabled not through the condition, disease, or disability but through society's response. This suggests that the way dementia is perceived comes from the way we perceive the self and how our society responds to the changed self. According to SCOPE, UK's leading disability charity, "the social model of disability says that disability is caused by the way society is organized, rather (than) by a person's impairment or difference" (Scope 2017). This leads to the final discussion of visualization of dementia at different levels: the domestic level, the community level, and the urban level.

Objects with dementia

In dementia care, the ruling paradigm is Kitwood's person-centered care (Kitwood 1993), which starts with "seeing the person with dementia as an individual with rights and a need for sensitive interaction" (Brooker 2004) both in their care and in the way they are treated in society. Though person-centered care can mean different things, it can be summarized by the VIPS acronym: (V) aluing people with dementia and those who care for them; Treating people as (I)ndividuals; Looking at the world from the perspective of the (P)erson with dementia; A positive (S)ocial environment in which the person living with dementia can experience relative well-being.

Empathy is one of the key components of person-centered care. To try to gain insight in the way a person with dementia perceives the world is the stepping-stone to empathy. As the empathy-altruism hypothesis (Batson et al 1991) states, feelings of empathy toward another human being will evoke altruistic motivations and thus empathy seems to be key to acting in the interests of persons with dementia.

Movies such as *Still Alice* or the French movie *Amour* try to tell the story of life with dementia, opening up this fragile topic to a mainstream audience. Although these provide an insightful look into the world of a person with dementia, it is still hard to appreciate living with dementia. Direct contact and spending time with a person with dementia is one effective, but time-consuming form of gaining empathy (Lindsay et al. 2012).

The Open Dementia project intended to find an easily reproduced way to have participants better understand the world of a person with dementia, or even let citizens immerse themselves in the world of dementia. The end-goal is to have participants change their response when confronted in day-to-day interaction with persons with dementia.

From this care paradigm and the notion of empathy, we chose to conceptualize the toolkit to engage the participants actively through "acting out" (Stethe & Baernstein 2006) elements of dementia and evoke "resonance" feelings (Halpern 1993) (feeling as though you have dementia). We developed eleven sets of "demented objects" that can magically dement the participants temporarily (Figure 8.3). These "demented objects" can help people to experience dementia in three ways:

- Disabling tools—stimulating tools to disable your capability;
- Confusing tools—twisted tools to make users confused;
- Performance tools—disrupting games for users to "perform" being demented in a group.

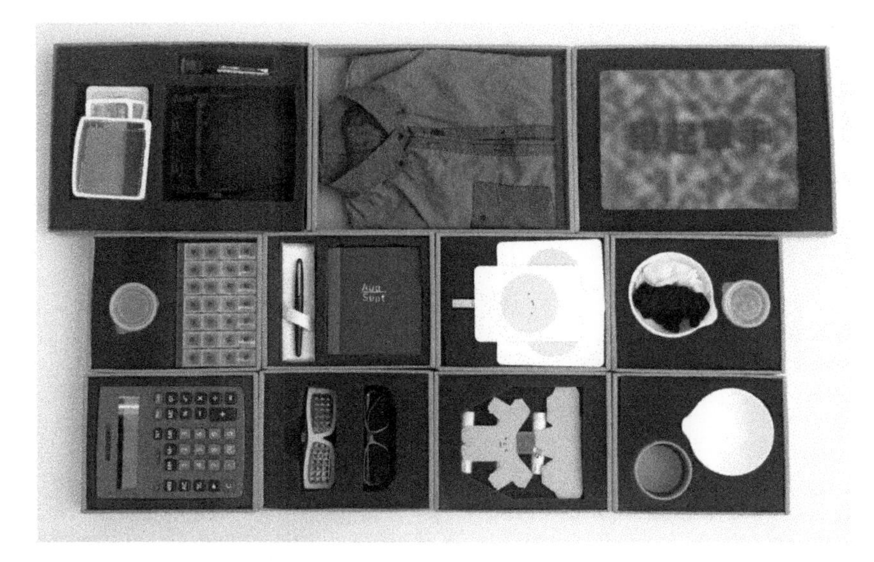

Figure 8.3 Dementia Experience tools—Demented objects.

Each of the "demented objects" corresponds to a symptom of dementia, and can temporarily cause dementia symptoms in the participant. Table 8.1 shows how the eleven demented objects can make people experience dementia.

Traditional empathic tools focus on stimulation of a specific physical or mental impairment. A good example is Ford's Third Age Suit, which gives the wearer the reduced mobility or impaired eyesight of a 100-year-old person. Simulating a cognitive condition such as dementia is more complex. Moreover, empathic tools that focus on physical and bodily experiences may limit the possibility of gaining empathy, as they disregard the cognitive, mental, or social consequences of a certain condition. The challenge of replicating the cognitive condition of dementia poses both a challenge and a possibility.

The "demented objects" in the toolkit mimic everyday situations (like using an elevator) or artifacts (like a sign or a pillbox). There is, however, a "twist" or a bit of magic involved in the use of the objects or the performance of the everyday situations: the seemingly normal pill box seems to have its own logic (mixing up days) and its instructions turn out to be illogical. For example, in the tool focusing on memory loss, the participant is asked to write down a complex series of events in a diary. In the course of doing this, one has to go back reviewing earlier dates only to find out that they have disappeared from your agenda. By using "magical ink" that disappears after five minutes, the tool causes a feeling of loss and bewilderment similar to what a person with dementia feels when confronted with their failing short-term memory.

Table 8.1 The eleven games with the demented objects

Type of tools	Activity name	Corresponding symptoms	Activity
Disabling tools	1. 迷失的眼鏡 (Vision-limiting glasses)	Decline in orientation	Participants wear disorienting glasses, limiting their view to only one side. The participants are asked to find cards, which are scattered, about the room by the other participants.
	2. 出門帶啲乜 (Pick Me Up before You Go)	Visual and spatial problems	Participants wear a pair of special glasses that block vision through reflection. They are asked to pick something essential for going out.
	3. 執唔執到豆？ (Sort the Beans)	Decline in motor planning	Participants wear gloves to reduce the sensitivity of their fingertips and sort beans into different bowls.
Confusing tools	4. 日期與活動 (Date and Activities)	Memory loss	Participants are asked to mark down several appointments in a notebook. But the ink disappears in a few minutes, which makes the participant unable to read their notes when asked to do so later.
	5. 齊齊計數 (Let's Calculate)	Decline in problem-solving skills	Participants are asked to do simple calculations, but they are provided with a rigged calculator, which makes it impossible to perform the task.
	6. 準時食啱藥 (Take the Right Pills)	Decline in judgment	Participants are asked to sort pills into a typical multi-slot pillbox, with tedious and confusing instructions.
	7. 製作腦人 (Making the Brain-person)	Misusing objects	The participants are asked to use the glue-pen provided to make a paper model of the Brain-person. But only one of the glue-pens is real glue; the others are stuffed with lipstick or candle wax.

Table 8.1 Continued

	8. 著襯衫 (Wearing it Right)	Decreased coordination and motor function	Participants are asked to wear and button up a long-sleeved shirt, but the buttons do not align with the buttonholes and the collar does not fold properly.
Performance tools	9. 做到啲乜 (What can you do?)	Difficulty following instructions	One of the participants will be the "instructor" and another participant will be asked to stand near the instructor and act out gestures shown in the instructor's cue cards. The cue cards show different information depending on the distance of the viewer. Hence the spectators will find it strange that the participant always performs something different from what the cue cards suggest.
	10. 有口難言 (Charades)	Difficulty communicating	A participant is asked not to speak, and to communicate to other participants that he or she is suffering from constipation.
	11. 數銀仔 (Counting the coins)	Decreased ability to focus or concentrate	One participant is asked to sort numerous coins into different bowls, while another participant is asked to distract and confuse the person who is counting by murmuring other numbers into his or her ear.

Using magic and performance to embrace dementia as culture

The tools discussed in this chapter were partly set up by a nonprofit organization that researches dementia and has run a care home for dementia patients since 2000. Its main goal is to promote dementia care and the knowledge of dementia in general. The center also focuses on the training of formal and informal caregivers and the education of the general public. For these last two objectives, the center reached out to two of the authors to see where design can aid in these goals. The main project question was: How can design aid in (1) giving an insight into what dementia is; (2) helping a general audience understand that the prevalence of dementia is quite high and that persons with dementia are thus an integral part of our society? By providing these insights, the toolkit is intended to raise empathy for people with dementia.

Entering the magical world of dementia

To overcome the challenge of understanding dementia, we used the notion of magic. Magic can be defined as "mysterious tracks: a quality that makes something seem removed from everyday life, especially in a way that gives delight" (New Oxford 2001), taking into account that which goes beyond the everyday life. Further, magic is defined by cultural anthropologist Kottak (2004) as the "use of supernatural techniques to accomplish specific aims." Keesing and Strathern's (1998) definition focuses on how magic "represents human attempts to manipulate chains of cause and effect between events that to us are unrelated, in ways that to us are irrational."

From the last two definitions we borrowed the notions of "supernatural" and "irrational." While the latter can be seen as a negative term, both focus on that what is different from normal, cannot always be explained logically, or goes beyond what is natural. Combining these three definitions we see a tension between the everyday and the supernatural, the rational and the irrational, the normal and the abnormal. The design team used these frictions as a starting point, trying to make artifacts that would play with all these tensions, being everyday and out-of-the-ordinary, rational and irrational.

Performing dementia

The act of performance is important for "the demented objects." The objects or everyday situations are not merely used, but are performed according to instructions (a script), with some participants in the role of the person with dementia while others become the spectators responding to the person's behavior. Performance is an ideal tool which takes the participants into a magical world, and, just like characters in traditional theater, their perspectives of the world are different from those of the spectators.

Through the performance, the participants not only physically feel the struggle of everyday tasks for a person with dementia, they also feel the frustration of being misunderstood, and the inability to communicate. For example, using the oddly buttoned shirt or calculate with the tricky calculator (Figure 8.4), participants would be performing something familiar. After all, the struggle of dementia is not only physical, or physiological, but also social and interpersonal, and it is of the utmost importance for the people around demented person to be aware of this.

Binder & Foverskov (2010) have already related design to performance as well as to the imaginary world and everyday life. Developing the theory of

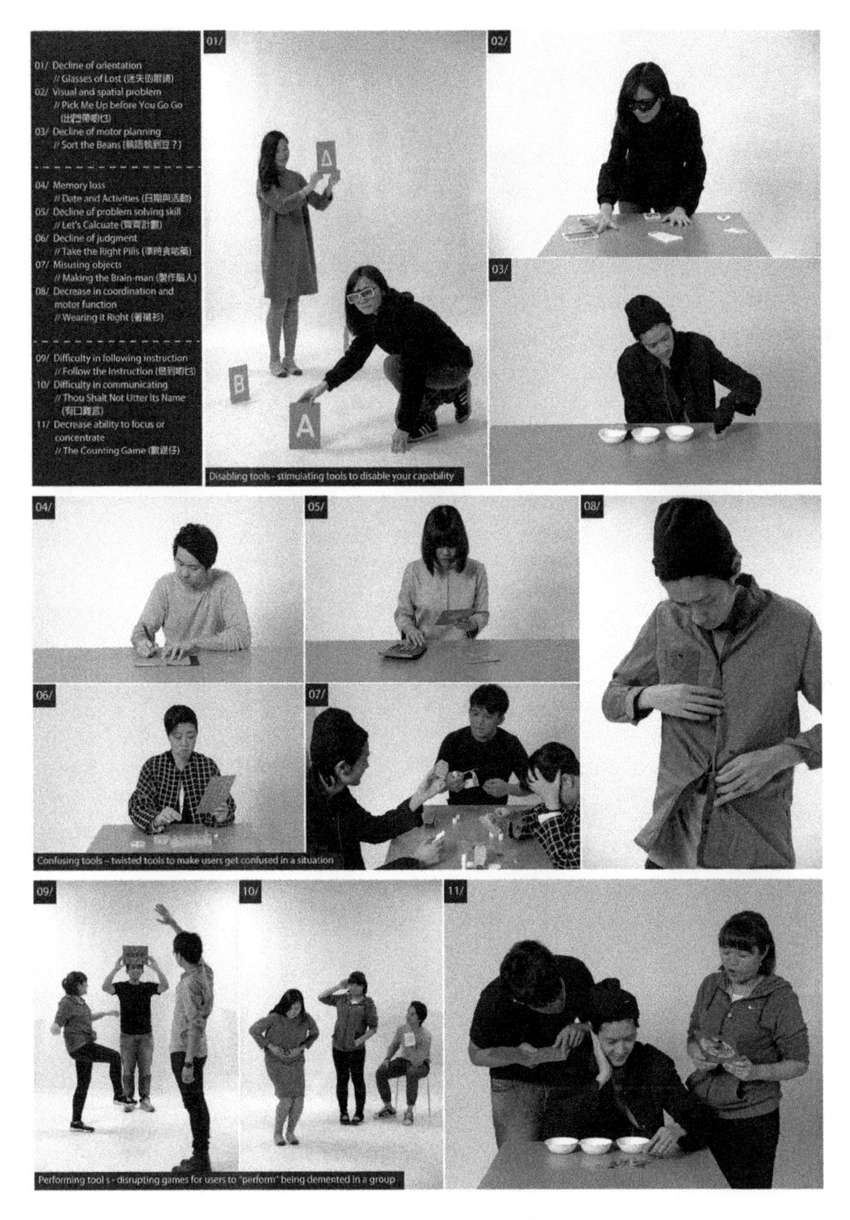

Figure 8.4 Performing the Dementia Experience tools.

symbolic interactionism and Victor Turner, Binder & Forversfov argue that "design as performance is precisely to connect the multifacetted role-playing of the everyday with the playful exploration of the 'what-if' of the theatre." The "demented objects" tap into this relation between design tools and theater, and at the same time the imaginary (magical) world and the everyday.

Conclusion

In 2015, we were asked to research, design, and prototype a set of "empathy tools" to enable people to better understand the illness of dementia. From its launch in April 2016, the toolkit was rolled out for training across Hong Kong communities. The Open Dementia project opens up a new way of viewing the culture of care. Design research as a new discipline could contribute to a new approach to aged culture as well as linking different generations and professions to co-create a better future and come up with innovative and holistic ways to tackle aging-related matters. Care would no longer be standardized, but the product of the co-creation process.

This particular project shows the potential of the development of the concept of "culture of dementia," which aims to change people's perception of the condition. It tries to foreground how joy and love can have a place in the life of a person with dementia and how meaningful, humoristic, and positive interactions can be omnipresent in daily life. By heralding this positive perspective, the research aims to inspire designers to develop more appropriate designs to address this mystery while other experts work on cures. For example, could designers create a storytelling tool for carers to capture the patients' happy moments? Can a tool help us to enter the "magical world" of dementia, to see things differently and create a different world after the experience?

Design and design research could also take the concept of aged culture or "culture of dementia" and use the ingenuity of everyday life that we believe could be captured and then inspire design and innovation.

Acknowledgment

We would like to thank HKDI DESIS Lab Graduate Trainees (Greta Kwok, Louise Wong and Cyril Lee) and administrative and financial support of HKDI (Hong Kong Design Institute). Special thanks is also given to our content provider, collaborator, and client, Hong Kong Jockey Club Centre of Positive Ageing, which is Asian expert in dementia research and a care provider.

References

Batson, C. Daniel, et al. (1991), "Empathic Joy and the Empathy-Altruism Hypothesis," *Journal of Personality and Social Psychology*, 61 (3): 413.

Bazalgette, Z., et al. (2011) *Coming of Age*, Demos. https://www.demos.co.uk/ accessed July 26, 2017

Binder, T. and Foverskov, M. (2010), "Design as Everyday Theatre," in J. Halse, E. Brandt, B. Clark, and T. Binder (eds.), *Rehearsing the Future*, København: The Danish Design School Press, 204–05.

Brooker, D. (2004), "What is Person-Centred Care in Dementia?" *Reviews in Clinical Gerontology*, 13 (3): 215–22.

Halpern J. (1993), "Empathy: Using Resonance Emotions in the Service of Curiosity," in H. Spiro, M. G. McCrea Curnen, E. Peschel, D. St James (eds.), *Empathy and the Practice of Medicine*, New Haven, CT: Yale University Press, 160–73.

Hashmi, M. (2009), "Dementia: An Anthropological Perspective," *International Journal of Geriatric Psychiatry*, 24 (2): 207–12.

Keesing, Roger M. and Andrew J. Strathern (1998), *Cultural Anthropology: A Contemporary Perspective*, 3rd ed., New York: Harcourt Brace.

Kitwood T. (1993), "Towards a Theory of Dementia Care: The Interpersonal Process," *Ageing and Society*, 13 (1); 51–67.

Kottak, Conrad P. (2004), *Anthropology: The Exploration of Human Diversity*, 10th ed., New York: McGraw-Hill.

Lee, Y. (2012), *The Ingenuity of Ageing: For Designing Social Innovation*, supported by the Department of Business, Innovation and Skills (BIS) and Royal College of Art, London UK, ISBN978-1-907342-46-2.

Lindsay, S., Brittain, K., Jackson, D., Ladha, C., Ladha, K., and Olivier, P. (2012), "Empathy, Participatory Design and People with Dementia," Presented at the *Proceedings of the 2012 ACM annual conference on Human Factors in Computing Systems*, ACM, 521–30.

Longmore M., Wilkinson I. B., and Rajagopalan S. (2005), *Oxford Handbook of Clinical Medicine*, Oxford: Oxford University Press.

New Oxford Dictionary of English (1998, 2001), 1111. Oxford University Press, UK.

Padden, C., Humphries, T., and Padden, C. (2009), *Inside Deaf Culture*, Cambridge MA: Harvard University Press.

SCOPE (2017), *The Social Model of Disability*, access via http://www.scope.org.uk/about-us/our-brand/social-model-of-disability

Stethe uyseusingpien, K. A. and Baernstein, A. (2006), "Educating for Empathy," *Journal of General Internal Medicine*, 21 (5): 524–30, http://doi.org/10.1111/j.1525-1497.2006.00443.x

9

Cities of Homefullness: A Proposition

Neal Haslem, Keely Macarow, Guy Johnson, and Marcus Knutagård

Introduction

This chapter introduces *Homefullness*, an art and design-led response to the housing crisis. It then describes current housing conditions in two cities on opposite sides of our world: Melbourne and Malmö. *Homefullness* is a multidisciplinary art and design-led inquiry into the ongoing, seemingly intractable issue of homelessness and housing stress. It investigates how art and design processes and artifacts, applied through co-design methods, can work with manifold stakeholders to produce innovation in response and conceptualization of social issues and, through this, inform future social policy and planning. The design principles and philosophy underlying *Homefulless* as a co-design project are discussed. In addition, the latest iteration of the *Homefullness* project, 'Cities of Homefullness', is examined. This project aims to provide an aspirational declaration for cities to confront the injustices of homelessness and housing and to imagine and co-design sustainable, equitable, and creative housing strategies.

The *Homefullness* project

Levels of housing instability, homelessness, social dislocation and unrest are a concern for cities around the globe. Our project, *Homefullness*, has grappled with this issue since it was first presented in the Homelessness Design Challenge, exhibited in Melbourne's Federation Square in 2012 (Australian Design Review 2011). The first move of the project was to re-orient issues of homelessness and housing stress by introducing a new word, and with it a concept: homefullness. Through a simple act of naming, *Homefullness* deliberately confronts the intractable housing issues which seem almost a necessary part of cities. With *Homefullness* the focus is shifted speculatively toward an imagined city that maintains a state of homefullness as a necessity for all its inhabitants.

The basic premise of the project is that art and design processes (and material artifacts; see Figure 9.1 the *Homefullness* manifesto tea-towel) can enable situations of human interaction that allow the re-imagining of contemporary conditions. This collective re-imagining—and the collaborations

Figure 9.1 The first *Homefullness* artifact "Homefullness #1" a tea-towel printed with the *Homefullness* manifesto (photo Neal Haslem).

and communities that are created through it—opens consciousness, collectively, toward alternative housing futures for our cities.

The project involves designers, artists, sociologists, social workers, and housing researchers as a core group and acts to facilitate an ongoing conversation through which all stakeholders—individuals and social entities—meet to produce innovative responses to housing issues.

Homefullness asks how art and design methodologies can activate ideas and motivate community programs to move toward affordable housing for all. Figure 9.2 shows one of these discussions, the *Homefullness* roundtable from late 2015, during which diverse stakeholders working on, and affected by, issues of homelessness and housing stress in both Australia and Sweden, met to explore innovative tactics and responses to these complex issues.

The project creates spaces that bring together different parties in an enduring conversation about what might constitute homefullness. These are spaces of transdisciplinary knowledge, beyond specific disciplinary boundaries and epistemologies; they allow new connections, bridges, and generative collaborations between all parties.

Cities of Homefullness, the latest move for the *Homefullness* project, asks cities to declare their intention to move toward a state of homefullness. *Cities of*

Figure 9.2 *Homefullness* roundtable at RMIT University, Melbourne, Australia, in December 2015 with visiting researchers from Sweden (photo Neal Haslem).

Homefullness remains propositional; it is a *move toward*, it is an *aim*, it is a *collective agreement* that homefullness is a shared value in an ongoing conversation.

The problem of homelessness and housing stress in Melbourne and Malmö

Although historically people have moved to cities to improve their lives, inequality among those living in cities remains a challenge. Cities that successfully manage these issues are those that provide accommodation, and support the establishment of homes, households, a sense of belonging, and community for all new arrivals (including refugees and migrants)—what we term "homefullness." How can homefullness be theorized, practiced, and integrated into the cities of Malmö and Melbourne?

Melbourne is the second largest city in Australia with a population over 4,500,000. It is located in the state of Victoria on a bay in the south east of the continent and has a large suburban sprawl that covers 9,990 square kilometers. Malmö, on the southwest coast of Sweden, has a population of 320,000. Malmö is very close to Copenhagen, Denmark, with a bridge joining the two cities since 2000. While Melbourne and Malmö have vast differences in size, they both have crises with homelessness and an extreme lack of housing affordability. Although the crisis is different in each city, authorities in Melbourne and Malmö react to public tensions around homelessness in similar ways.

Over recent years, homelessness has become more visible in Melbourne. In September 2016, the City of Melbourne counted 247 rough sleepers in the city, an increase of 74 percent from two years earlier (City of Melbourne 2016). A few months later a flood of media reports suggested the City of Melbourne was in the midst of a "homelessness crisis." City councilors and politicians reacted quickly to the press reports, but not always sensibly or with compassion. In February 2017 the Melbourne City Council attempted to introduce a by-law that banned camping in the city, effectively outlawing rough sleeping, while the Victorian state government's response focused on the provision of temporary accommodation and support.

Malmö's homelessness crisis emerged earlier. After the Million Homes Programme (1965–74), homelessness in Sweden declined dramatically (Hall and Vidén 2005). When homelessness returned to Sweden in the late 1980s the profile of the homeless population had changed. In 2005, there were

694 homeless adults in Malmö. By 2016 that number had increased to 1,740, of whom 30 were sleeping rough. In addition, there were 887 children who were homeless. In just over a decade the total number of homeless people in Malmö increased by over 250 percent.

During the past decade, Swedish authorities have explained the rise in homelessness largely in structural terms. They point to the impact of radical changes in housing policy in 1991 (Hedin et al. 2011) that led to a highly deregulated housing market. Despite considerable population growth in Malmö the construction of new buildings has not kept pace.

Many people deemed homeless in Sweden live in apartments sub-let from social services. This system is referred to as the secondary housing market. Tenants are subject to strict regulations, and can be evicted at a week's notice. Most of the people in this group (just over 830), often referred to as the structural homeless, were born in another country and most homeless children belong to this category. Most are on income support, which effectively excludes them from the private rental market and traps them in the secondary housing market (Benjaminsen and Knutagård 2016).

In recent years homelessness has been exacerbated by the humanitarian crisis predominately caused by the war in Syria. During 2015, over 160,000 asylum seekers entered Sweden, most of them through Malmö. This led to more restrictive border controls, dramatically slowing the commuting between Sweden and Denmark. This made cross-border travel for employment impossible. Asylum seekers were pushed back to the country where they first arrived in Europe. This made Swedish municipalities responsible for housing refugees. Competition for scarce housing increased and municipalities set up emergency shelters in temporary housing alternatives. The municipalities have continued to use temporary housing rather than provide permanent housing.

In responding to the homelessness crises, authorities in both Melbourne and Malmö continue to apply "last resort" solutions inappropriate for people who have only recently found themselves homeless (Knutagård 2009). Whenever homelessness increases, night-shelters and other types of emergency housing become a recurrent solution (Knutagård and Nordfeldt 2007). These sorts of solutions can exacerbate the issues in the long term.

In Melbourne, despite a media focus on the homeless who are sleeping rough, the majority of homeless people live temporarily with friends, in boarding houses or caravans, or in severely overcrowded dwellings (Australian Bureau of Statistics 2012). While the public tends to think that mental health and addiction are the primary causes of homelessness, for most homeless people the primary problem is a lack of affordable housing. Australian housing is among the most expensive in the world. Rising house prices deter entry into the housing market for lower and even middle-income groups. This puts increasing pressure on the private rental market, which comprises nearly 25 percent of Australia's housing stock. In Australia, renting is not considered a long-term tenure in its own right. There is little discussion of security of tenure for renters. Landlords are legally able to issue 120-day "no reason" eviction notices, irrespective of the length of time the tenant has been in the property or the condition they have kept the property in.

High housing prices, the tight private rental market and the lack of security of tenure drive inequities in housing, which are further compounded by a lack of social housing. Unlike Sweden, social housing in Australia has always been limited, amounting to around 5 percent of the nation's housing stock. Despite strong evidence that public housing offers the strongest protection against homelessness and housing instability (Johnson et al. 2015), Australian governments have neglected public housing. From the mid-1990s, public housing declined in real terms and as a percentage of the nation's housing stock (Groenhart and Burke 2014).

In Australia the primary response to homelessness is through Specialist Homelessness Services (SHS), of which there are around 1,500 across the country. SHS typically provide case management for short- or medium-term temporary accommodation. High demand means that many people do not get into temporary accommodation and those that do are often forced to stay for long periods because there is no alternative. Evaluations of the SHS have found that a lack of exit points was the major factor undermining the effectiveness of the program.

The need for homefullness

For many people in Australia home ownership, what was once referred to as the "Great Australian Dream," is increasingly unlikely. The housing crisis continues unaddressed. The current concept of housing as an investment accelerates the boom in prices and loses sight of the meaning of housing and home. There are concerns that any sudden change to policy might induce economic shock.

It is clear that contemporary society needs to reimagine the way it views housing if it is going to be able to respond to the current crises in homelessness and housing stress. When individual economic benefit remains a central motivation, it is difficult to conceptualize the planning and building of housing for any other reasons. Australian housing policy responses continue to be narrowly focused on short-term economies. It is important that we incorporate energy efficiency, sustainability, and adequate physical and cultural infrastructure into all new housing. In addition, it is important that we move toward more sustainable future-proofed models for housing which are resilient to and help counteract extreme weather events, economic insecurity, and the political extremism that continues to fuel social, personal, cultural, and political uncertainty and vulnerability.

The reimagining and development of the housing that we desperately need for our cities must cross sectors, governance, opportunities, cultures, and language and include people from diverse communities and expertise. The collective imagining, co-design, and development of a community of homefullness (rather than one of homelessness) provides a strategy for this change.

Homefullness in our cities

What could it mean if we were to declare homefullness as a necessity for our cities? What would this mean for our ways of living and acting in the world? If we were to use words and enact deeds that were positive and affirmative, would this mean that we might make a shift to our personal thinking and everyday lives? Would these small changes lead to wider changes in the ways that we described, organized, and developed our housing and our communities?

A consequence of the commodification of housing is a separation of housing from social relations. Yet adequate housing is crucial to personal and social inclusion and cohesion. A secure home allows individuals, families, households to have personal, communal, physical, and intimate relations. It provides an abode to grow, relax, nourish, commune, seek solace, and party. We can live out the narratives of our daily lives in the knowledge that we know we will wake, tend to our ailments and illnesses, return from work and school, cook our evening meal, and sleep at night.

With this in mind, it is important that we turn to new ways of thinking and acting in our cities toward housing. We propose that we discuss, plan, develop, and build cities of homefullness where housing is focused on and intrinsic to community well-being, creativity, engagement, development, and empowerment. How might this work? Housing as it is currently designed, planned, and purchased continues to involve a limited number of actors. Instead, the *Homefullness* project proposes that co-design, with its capacity to support multiple viewpoints and potential for innovative ideation, provides a way to move away from current limited concepts of housing, which is primarily viewed as a financial commodity.

Homefullness and design practice

Human-centered design (and its close relative user-centered design) arose through a need to produce better technologically driven artifacts. As information technology developed in the late twentieth century, it became clear that although the technology and its functionality were increasing, it was not always user-friendly. Products were designed and implemented with a focus on the product and its purpose rather than the people who needed (or were required to) use it. Human-centered design is a conceptual turn from privileging the *foreseen use of a product* toward privileging *the potential users of that product*. Human-centered design thinks about how designers can work with the potential users/humans of products in order to design better "products" (Robertson and Simonsen 2012).

Originally the products being re-imagined with human-centered design were computers, computer programs, phones, and other technological devices. These products, particularly the digital ones, lacked an intrinsic usability and so required designers to find new ways for humans to live and work with them. Methods of prototyping (workshopping "work-in-progress" products), empathy-mapping (thinking and visualizing what the users might want/need), persona-mapping (imagining what types of users might want the product and what their needs might be), cultural probes (designing artifacts which are distributed among stakeholders to collect cultural and personal understandings), focus groups and interviews, and attention to analyzing the "data" that such methods produced (customer journey maps) were all developed in order to enable this turn to the user. As the methodology of human-centered design has gained success the individual methods it has generated have been borrowed by other domains such as architecture, urban design, communication design, media, and social services. These methodologies are sometimes applied from a purely economic standpoint (how do we design a product with strong market appeal?) and sometimes with broader aims (how do we use design to create a better world for human beings to live, work, and flourish in?).

Participatory design, on the other hand, extended from an emancipatory political standpoint that designed products and spaces should be designed with input from the people who needed to use them (Robertson and Simonsen 2012). Initiated through worker's rights movement, this brought end-users into the design process. Like human-centered design, participatory design developed various methods to bring potential users of services, systems, and products into the design process at various points. Participatory design identifies the designer as a *facilitator* rather than a *definer*, and the roles of ideation and design iteration are shared with end-users. Participatory design is applied in various degrees depending on the situation, from a strict and thorough incorporation of users throughout design and production to more moderate applications that involves some user participation in the design process.

Co-design and co-creation are terms for practices that have arisen from both human-centered design and participatory design. Co-design sees that any aim to design change in the world necessarily involves the people for whom that change is intended. It requires "end-users" to have a say in decisions before any "concrete starts to pour." The collaboration produced through co-design brings about a collective, discursive process that guarantees a better outcome, more suited to a situation based on the different experiences of different stakeholders. For the *Homefullness* project another aspect is important: the sharing of responsibility and the openness to other voices brings a broader understanding and allows diverse viewpoints to co-exist and be respected. Allowing new conceptualizations and new relations to become present becomes the most critical outcome of the process.

Co-labs are extensions of a co-design process in which a "living laboratory" is put in place after needs have been identified. This space is facilitated by designers and other empowered stakeholders in a particular design space (e.g., urban agriculture) and allows manifold opinions, ideas, political standpoints to be workshopped, leading to potentially innovative project ideas and bringing community to the issues at hand.

Homefullness applies co-design and co-lab principles. Our initial premise imagines homefullness—as opposed to the existing issues of homelessness and housing stress—as a shared aspiration. From this future scenario, our concept "steps backward" toward the present by providing opportunities for different stakeholders to become part of the conversation of homefullness and asks "what is homefullness?" and "How might we move towards homefullness?."

The *Homefullness* research program was developed by art, design, social science, and housing activist researchers in Sweden and Australia to engage in international dialogue, public conversations, and creative intervention. Since 2012 we have presented exhibitions, roundtables, symposia, and papers to spark conversations around homelessness and housing stress in Melbourne, (Australia) and Stockholm, Malmö, and Helsingborg (Sweden). The first event was a public screen-printing of posters proclaiming the *Homefullness* "Manifesto for Full Housing" at Melbourne's Federation Square in 2012 (Figure 9.3). Passers-by were invited to watch the printing of the manifesto and graphic novel micro-narrative provocations around the theme of homelessness and housing stress. Some people elected to enter into conversation about the project and some elected to help with printing or hanging out freshly printed tea-towels to dry. While the manifesto is declarative and singular in its aims, the project itself is designed to create a space within which the theme is raised for consideration, reflection, and discussion.

In Open for Inspection, West Space Gallery, Melbourne, 2014, a mixed media installation of artifacts, a floor drawing and video were exhibited on and around the theme of homelessness and housing stress in order to "set the scene" for a number of group discussions and conversations. At times these conversations were free ranging, allowing people to speak about their experiences or air their opinions, and providing spaces to allow housing service providers, architects,

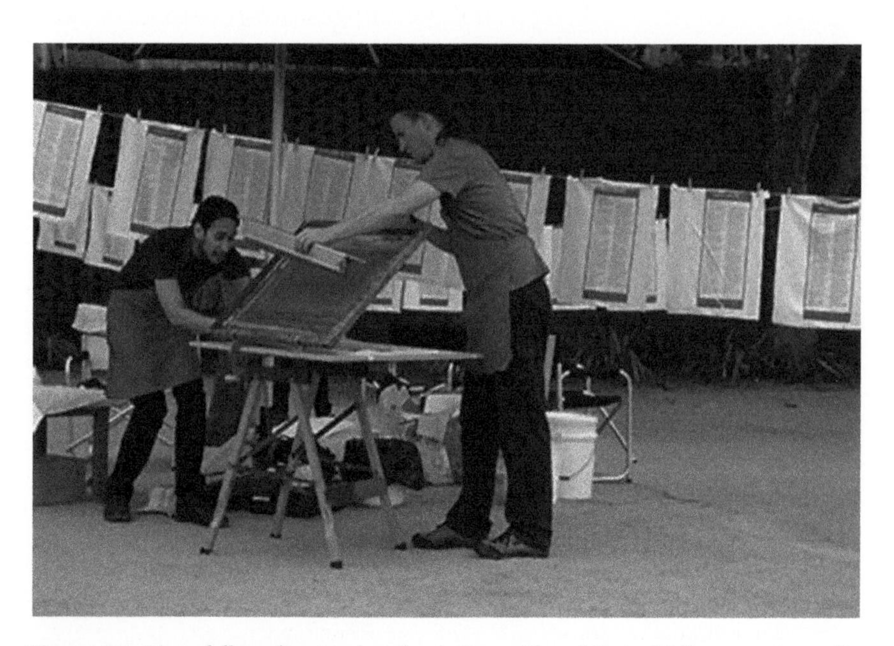

Figure 9.3 *Homefullness* live tea-towel printing with public in Melbourne, Australia, in April 2012 (photo Kirsten Haydon).

urban planners, and activists a public forum through which to explain their practice and motivations. In these moments art and design are being applied in order to facilitate co-design spaces for innovation.

Homefullness does not claim to have all the answers to its questions. Rather, the project provides the means through which the issues of homelessness and housing stress can be discussed and re-imagined. We believe that it is through creative intervention and critical discourse that questions about inclusive ways to approach housing are not only "kept alive" but can also be opened up in new and productive ways. In this way *Homefullness* has over the last six years reappeared in various guises, both in Melbourne and Malmö, in order to facilitate an ongoing conversation about housing needs and aspirations. Design artifacts (e.g., household tea-towels) are used to set the theme of the conversation and provoke response and discourse allowing the expression of various experiences of this complex contemporary issue to co-exist.

Cities of *Homefullness*

Cities of Homefullness, as the next iteration of the *Homefullness* campaign, brings the entity of the city directly into the discussion. Again, through simple art and design devices and artifacts (Figure 9.4), the project proposes to provide space for a conversation to be maintained and developed within the lens and scope of our cities and their diverse communities.

Cities of Homefullness is a co-design project, activating moments within the cities in which, and through which, the conversation and movement toward *Homefullness* is made. In declaring themselves as *Cities of Homefullness* Malmö and Melbourne would also declare themselves to be "living labs" which include manifold voices, opinions, methods, and understandings aimed to arrive at a better understanding of the conditions of *Homefullness* and the activities and systems which might be put in place to achieve it.

The *Homefullness* project, in this newest iteration proposes that we discuss, plan, develop, and build cities of homefullness within which housing is seen as intrinsic to community well-being, creativity, engagement, development, and empowerment.

Through the *Cities of Homefullness* proposal the cities of Malmö and Helsingborg have started discussion around participatory design and participatory research. One of the projects initiated is a service-user participation through dialogue.

Figure 9.4 Proposed Cities of *Homefullness* flag. Malmö, Sweden, during *Homefullness* roundtables during April 2016 (photo Neal Haslem).

Dialogue meetings have been carried out in all the different housing alternatives within the social housing program in Helsingborg. A "future workshop" was held on different aspects of homefullness: creating safe housing conditions, inclusive work programs, and peer-support groups. The *Cities of Homefullness* project has made connections with established participatory projects on gap-mending strategies, where service-users' experience is included and actors are working on equal terms to change the existing system (Heule, Knutagård and Kristiansen 2017). The change process takes time, but already signs of change are visible. Formerly homeless people are included in decision making, planning, and reorganization of the social housing program. The methods used are a mix of dialogue forums, workshops, and creative projects. One example is a collection of photographs that different service-users within the social housing program have taken of artifacts and other objects that symbolize their home and sense of home. The photographs will be published as a magazine, using similar layout and style as the popular types of home-style magazines. The idea is to challenge the discourse of what constitutes a home and to bring homeless people's experiences to the fore.

In March 2017, the Victorian state government released a series of housing initiatives to address homelessness, housing disadvantage and the lack of housing affordability in metropolitan Melbourne. These initiatives include packages to provide supportive housing for homeless people and rough sleepers (Foley 2017), a billion-dollar loans scheme running at a lower interest rate for housing associations to borrow funds to build new homes (Pallas 2017a), 100 new social housing dwellings in established suburbs (Pallas 2017b), long-term leases for renters (Andrews 2017), and the rezoning of 100,000 lots of land on the edges of Melbourne to allow for the development of new suburbs. These housing programs aim to address current housing problems in Melbourne. However, what appears left out of these new policies and packages for housing is the relational, generative, and discursive importance of community. While we appreciate the gesture and value of these Victorian government packages, we hope that an inclusionary participatory approach is taken to their development. We suggest that community members should be at the center of the planning, design, and development of new housing, resources, and facilities. If a co-design framework and integrity are applied to these new suburbs and housing projects, new residents and community members will be able to shape and develop the housing, amenities, and spaces that they will use, look after, enjoy, and appreciate. This is the essence of *Homefullness*.

Conclusion

Cities of Homefullness is propositional. However, as a proposition it is also a provocation. The *Homefullness* project is ongoing and will work toward the uptake and declaration, at a city-wide scale, of the aspiration for *homefullness*. The *Homefullness* project demonstrates how art and design processes, applied with co-design methods, stimulates dialogue-driven innovation within the diverse stakeholders involved in complex social issues. The project allows different understandings and responses to be brought together in dialogue. Through this it provides generative events during which different stakeholders are exposed and confronted by foreign ideas and concepts. The key finding of the *Homefullness* project so far has been the potential for art- and design-facilitated dialogue between diverse stakeholders to allow activation of innovative understandings, conceptualizations, and, ultimately, actions. Examples like the Housing First initiatives in Sweden (Knutagård 2017; Knutagård and Kristiansen

2013) have achieved impressive results through the simple but fundamental change of abandoning the traditional "staircase" model (which provides housing incrementally and only if new tenants stick to a series of programs) by providing permanent housing in the first instance. This is an exemplary act of homefullness. Through these and other acts, small and large, the conversation—and the process of re-imagining—continues. Our hope is that our communities and governing bodies will work toward becoming cities of homefullness and move us toward an enabling, inclusive, sustainable, and creative housing future.

Funding from The Swedish Foundation for International Cooperation in Research and Higher Education (STINT) has helped make the *Homefullness* project collaboration possible.

Acknowledgments

The *Homefullness* project is a collaboration involving art, design, and housing researchers based in Australia and Sweden including Mick Douglas, Hélène Frichot, Neal Haslem, Per-Anders Hillgren, Rochus Hinkel, Guy Johnson, Marcus Knutagård, Keely Macarow, Margie McKay, and Mim Whiting.

References

Andrews, D. (2017), *Long-Term Security for Tenants and Landlords*, Victoria State Government, March 2, 2017.

Australian Bureau of Statistics (2012), *Census of Population and Housing: Estimating Homelessness*, Canberra: Australian Bureau of Statistics.

Australian Design Review (2011), *Design Challenge 2011: Homelessness*, Australian Design Review, viewed 1 July 1, 2017, https://www.australiandesignreview.com/event/14871/

Benjaminsen, L. and Knutagård, M. (2016), "Homelessness Research and Policy Development: Examples from the Nordic Countries," *European Journal of Homelessness*, 10 (3): 45–66.

City of Melbourne (2016), *Street Count 2016 Final Report*, Melbourne.

Foley, M. (2017), *Giving Rough Sleepers A Path Towards Home*, Victoria State Government, January 27, 2017.

Groenhart, L. and Burke, T. (2014), "Thirty Years of Public Housing Supply and Consumption: 1981–2011," *AHURI Final Report Series - Project: The Interrelationship between Structural Factors and Individual Risk Factors in Explaining Homelessness - AHURI Final Report No. 231*, vol. 231.

Hall, T. and Vidén, S. (2005), "The Million Homes Programme: A Review of the Great Swedish Planning Project," *Planning Perspectives*, 20 (3): 301–28.

Hedin, K., Clark, E., Lundholm, E., and Malmberg, G. (2012), "Neoliberalization of Housing in Sweden: Gentrification, Filtering, and Social Polarization," *Annals of the Association of American Geographers*, 102 (2): 443–63.

Heule, C., Knutagård, M., and Kristiansen, A. (2017), "Mending the Gaps in Social Work Education and Research: Two Examples from a Swedish Context," *European Journal of Social Work*, 20 (3): 396–408.

Johnson, G., Scutella, R., Tseng, Y., and Wood, G. (2015), "Entries and Exits from Homelessness: A Dynamic Analysis of the Relationship between Structural Conditions and Individual Characteristics," *AHURI Final Report Series - Project: The Interrelationship between Structural Factors and Individual Risk Factors in Explaining Homelessness - AHURI Final Report No. 248*, vol. 248, pp. 1–67.

Knutagård, M. (2009), "Skälens fångar. Hemlöshetsarbetets organisering, kategoriseringar och förklaringar. [Prisoners of reasons: organization, categorizations and explanations of work with the homeless]," Lund University.

Knutagård, M. (2017), "Innovationer i välfärden – Mending the Gap [Innovation in Welfare – mending the gap]," in A. M. Støkken and E. Willumsen (eds.), *Brukerstemmer, praksisforskning og innovasjon*, Kristiansand: Portal forlag, 89–106.

Knutagård, M. and Kristiansen, A. (2013), "Not by the Book: The Emergence and Translation of Housing First in Sweden," *European Journal of Homelessness*, 7 (1): 93–115.

Knutagård, M. and Nordfeldt, M. (2007), "Natthärbärget som vandrande lösning. [The shelter as a recurrent solution to homelessness]," *Sociologisk forskning*, 44 (4): 30–57.

Pallas, T. (2017a), *Reform, Growth and Better Outcomes for Social Housing*, Victoria State Government, February 23, 2017.

Pallas, T. (2017b), *Unlocking New Communities and Affordable Housing*, Victoria State Government, February 28, 2017.

Robertson, T. and Simonsen, J. (2012), "Challenges and Opportunities in Contemporary Participatory Design," *Design Issues*, 28 (3): 3–9.

10

Learning from Parramatta Girls Home: Tactics and Practices for Strategic Design in the Margins

Lily Hibberd

The purpose of this chapter is to critique how design has affected the organisation of Australian child welfare institutions and impact of this on the lives of former residents in the care of the state. This analysis specifically situates the methods and tactics of a collective of former residents of Parramatta Girls Home—the Parragirls—within a strategic design paradigm. Hill elaborates (2012: 11) that strategic design "is focused on the systemic redesign of cultures of decision-making at the individual and institutional levels." Significant to this domain of design research is the emergent notion of design for social innovation, which Manzini (2015) defines as a field of possibility in an enabling and dynamic social ecosystem. In the context of institutional and post-institutional care, the potential of this new thinking is even more crucial. Former residents of welfare institutions have been and remain excluded from decision-making across plural political, government and social structures; where their capacity to provide expertise from their intimate experience of institutions would be a game-changer in particular for ethical heritage interpretation, welfare services, community engagement and more complex and rich ways of including marginalised institutional memories in the annals of public history. In this framework, design shifts the locus of power from a confined college of experts to a human-centered methodology of collaborative, responsive and adaptive approaches that are able to develop better social outcomes.

Along these lines, under the auspices of the Parramatta Female Factory Precinct Memory Project (2017), since 2012 the Parragirls have generated an array of community and creative projects on the site of the former Home. Taken singly or seen through a particular theoretical lens these projects could be categorised as either contemporary art, activism or social history but this is a radical reduction and suppression of the magnitude and the deeper questions underlying their work: What motivates Parragirls to return and occupy a place of personal and public conflict after more than fifty years? And why have the women specifically developed strategies to transform this traumatic institutional place into a space of care? In order to contend with these layered temporal, emotional and social complexities, this text consolidates design strategies developed across the life of the Memory Project to contribute to an expanded view of strategic design, particularly how Parragirls have employed certain "tactics" (conceived after de Certeau 1984: xix and 130) to form part of a design methodology where the institutional "space" of Parramatta Girls Home "appears once more as a practiced place." This chapter moreover aims to document the Parragirls' contribution to improved design approaches to post-institutional care and structural reform appropriate to the repercussions of enduring systemic failings as revealed in the Royal Commission into Institutional Responses to Child Sexual Abuse (Commonwealth of Australia n.d.) which have allowed for the abuse of children in the care of the Australian welfare system.

This two-part analysis begins with *the "dark" margins of child welfare* where I define the underlying structures of marginalization within Australian child welfare and its relevance to strategic design, drawing on the work of Hill (2012). I then examine the methods Parragirls have developed in line with de Certeau's (1984: xiv) conceptualization of "ways of operating," as part of a strategic design approach crucial to the contemporary reform of state welfare systems. In *memory to action* I provide case studies of the Parragirls' use of memory as a "tactic" (de Certeau 1984: xii) to subvert the rituals and representations that institutions impose upon them. I finally describe how Parramatta Girls Home functions as a touchstone for cultural change—that not only cares but restores and repairs social equity and justice in the very place where it was lacking. Throughout in this chapter, I foreground the work of Parragirls, chief among them the vision and leadership of PFFP Memory Project director Bonney Djuric (as pictured in Fig. 10.1). The innovation underpinning this text is the result of the Parragirls' collective response to institutional care, even though—and crucially because they are not seen as experts—their work remains otherwise overlooked.

Figure 10.1 Bonney Djuric outside Parramatta Girls Home, 2012, photo Lily Hibberd, courtesy PFFP Memory Project.

The "dark" margins of child welfare and designing for visibility

In the convergence of design and social organization, the word "margin" carries a dual meaning. A margin is the empty space around a page; a physical border in a design context. A social margin is however a zone or condition that excludes people from mainstream society. In both cases, margins are integral to the whole design and as such may seem invisible or unintentional. Despite the passage of almost forty years, de Certeau's claim (1984: xvii) that "Marginality is today no longer limited to minority groups, but is rather massive and pervasive" is all the more pertinent in our present era of global border protection and the increasingly visible politics of social and economic division. On this basis, a case can be made for the importance of making the margins a visible and carefully considered element in the strategic design of the social ecosystem, what Manzini (2015: 121) calls "designing for visibility."

State-run institutions such as Parramatta Girls Home are part of a historical paradigm, which originally centralised the controlled "care" of child welfare subjects. Australia's colonial welfare institutions were established on practices of marginalization and institutionalization—combining the "total institution" (Goffman 1961) with the "disciplinary society" (Foucault 1991). Australian child welfare is arguably founded on the colonial conception of welfare subjects as a social burden, to be rendered invisible and powerless within disciplinary institutions; ideas that remain widely accepted as part of the contemporary juvenile justice system. Nonetheless, how can a system of care deliver violence on its subjects? In its dual sense, care can be a burden: we can care for someone or something or hope to avoid troubles—to be care-free. As such, the notion of care raises complex and contradictory ideologies that underpin the success or failure of a society to care for its own.

The Royal Commission (Commonwealth of Australia n.d.) has uncovered the nature and extent of sexual abuse at Parramatta Girls Home, with a predominant emphasis on the culpability of individual former superintendents. But the problem of how to deliver reparative care to victims in the aftermath is, by the Royal Commission's own admission, deeply problematic, as suggested in the 2015 report "Redress and civil litigation" (Commonwealth of Australia 2015: 5): "In our view, the current civil litigation systems and past and current redress processes have not provided justice for many survivors." This seemingly unbridgeable gap between immutable and plural systems and reparative justice could be more productively addressed through Hill's (2012) concept of "dark matter," which he defines (2012: 50, 52) as the "architecture of society"; the underlying and unseen, "otherwise amorphous, nebulous yet fundamental" networks of "organizations, culture, and the structural relationships that bind them." In essence, the current situation of the Australian welfare system and the challenges for its reform are due to the deeply entangled web of dark matter. By way of solution, Hill (2012: 62, 87) proposes that strategic design can be deployed as a "cultural act" and applied at the level of social and policy design to wrestle with this "dark matter in order to outline a more constructive set of trajectories for society."

For people burdened with social disadvantage, mental health issues, disability and experiences of abuse as well as the taint of criminality, the long history of punishment and marginalization is an apparent dark matter. The fact that Parramatta Girls Home was closed in 1974 does not remove the sense of this burden, which is an encumbrance to the need for the full recognition and remit of justice for the unwarranted punishment and abuse that this institution systematically meted out on its residents. These events impact on the present lives of these women and the tendency to bury their experiences in history is precisely why Parragirls are now actively engaged in operations that redefine how the Home and state welfare is represented and operates in the present. Their struggle is not only with governments and welfare agencies but with the marginalization maintained in a paradoxical public imaginary of state care under what Djuric (2011: 11) calls the "Guise of Benevolence," a paradox of care that effectively renders the human rights of its subjects invisible.

The work of the co-founders of Parragirls, Bonney Djuric and Christina Green, is remarkable for the strategic design approaches they have developed to make the dark matter of the child welfare system publicly visible. An illustrative example is the "Talking Circles" program, which Green conceived in 2013. Combining dynamic and open approaches to education, social history and psychology, this program exemplifies a strategic design methodology, which according to Hill (2012: 11) is "focused on the systemic redesign of cultures of decision-making at the individual and institutional levels." Talking Circles subverts the controlling institutional paradigm to promote interpretive, open and collaborative knowledge production, in contrast to the way that decision-making is usually applied to institutionalised people.

Green's program first of all invites participants take a short self-guided walk of Parramatta Girls Home with insights (scripted by Green) into its institutional and Aboriginal history and Indigenous flora, after which the group convenes in the Memory Project's on-site workshop. Then small parties or "circles" are assembled. A facilitator is present. Topics of conversation are not provided. Instead, the facilitator shapes a conversation (Green 2013) that is "open to possibilities and new lines of inquiry or action," to foster a "process of thinking outside the square . . . embracing multiple and diverse scenarios." Green (2013) states that Talking Circles' purpose "is to give people an opportunity to interact around key ideas or specific areas of interest . . . [which can be] informal and discursive, or structured and task-oriented." She emphasizes (2013) that the primary intention, "is to find a common ground of shared meanings and experiences in which differences are recognised and respected" and that this flowing process aims to create a kind of "collective intelligence around the stream" and "embody a spirit of openness to new knowledge." And this, in Green's words, is "where cycles of conversation begin."

Talking Circles demonstrates an assemblage of a complex array of knowledge to create an open-ended, dialogical learning situation that encourages non-experts to work in what Manzini (2015: 67) calls "dialogic cooperation." Manzini (2015: 37) describes this emergent approach as a dynamic interaction between two poles of design producers. On one hand, "diffuse design" is put into play by non-experts in their "natural designing capacity"; on the other, there is the "expert design" of professionally trained designers. As design becomes increasingly relevant to sociocultural ecosystems, Manzini (2015: 122) claims that collaboration between expert and non-expert design is principal to designing for social innovation.

Talking Circles is also an illustration of de Certeau's concept of "ways of operating" (1984: xiv) that "constitute the innumerable practices by means of which users reappropriate the space organised by techniques of sociocultural production," in this case the reorganization of dominant knowledge production for institutional care. Green's program design subverts hierarchical modes of knowledge production in an institutional context. For example, Goffman (1961: 47–48) outlines how the practice of mortification implies that institutional subjects are more likely to be told what to think rather than being given opportunity to generate autonomous, new thought. Green transforms this institutional knowledge order to offer a model of human-centered, collective knowledge production, to learn not *about* but *from* the Parramatta Girls Home site.

This model is not only appropriate for activities at the former Girls Home but could also be applied at other locations where the nature of its educational constituency requires a non-authoritative and generative design approach. Fundamental to Green's program design is the fact that someone with direct experience of the disciplinary welfare has conceived this work. This also highlights the need to empower marginalized people as experts: to legitimise them as knowledge producers and agents of social transformation. "Diffuse" approaches to social programs have the potential to create openings for otherwise invisible or marginalized people and communities to become actors for change.

But inherently marginalizing structures cannot begin to care of their own accord, they need to be reformed if not disassembled from the foundations of a society. What is therefore required is a process of deep analysis that coheres all the issues and structures at a "meta and matter" level across the systemic scale, an approach Hill (2012: 100) maintains is about "designing both the matter (the objects, spaces, services) at the same time as the meta (the context, the organisation, the culture)." The "meta and matter" approach is well established in Memory Project practices such as Green's Talking Circles, which takes as its material not only marginalization and but the invisible matter of trauma embedded within Parramatta Girls Home to provide insight into future use of decommissioned institutional buildings and sites of care.

Memory to action: Transformational memory tactics for social change

In *The Practice of Everyday Life* de Certeau (1984: xii–xix) outlines the operational difference between strategy and tactics. He defines strategy as "a calculus of force relationships when a subject of will and power . . . can be isolated from an environment." A tactic according to de Certeau (1984: 38) "insinuates itself into the other's place, fragmentarily" so that "a tactic is determined by the absence of power just as a strategy is organised by the postulation of power." Tactics thus arise directly out of resistance to institutional power where, as de Certeau argues (1984: xii), "the weak are seeking to turn the tables on the strong."

This section examines approaches to memory work as a set of tactics for the critique of care in an institutional and post-institutional setting. Its focus is to draw a comparison with de Certeau's analysis to the relationship between care as a function of government strategy and the tactics of care Parragirls have developed in response to their lack of power as subjects of state welfare. de Certeau (1984: 37–38) further explains the military geneses of the concept of tactics, noting that, whereas a strategy is developed from a Panoptic perspective (at a distance), tactics are produced as a result of "combat at close quarters," where there is "delimitation of an exteriority." An operation in close proximity to an action thus occurs in direct response to what de Certeau (1984: xiv) calls the "violence of order." de Certeau's cornerstone argument is that tactics are part of wider practices of everyday life, as users or unrecognised producers (in contrast to consumers) transform places defined by (1984: xix) "political, economic, and scientific rationality." Transferring de Certeau's analogy to the context of Parramatta Girls Home reveals many parallels. Djuric (2011) provides a comprehensive account of the Panoptic order of the Home in its ritualistic and punitive control of the children in its care. Without vision or visibility beyond the walls of the institution, the only "opportunities" available to its adolescent residents were tactical: secret codes, bonds, and shared rituals. The tactics of resistance Parragirls deployed during the period of the Home's operation are either unknown or poorly understood outside of the Parragirls community. It is however the contemporary turn that Parragirls have taken to contend with and reappropriate their memory of past violence and resistance as a tactic to force open its present-day forgetting that is of interest here.

The 2016 project *Living Traces* exemplifies de Certeau's notion of tactics (1984: 37–38) being produced from "combat at close quarters" as the Parragirls retrace and reclaim memory through the return to and touching of the Home's tangible vestiges. Over the years since 2006 that the women began to gain access to buildings that were previously off-limits, Djuric remarked how many Parragirls determinedly sought out very specific locations in former isolation and punishment cells. What they hoped to find were "scratchings": words, names, or acronyms written in coded language, a syntactic network of care among a society of captives. According to Djuric (2011: 154), "The lover system came with its own language, ILWA (I Love Worship Adore/Always), or TID (Till I Die), or SML (Send My Love) or a girl's initials or number inserted in a heart shape, was all part of the "secret code." These marks (see Fig. 10.2) were covertly scored while in solitary confinement as an act of solidarity and—given the risk of violent or solitary isolation punishment—in defiance of the institutional regime. And this act of marking the site by girls who had no rights whatsoever (property, bodily or otherwise) precisely coincides with de Certeau's (1984: xxi) claim that a tactic "transforms another person's property into a space borrowed for a moment by a transient." Through *Living Traces* the women redeploy the deeper significance of these marks to rethink their relationship to the Home as a represented place and their present power relation to institutional care structures. There is also an aspect in which the project revives memory in the present, specifically living memory through tactility. Coming into close proximity with the former institution—its confines, constricts, textures, and smells—and touching a mark made in secret, perhaps lost to time over fifty years, is an example of memory in action, namely the lasting power of embodied memory for the institutional subject. The tactile memory embedded in these scratchings also connects every single person who passed through the institution; an otherwise nameless and powerless collective.

Living Traces brought together large groups of Parragirls for collective workshops in the former classroom block at the Home. Of particular note is the way in which the difficult, traumatic and even conflicting memories were handled. While the subject of scratchings for some former residents calls up a dissenting or fighter's narrative, for many these marks are scars; triggers for

Figure 10.2 Bonney Djuric tracing scratchings, Parramatta Girls Home, 2012, photo Lily Hibberd, courtesy PFFP Memory Project.

palpable memories of terrifying isolation and fear, and literally as traces of scars on the body. Memories such as these can clash in the present: no-one recalls or even wants to remember pain in the same way, let alone reconstruct it even if collectively from the rubble of the past. For de Certeau (1984: 108) "The dispersion of stories points to the dispersion of the memorable as well. And in fact memory is a sort of anti-museum: it is not localizable." Where then to place these memories? Scratchings on the walls of the Home are more complex than evidence; they are redolent and sentient mirrors of past events transformed through and with the present body and mind. In this context, the women undertook a subversive mnemonic tactic of working in the presence of this memory (in a room where the pins some used to scratch codes into their skin are still turning up in the carpet), thus visualizing without verbally addressing traumatic memory but giving it a space all the same.

The collagraph-intaglio print technique adapted for the situation is an excellent example of a form open to transformative and embodied memory, whose malleable yet traceable form and function harkens to Freud's (1950) allegory of the Mystic Writing Pad. For the purposes of *Living Traces*, a simple piece of timber was prepared with a thick layer of plaster for each artist (as seen in Fig. 10.3), in which marks, images, or impressions could be inscribed. A wide range of responses flowed from the women, ranging from patterns, signs, and abstract arrangements created from pressed fabrics, images both specific to the institution and its past as well as personal pictures of beauty (pets and flowers). Rather than being confined to the past, these works made an explicit statement

Figure 10.3 PFFP Memory Project Jenny McNally with intaglio print, Living Traces workshop, 2016, photo Catherine McElhone, courtesy PFFP Memory Project.

Figure 10.4 Print by Gypsie Hayes from "Living Traces" artist book, 2016, photo Lucy Parakhina, courtesy PFFP Memory Project.

of mnemonic liberation from the institution, as if the marks they were making into that present-day surface—more than fifty years later—were the scratchings of liberated subjects no longer defined or confined by the Girls Home.

These prints then formed a canvas for the superimposition of archival materials drawn from Djuric's extensive research. This collection included photographic documentation of hundreds of scratchings from the Home, child welfare records, and old handwritten texts from other Parragirls. The resulting prints are a palimpsest of layered texts, textures, and references (for example in Fig. 10.4), they also interrogate the veracity of official history: questioning the records produced by state agencies who control and generate the facts and stories that determine public history. And for Parragirls this endeavor is much more than personal struggle; it is a question of restorative justice, as Jenny McNally explains:

> At the stroke of a pen, my life changed forever. As children what happened affected our lives in profound ways. Back then we never got the chance to read what was recorded, to correct or dispute it, or to add our own voice . . . The only way we could express ourselves was to scratch words into the walls or onto our bodies. Now a lifetime later, we revisit those marks, we read what was written about us and we are responding in our own ways to set the record right. (Djuric and Hibberd 2017)

Through *Living Traces* the women challenge the notion that records of the past are indelible for two reasons. First, the documents welfare departments hold on the women remain the property of the state (and, until recently, were largely inaccessible to former residents). Second, the content of these records can be anomalous with personal memory (and, as many women say, riddled with errors and fallacies). While the Royal Commission into Institutional Responses to Child Sexual Abuse (Commonwealth of Australia 2016) has specifically undertaken to examine institutional recordkeeping practices and "how these practices could be improved for children in the future", thus far no opportunity has been offered to enable former welfare subjects to contest let alone rectify their own records.

In this work Parragirls enact series of tactics to repair the fractious breach between inaccessible and contested state archives and their lives; to amend the record, if only for themselves. The most crucial tactic to emerge from this project however involved designing a conceptual space—a space in de Certeau's (1984: 130) sense of "practiced place"—in which otherwise inadmissible evidence of memory can be produced. The potential for the generation of new memories from old is vital in the context of past trauma, which public memory unfortunately tends to compound with its appetite for stereotyped national narratives. But Parragirls have established a space where memory can be evoked as a tactic of memorial disruption and destabilization, for which de Certeau (1984: 108) provides the analogy of "the awakening of inert objects . . . which, emerging from their stability, transform the place where they lay motionless into the foreigners of their own space." For example, prior to this project Parragirls scratchings were considered less than worthless, even defacements, but *Living Traces* has given these marks renewed and vital, living significance for Parragirls. Even so, the last of these remaining marks threaten to be erased as New South Wales Government advance its Parramatta North Urban Transformation plan, a struggle that is ultimately emblematic of the power dynamic that institutions have to marginalise or neutralise memory, and how strategic design on the other hand can be deployed as an emancipatory mnemonic tactic. The present interpretation and future use of such a significant public site, particularly its proposed adaptive re-use, requires an integrated design practice that overthrows such forgetting and neglect through an ethos of care in action.

Conclusion

At Parramatta Girls Home past injustice provides the impetus from which to envisage approaches to strategic design that provide a framework for future care. While this chapter inevitably contends with the extreme case of a former place of punishment and state-sanctioned violence as well as its aftermath, this study offers a range of new perspectives for strategic design. Parragirls believe the Girls Home is a site from which we must learn—a place of living history and a touchstone for national memory, welfare reform, and restorative justice. This is the driving ethos for the collective work of the Parragirls, which offers a significant catalogue of practical tools and tactics for implementing social change, not *as* design but *through* design. Expanding the discipline of strategic design to embrace innovations emerging from otherwise overlooked producers such as the Parragirls could generate a dynamic new collaborative knowledge ecology within which practitioners (across urban, architecture, landscape, and many other disciplines), policymakers, and creative producers might rethink and transform the way we design systems care for the future.

Biography

Lily Hibberd is an artist and writer and DECRA Research Fellow at National Institute of Experimental Arts, UNSW, Sydney. She is Creative Director and cofounder with Bonney Djuric of Parramatta Female Factory Precinct Memory Project. Together they develop and facilitate creative projects with former residents of Parramatta Girls Home. Lily curates Memory Project onsite exhibitions and public programs and produces collaborative video and performance works with Parragirls. She is coauthor with Djuric of numerous publications. Lily Hibberd is the recipient of an ARC Discovery Early Career Researcher Award Scheme to research new digital media representations with Parragirls. This research led Lily to co-produce the 3-D immersive cinema project "Parragirls Past, Present" at UNSW EPICentre for The Big Anxiety: festival of arts+science+people 2017 in collaboration with Parragirls and UNSW media artists.

References

Commonwealth of Australia, Royal Commission into Institutional Responses to Child Sexual Abuse, *Terms of Reference*, n.d. Available online: www.childabuseroyalcommission.gov.au/about-us/terms-of-reference (accessed August 17, 2017).

Commonwealth of Australia, Royal Commission into Institutional Responses to Child Sexual Abuse, *Redress and Civil Litigation Report*, September 2015. Available online: https://www.childabuseroyalcommission.gov.au/redress-and-civil-litigation (accessed July 30, 2018).

Commonwealth of Australia, Royal Commission into Institutional Responses to Child Sexual Abuse, *Records and Recordkeeping Practices Consultation Paper*, September 2, 2016. Available online: childabuseroyalcommission.gov.au/getattachment/f7289d7c-52e7-4143-a6ed-1aa149263eaf/Consultation-Paper (accessed March 17, 2017).

de Certeau, M. (1984), *The Practice of Everyday Life*, trans. Steven Rendall, Berkeley: University of California Press.

Djuric, B. (2011), *Abandon All Hope: A History of Parramatta Girls Industrial School*, Perth: Chargan My Book Publisher.

Djuric, B. and Hibberd, L. (2017), "At the Stroke of a Pen, My Life Changed Forever," Featured news, International Coalition of Sites of Conscience. Available online: www.sitesofconscience.org/en/2016/03/living-traces-parramatta-female-factory-precinct-memory-project/ (accessed February 21, 2017).

Foucault, M. (1991), *Discipline and Punish: The Birth of the Prison*, trans. A. M. Sheridan Smith, London: Penguin.

Freud, S. (1950), *A Note upon the "Mystic Writing-Pad,"* in *Collected Papers*, vol. V, London: The Hogarth Press, 175–80.

Goffman, E. (1961), "On the Characteristics of Total Institutions," in *Asylums: Essays on the Social Situation of Mental Patients and Other Inmates*, New York: Doubleday Anchor, 1–124.

Green, C. (2013), *Talking Circles*, unpublished PFFP Memory Project description.

Hill, D. (2012), *Dark Matter and Trojan Horses: A Strategic Design Vocabulary*, London: Strelka.

Manzini, E. (2015), *Design, When Everybody Designs: An Introduction to Design for Social Innovation*, trans. R. Coad, Cambridge, MA: MIT Press. Available online: www.jstor.org/stable/j.ctt17kk7sv (accessed August 17, 2017).

Parramatta Female Factory Precinct Memory Project (2017), pffpmemory.org.au, www.parragirls.org.au/ (accessed February 12, 2017).

11

Nurturing Forth: Designing Careful Futures in a Small Arctic City

Andrew Morrison, Maria Bertheussen Skrydstrup, Angeliki Dimaki-Adolfsen, and Janike Kampevold Larsen

Introduction

It's now over a hundred years since the Grand Hotel in Vardø opened its doors on a small island just off the coast of northern Norway. At that time Vardø was one of the richest towns in the Norwegian arctic. With a long history of trade with Northwest Russia, since the 1850s Vardø had made its fortunes from the rich fishing fields of the region's ice-free waters. On opening, the Grand was a cultural landmark and probably the most advanced facility of its kind at the time, with a rooftop terrace, window frames inlaid with mirrors, imported chandeliers, and lighters built into the tables in the lounge. At its zenith, Vardø had a population of 4,000 and a harbor so busy that children reputedly went from one side to the other by clambering across fishing vessels.

Following the occupation of the town and the hotel by the Nazis in the Second World War, the Grand lost much of its earlier appeal. However, unlike much of the wooden structures of the town that suffered bombing and burning, this four story concrete building survived. Over its life, the building has functioned as a telegraph office, a pharmacy, and a municipal library. Since the Second World War, the Grand has operated as a hotel, the ground floor used by the town school, as offices for business, and as a venue for the regional museum. From the early 1970s, the Grand has been in the hands of family owners, the Bertheussens, (Figure 11.1). Since the 1980s, largely because of sustainability restrictions on fishing catches, Vardø has shrunk to about 2,000 inhabitants, with many empty buildings and a loss of pride.

The main paradox for the owners has been how to finance the renovation of such a massive building and to develop it as a source of income yet revive it

Figure 11.1 Vardø Hotel, northern Norway, 2016. (photo: Jonas Adolfsen)

as landmark of cultural activities in the town (Figure 11.1). When the family took over the Grand, it was used for electrical education, by a diving club, for band practices, and as a nightclub. The chequered uses to which the Grand has been put perhaps prepare it well for the changing climates of cultural survival in the Anthropocene. Today, the exterior walls, windows, doors, and roof have been fully restored thanks to support from Vardø Restored, a project that has succeeded in revitalizing numerous buildings through a community-centered initiative to revive and document key properties in the town (www.vardorestored.com; Figure 11.2).

Despite its demise as lucrative fishing town, Vardø is characterized by niche tourism, especially birding, daily visits by the *Hurtigruiten* coastal cruise ship, the successes of the Vardø Restored project, and a number of new investments, such as the municipal offices, swimming pool, and theater and meeting venues.

How then might a community-driven exploratory initiative on cultural innovation for sustainable future arctic living be put together and developed? In what ways might partnering of local citizens' expertise and that of external design

Figure 11.2 Historical and contemporary views of Vardø Hotel, Vardø Restored project. (www.vardorestored.com)

contributors be used to support local cultural expression and its ongoing life? In what ways might developments in social innovation hubs inform prototyping of a more culturally inflected venue?

Design and "a culture of care"

We offer an ethnographically informed account of the revitalization of the former hotel that has taken place through a process of negotiation and conjectural design within a large research project called Future North is centered on cultural landscapes of the future arctic. In harmony with the community project Vardø Restored, our aim as local citizens and visiting design researchers has been to move from calls for climate change resilience to shaping an emergent careful practice of finding new modes of constructive cultural engagement. Our attention has been on shaping a sustainable design for the Grand as what we term a "a cultural hub" suited to the character and context of this small arctic town (Figure 11.3). Our focus has been on developing "a culture of care" in and as cultural practice, and oriented to a future not founded on economic innovation only.

Designing "a culture of future care" is in many ways like engaging with living culture: it is dynamic, it is built through dialogue and through negotiation, and it emerges through its articulation, thereby voicing identity, asserting potential, and offering change over time. In our collaboration, culture is central to the participative building of alternate means to survival that cannot be based on resource extraction or unbridled development driven from the outside. In this design-oriented context building practices of social innovation (e.g., Ehn, Nislsson, and Topgaard 2014) and cultural innovation, we recall that Latour (2010: 487) challenges us to think and move cautiously from critique to composition.

Methodologically, such a composition has been nurtured over a period of five years as we have collaborated closely to build connections and exchange knowledge and experience between Vardø Restored and Future North. We have drawn together community activism and situated knowledge with action research, design-based pedagogy, and inquiry (Pink 2012). The resulting Vardø HUB project is the interests and concerns of local townspeople and external researchers coming together through a spirit of care for place. Such care of, in, and for place needs to be understood as a set of relations between place as

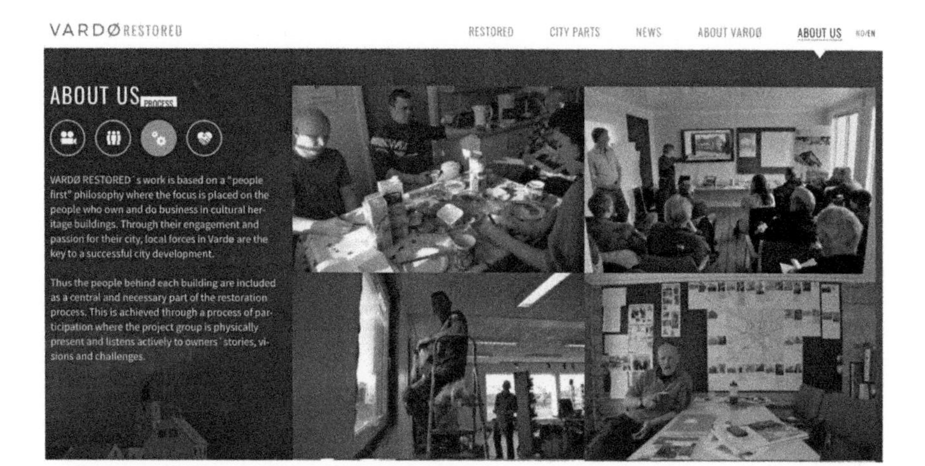

Figure 11.3 (Top) Participation and practices in Vardø Restored (Photos: Vardo Restored). (Middle and bottom) first floor of the Grand Hotel before reflooring and redesign as a space for flexible use; the second floor in the process of refurbishment in 2017 into potentially fourteen rooms with shared bathrooms for hire, with stairs to the top floor attic intended for conversion into four studios for artists, researchers, longer stays. (Photos: Jonas Adolfsen)

past/heritage and place as unknown and emergent in negotiating a seemingly precarious arctic future in the context of climate change. Such engagement has involved numerous visits from Oslo to the far north and the growth of common goals, activities and events, professional relationships, and friendships. Our collaborative weave of making, reflecting, learning, and understanding has come together around the exploratory connection of the *HUB* to physical and economic consequences. It has been mediated by visits, longer stays, numerous Whatsapp conversations, and SMS exchanges, and discussions about examples of other sites and projects shared between us on Facebook.

Arguments for linking the practices of design and culture that are meshes of the social and the technical, the creative, and innovative (e.g., Balsamo 2011) have also appeared in Science Technology Studies notably through the work of Mol (2008) on care (Mol, Moser and Pols 2010). Latour (2004, 2010) has further argued that we need to pay attention to how to think about materiality and facts in which "things" are also agentive and connected to material ordering (Denis and Pontille 2015). Latour (2004: 232) distinguishes between matters of fact and of concern, and signals a need to go beyond the division of objects and things. Attention to "matters of care" as he terms it, has also been central in our work where a co-creative design journey has involved a large building whose exterior has been expertly secured against the elements. Care is a matter of both reaching into possible futures speculatively, and also ethically where it entails relations between human and nonhuman (Puig de la Bellacasa (2017)). For Puig de la Bellacasa (2011: 100), "The notion of 'matters of care' is a proposition to think with." The thinking has had to do with developing a cultural perspective on care that extends to reaching into future spaces for cultural imagining and deliberative action in a small town within a changing arctic.

But what does it means to enact such participation when the mode of inquiry is speculative, and contains a mix of actants, human and nonhuman? What might attending to matters of care be transformed into discursively and locatively, through co-design activity and participation, when the intention is to address future concerns based on emergent practices that are unfolding in the present?

For Parreñas and Boris (2010) this is a matter of "intimate labors" in which politics, technology, and care are intertwined. Such labors are also crucially about understanding and exercising the ethics of care (e.g., Moore, 1999) that is sensitive to a diversity of needs. For Vardø this means designerly recommendations for everyday futures. In a sense this very local case needed to be negotiated on site and into emergent futures, with design-centered knowledge such as scenario building, anticipating service-related encounters for visitors to the Vardø HUB communicated through design workshopping, sketched alternate room uses, and event designs to work with the spatial and performative material potential of the location and the built. The design considered what "repair might mean" (e.g., Jackson, 2014), extending beyond this into a mode of social provisioning with acts of situated care in a twenty-first-century setting (Cumbers, Davis, and McMaster 2015) in which aspects of participatory urbanism, and shared making might come to the fore. This would be not merely in terms of design materiality but also material design practices that would provide means to self-propagation and resilience as the *HUB* comes into its own, performatively and productively, and especially through a mode of "making itself."

As Mathews (2014) argues in his design of a new service development model, this needs to be seen in terms of building the intersections and interrelations in a mesh of actions and activities that are experiential for participants. In our case this involves visitors and local actors in the orientation, offering, and outcomes of what is designed with care, for careful futures and in caring for a potential development of locally and externally connected "cultural tourism." Our work needs to be understood as part of a wider engagement in the Future North project, with legacies and contemporary policies concerning "Arctic architectures" (Hemmersam 2016). For us in Vardø—intimidated as we all were by the sheer scope of the hotel's rooms, floors, and possible uses—an Arctic architecture is best identified and constituted through "place specific Arctic urbanism" (Hemmersam and Harboe 2016). This is a form of urban co-design and engagement in which local community organizers and motivated use can together define possible future uses and activities.

Nurturing careful culture in context

As Tronto (2010) argues more broadly, today in the Arctic we are faced with the challenge of creating caring institutions. This is difficult to achieve systemically in small arctic towns and settlements, even in Vardø with its airport and good road and sea links. Citizen engagement (Creighton 2005) is now a key aspect in shaping urban design and practices that are centered on the everyday and shared decision making. We need to take up the emergent discourses and experience of "engaged citizens" (Foth et al. 2011), drawing together expertise that is local and remote, physical and virtual, in developing a hybrid of physical cultural space and online virtual support. Davies and colleagues (Davies et al. 2012) propose that such deliberations need to shift their focus from the discursive to the experiential, material, and affective that together allow us to emphasize "material deliberation" in a wider societal frame.

The Vardø Restored initiative has sought to rescue and revive select properties in the town and to motivate community-building, shared expertise, and collaborative practices through a bottom-up approach to urban renewal, supported by a regional bank and the municipality. The project provides considerable evidence of how locally generated action can tackle the challenges of a shrinking Arctic town where numerous properties are in need of restoration and lie empty. The project worked to restore selected landmark buildings, such as the North Pole Bar (http://vardorestored.com/en/project/nordpol-kro/). The Vardø HUB came into being after long conversations and scenario workshops about different development options and potential business models; visits to regional and local offices of the national innovation funding agency Innovation Norway; various social innovation and maker space sites; and requests for full occupancy from the Globus data sensing and strategic management facility located on the island. For the owners, making an appropriate and careful decision to ensure a culturally dynamic outcome was a pressured, tiring, and challenging process that involved mapping the various options against one another and against existing and potential resources (Figure 11.4). One of the key roles of the design researchers was to familiarize the owners with these options and to unpacking models of making outside the immediate ones on offer.

Along with the recent boom in social media there has been a growing interest in online action, making, maker spaces, and communities (e.g., Hargreaves and Hartley 2016), connected to emergent technologies such as Additive Manufacturing and fablabs as well as DIY media and citizenship (Gauntlett 2011; Ratto, Boler and Deibert 2014). Interest has grown in cultural and expressive critiques of technology through local action, emergent socio-material practices, and fostering sustainability through co-creation (e.g., Fleischmann 2016). Within HCI, arguments have also been advanced for the enactment of care through communities of makers (Ratto 2011; Toombs, 2015) and hacker spaces (Toombs, Bardzell, and Bardzell 2015).

Figure 11.4 Members of the two projects discussing options for the conversion of the top attic floor (From left to right): Maria Bertheussen Skrydstrup (owner, hotel), Heather Moore (consultant), Angeliki Dimaki-Adolfsen (designer), Janike Larsen (project leader, Future North), Jonas Adolfsen (architect, photographer), and Svein Harald Holmen (project leader, Vardø Restored). (Photos: Andrew Morrison)

The emergent ethos of maker communities has been taken up more strategically through the targeted funding of social innovation programs that support and shape commercial, collaborative entrepreneurship. The establishment of maker spaces for "social innovation hubs" has been taken up across Norway. Many of these initiatives are founded on DIY principles, yet are usually geared toward commercial advantage rather than cultural innovation, and do not connect to maker communities and distributed social media where knowledge is shared and sown. Hubs may offer touchdown spaces, venues for start-ups and for workshops, but they are not necessarily designed to connect these often separate initiatives, leaving them to the logic of a neoliberal, market-driven framing of innovation (Julier 2017). This is a core notion in the promotion of training, business, and innovation strategies, headed by the national entity Innovation Norway. Its program has funded venues such as the Impact Hub in Bergen (http://bergen.impacthub.net, see Figure 11.5) with its demarcation of values and activities that provide jobs and entrepreneurial skills.

The conceptualization of cultural hubs echoes much earlier community arts projects and centers where cultural production, exchange, and critique were central. The research literature has little on cultural hubs from a design perspective (e.g., Fushan 2011) and how a small community might develop a sustainable culture of care suited to its own setting and history. Further, this work is seldom framed in terms of design and less so in terms of how possible, potential, likely, and resilient futures of cultural articulation might be shaped and voiced. Special interest groups online and in specific places do arrange themselves and build and exchange their knowledge, products, expertise, and experiences. Well into our work we came across other projects, such as Casa Jasmina in Italy, with its focus on open source software in taking the Internet of Things into the home (http://casajasmina.arduino.cc/about/).

Nurturing a culture of care and a careful enculturation of "building" has been strongly influenced by the physical structure and costs of alteration, restyling and redesign of the Grand in Vardø. It looms large over the town, the first main structure one sees on arriving in the town via the road tunnel from the airport. The design of a cultural hub, the facilities, the services, interactions and process, management, presence, and a nurturing of a careful process takes time. It also needs the engagement of local inhabitants. The use of social and web media in the process needs to be designed with care and foresight as part of an unfolding, interconnected and yet distributed future for the Vardø HUB. This sort of "maker space" includes the unfolding processes of generating, learning, and sharing aspects and experiences in nurturing a culture of care that creates its character

Figure 11.5 Related examples of hub-based initiatives Sentralen and Impact Hub Bergen in Norway's two largest cities in 2017. (screen grabs from websites)

along with a related community of hope and sustenance (see Figure 11.6). We are now engaged in a wider a process of "augmented deliberation" (Gordon and Manosevitch 2011) that serves to connect virtual and physical to engage communities for urban planning.

Next the Vardø HUB will develop a website for visitors, highlighting birding, the local fortress and the award-winning Steilneset monument that memorializes the seventeenth century witch trials and executions. In making connections

Figure 11.6 (Top) Rasmus Skrydstrup showing his work in Trondheim cathedral in a discussion about designing a new kitchen as part of Vardø Restored. (Bottom) Angeliki and Andrew sketching, over dinner at one of Vardø's two Thai restaurants.

between tourism and culture as a mode of cultural mapping between space and place (Panofsky and Kellett 2015), we need not only to take up but also carefully orchestrate the further uses of online participation tools for contemporary public participation (Evans-Cowley and Hollander 2010). These are design elements in a wider communicative and cultural ecology of experience.

Conclusions

"Nurturing forth" refers to a gradual process of careful negotiation about how to work toward providing a cultural space and a potentially long-term platform for community interests and engagement in an island Arctic town. The design of such a culture of care has been nurtured through dialogue, through site visits, by working through alternate suggestions, offers, and scenarios for a future space that would allow for a diversity of present and emerging needs (Figure 11.7). We have come to see the Grand as a hub for cultural expression and articulation, for

Figure 11.7 Result of collaborative community and town mapping activity at Vardø HUB by Future North, Vardø Restored and Amphibious Trilogies projects, November 2017.

the meeting of artists, tourists, students, and researchers, local activities such as work functions, seminars, and exhibitions. There has been talk of turning the kitchen into a bakery; the loft has been a potential home for the owners; the planned coffee lounge became a carpentry workshop. Options, potential uses, and actual interests and needs have entangled us in a complex process of negotiation.

One recent development has been a community workshop involving public participants and key stakeholders, including the Mayor, supported also by the Amphibious Trilogies project into extended choreography. The event explored the position and potential of the HUB. It drew on a variety of local and external experts. Together we discussed and projected the mix of needs of the islanders and visitors, the community and means to careful further collaboration. This included wider issues of similar towns and the added network potential for connecting with similar municipalities in the region.

The process and activity of responding to these possibilities has helped us see that there is more than enough potential and demand for generating a space that can be used flexibly and tailored to different needs of the town over time. The programme for gradual development, partly funded by layers of use, floor by floor, has proved to be workable, and has nurtured thinking spatially about project-based and changing uses and requests. In the location of just one Arctic town, not all of these transformations are yet realized or defined. They need careful design that nurtures their potential as part of designing a culture of future care.

Acknowledgments

The Future North project thanks Maria Bertheussen and her parents, and Rasmus Skrydstrup, Svein Harld Holmen, Matts Kempe, Heather Moore, and Sandra Kemp for their inputs, Jonas Adolfsen for his architectural inputs and photographic documentation of the building, Amanda Steggell from Amphibious Trilogies for fresh impetus to the HUB, and the town of Vardø.

References

Balsamo, A. (2011), *Designing Culture*, Durham: Duke University Press.

Creighton, J. (2005), *The Public Participation Handbook*, Hoboken: John Wiley & Sons.

Cumbers, A., Davis, J., and McMaster, R. (2015), "Theorizing the Social Provisioning Process Under Capitalism: Developing a Veblenian Theory of Care for the Twenty-First Century," *Journal of Economic Issues*, 49 (2): 583–90.

Davies, S., Selin, C., Gano, G., and Guimarães Pereira, A. (2012), "Citizen Engagement and Urban Change: Three Case Studies of Material Deliberation," *Cities*, 29 (6): 351–57, http://www.sciencedirect.com/science/Article/pii/S0264275116309519

Denis, J. and Pontille, D. (2015), "Material Ordering and the Care of Thing's," *Science, Technology & Human Values*, 40 (3): 338–67.

Ehn, P., Nislsson, E., and Topgaard, R., eds. (2014), *Making Futures*, Cambridge, MA: The MIT Press.

Evans-Cowley J. and Hollander, J. (2010), "The New Generation of Public Participation: Internet-Based Participation Tools," *Planning Practice & Research*, 25 (3): 397–408.

Fleischmann, K., Hielscher, S., and Merritt, T. (2016), "Making Things in Fab Labs: A Case Study on Sustainability and Co-Creation," *Digital Creativity*, 27 (2): 113–31.

Foth, M., Forlano, L., Satchell, C. and Gibbs. M., eds. (2011), *From Social Butterfly to Engaged Citizen*, Cambridge, MA: The MIT Press.

Fushan, N. (2011), "Designing a Twenty-First Century Cultural Hub to Build Community," *Grantmakers in the Arts Reader*, 22 (2): 1–5.

Gauntlett, D. (2011), *Making is Connecting*, London: Polity.

Gordon, E. and Manosevitch, E. (2011), "Augmented Deliberation: Merging Physical and Virtual Interaction to Engage Communities in Urban Planning," *New Media & Society*, 13 (1): 75–95.

Hargreaves, I. and Hartley, J., eds. (2016), *The Creative Citizen Unbound*, Kindle ed., Bristol: Policy Press.

Hemmersam, P. (2016), "Arctic Architectures," *Polar Record*, 53 (4): 412–22.

Hemmersam, P. and Harboe, L. (2016), "Place Specific Arctic Urbanism," Paper presented at *Arctic Frontiers Conference*, 25–29 January, Tromsø: Norway.

Jackson, S. (2014), "Rethinking Repair," in T. Gillespie, P. Boczkowski, and K. Foot (eds.), *Media Technologies*, Cambridge, MA: The MIT Press, 221–40.

Julier, G. (2017), *Economies of Design*. London: SAGE.

Latour, B. (2004), "Why Has Critique Run Out of Steam? From Matter of Fact to Matters of Concern," *Critical Inquiry*, Winter, 30: 225–48.

Latour, B. (2010), "An Attempt at a Compositionist Manifesto," *New Literary History*, 41 (3): 471–90.

Matthews, T. (2014), "The Experiential Mesh: A New Service Development Model for Designing Highly Experiential Services," in *Proceedings of 6th International Conference on Service Sciences Innovation*, CD-ROM, Taipei: Taiwan. Paper 62, 12 pages.

Mol, A. (2008), *The Logic of Care*, London: Routledge.

Mol, A., Moser, I., and Pols, J. (2010), *Care in Practice*, Transcript: Bielefeld.

Moore, M. (1999). 'The Ethics of Care and Justice'. *Women & Politics*, 20(2): 1–16.

Panofsky, R. and Kellett, K. (2015), *Cultural Mapping & the Digital Sphere*, Edmonton: University of Alberta Press.

Parreñas, R. and Boris, E., eds. (2010), *Intimate Labors*, Kindle ed., Stanford: Stanford University Press.

Pink, S. (2012), *Situating Everyday Life*, London: SAGE.

Puig de Bellacasa, M. (2011), "Matters of Care in Technoscience: Assembling Neglected Things," *Social Studies of Science*, 41 (1): 85–106.

Puig de Bellacasa, M. (2017), *Matters of Care*, Minneapolis: University of Minnestoa Press.

Ratto, M. (2011), "Critical Making: Conceptual and Material Studies in Technology and Social Life," *The Information Society*, 27 (4): 252–60.

Ratto, M., Boler, M., and Deibert, R. (2014), *DIY Citizenship*, Cambridge, MA: The MIT Press.

Toombs, A. (2015), "Enacting Care through Collaboration in Communities of Makers," in *Proceedings of CSCW'15*, New York: ACM, 81–84.

Toombs, A., Bardzell, S., and Bardzell, J. (2015), "The Proper Care and Feeding of Hackerspaces," in *Proceedings of CHI'15*, 18–23 April, Seoul, 629–38.

Tronto, J. (2010), "Creating Caring Institutions: Politics, Plurality, and Purpose," *Ethics and Social Welfare*, 4 (2): 158–71.

12

The Artwork that Remembers: Designing a Methodology for Community-Based Urban Design

Jordan Lacey, Ross McLeod, Charles Anderson, and Chuan Khoo

Introduction: Designing an artwork that expresses care

Designing memory

Care must begin with the creative practitioner, if the work itself is to have any chance of contributing to a culture of care. This chapter discusses the collaborative design of an interactive work of public art in Selandra Rise, a newly developed suburb in the City of Casey, on the outer fringe of Melbourne, Australia. In most instances, the development of new fringe housing estates treats the "site" as a blank slate. This rapid developmental approach, fueled by population growth, razes the land and ignores the history and stories with which the land is imbued, such as the long association of the land with the indigenous people of Australia, and subsequent agricultural production. New housing developments systematically empty out story and environmental richness, deleting memory and leaving disenchanting, vacant, and alienating spaces. The development process then tries to imbue a sense of community through public art objects, with which the new residents may have no connection.[1]

Against this background, the project attempts to work with the new residents in the creation of memory. Memory is generated through artistic processes, including interactive touch, the playback of site-specific field recordings and the generation of light and structural vibration. The aim is to contribute to the community's evolving attachment with their new suburb by creating a place

Figure 12.1 A render of the final artwork. Note the sensing strips on the central stone. Beneath the ground is infrastructure producing the vibration, sound, and lighting.

in which memories are held and generated through their interaction with the work, and by so doing, turning space into place through the interconnections formed between people and environment.

The artwork (see Figure 12.1) will appear as two small standing stones emerging from the plaza adjacent to the entrance of the Clyde North Community Centre. Concealed beneath this rock formation is electronic infrastructure, enabling a range of evolving and open-ended interactions between matter, environment, and people. Transducers vibrate large steel plates embedded in the ground, the local sounds of community emanate from speakers and lighting plays upon the landscape. A reciprocal relationship is formed between the artwork's data-collection methods and the human activity that influences the artwork's daily expressions. It is through the generation of memory that the interconnection between community and landscape is formed.

Designing the "Other"

Conceptually, the design team was driven by the concept of the Other—the creation of a living sculpture that interacts with the local community. We use the term Other to describe a being of care. The various elements of the artwork (described below) come together to produce a being that, through interactive design, remembers. The memory of the Other operates in three ways:

1. The artwork collects data based on the ways the community interacts with the work on a daily basis.

2. The artwork is populated with local sounds that the community have identified as representing their suburb.
3. At dusk the artwork uses its databank (memory) to play back a mixture of local sounds, in combination with vibrating ground structures and uplighting, to create its own reflection of the happenings of the day.

Beyond its technical components, the Other is a call for mystery. The team asked whether the artwork can become a sufficiently mysterious entity that local people may be drawn to understand it and to interact with it. Rather than being just another piece of plonk art (so common in suburbia), this integrated work becomes a part of place—a mysterious inhabitant. It is at the point of interaction that the artwork-as-other viscerally reaches, through sound and vibration, toward the community who might seek to understand it. The ground surface of the artwork vibrates in different ways depending on how it is touched. At dusk, field recordings and lighting join the vibrational expressions drawn from the community's interest in the work on that day. This is an attempt to challenge the functionalization of everyday life (Lacey 2016) by producing unique expressions that attempt to evoke a sense of mystery, curiosity, and desire. The artwork that cares is built on the idea that connecting with mystery or the unknown is an integral experience to human well-being, and the creation of the Other is an attempt to evoke in the community these very feelings in a highly functionalized environment.

Caring about the artwork means focusing on the smallest details for the entire creative process. It is easy for the practitioner to consider a work complete in itself, while moving their focus onto the next project. While this may well serve the practitioner's personal agenda, it does not necessarily serve the community whose environment is forever altered by the intervention. Attention to detail is a reflection of the care taken by the design team to ensure that the artwork operates at its optimum capacity. Potential flaws or inconsistencies that might detract from the experience of the community are identified through rigorous testing, leading, eventually, to a work that provides a seamless interactive environment. To maximize the potential of meaningful community relationships, the practitioner must be invested in the community and ensure their work is carefully and deliberately integrated into the site. There is no way to define exactly how a creative team might achieve this. But by paying attention to the details of the evolution of the discussed artwork, a creative interdisciplinary team can work toward meaningful experiences that connect place and community.

Council-design team relations

The artwork commission was part of the design of the Clyde North Integrated Community Centre and Town Square in Selandra Rise, a new residential community located in the southeast growth corridor, 52 km from Melbourne's central business district. Selandra Rise is the result of a collaborative partnership between the property developers Stockland, the Metropolitan Planning Authority, the City of Casey, the Planning Institute of Australia (Victorian division) and the VicHealth health promotion fund (Nicholls, Phelan, and Maller 2015; Maller, Nicholls, and Strengers 2016). A key focus of the new development was to implement best practice planning for health and well-being and to assess the planned development's impact on the community. As a result, the development was planned to assure easy access to parks, pathways, and bikeways. However, Selandra Rise's physical isolation from the city and major shopping centers combined with the provision of a limited bus service meant that the majority of residents have long commutes to work and often require two cars to service the household. This is an issue as working adults are absent from home for long hours each day "reducing time they can spend with families, participate in community activities or exercise" (VicHelath 2016: 3), and the cost of managing motor vehicles can create a financial strain on households.

Selandra Rise's demographic is a rich multicultural mix: 42 percent of its population had lived in Australia for five years or less, 29 percent for 6 to 10 years. The main countries of origin are India (24%), Sri Lanka (19%) and Mauritius (9%) (VicHealth 2016). A large proportion of these households are young couples with children. The other major component of the local population is retirees. A retirement village is adjacent to the community center site, one of over 14 retirement facilities in the Clyde North area. As the local population will grow by 100,000 people over the next 10 years, addressing the physical isolation and cultural diversity of the inhabitants is a key challenge for local council and community organizations.

With these demographic issues in mind the Clyde North Community Centre was intended to provide space for community service organizations, and for community groups to come together. Central to the vision for the Community Centre and the adjoining plaza was the desire for a site-specific interactive artwork that would engender a sense of community engagement. The briefing document from the Arts Development Officer at the City of Casey called for the design, fabrication, and installation of an artwork that would play with the notion of poetics in public space and express public interaction in a physically experiential way.

The council's plan for the development of the artwork was to break away from the usual tendering process and instead employ a collaborative approach in which the council's public art, landscape architecture and design teams would work closely with an art and design-based research team to establish a fruitful exchange of ideas. Serendipitously, the Augmented Landscape Laboratory (ALL), an interdisciplinary team of artists and designers at RMIT University's School of Architecture and Design, had been recently established. At the time, ALL was prototyping strategies for the development of interactive systems that could generate affective environments in public spaces. The ALL team members were proficient in designing with a range of ephemeral materials including sound and light, and their interconnection through interactive data-based systems.

The ALL proposed a series of collaborative design sessions between the researchers and the design team at the City of Casey to establish the parameters of a creative methodology through which design decisions could be made. The process involved a lengthy period of familiarization with the issues surrounding the community, the site, and the nature of interactive design by all parties. This process ensured that the artists, designers, landscape architects, and the community engagement staff at the council had a common language through which to discuss the development of the design.

The research team successfully argued that there is a much better chance of creating integration between artwork and built environment, and of generating real community engagement, if the artwork feels like a part of place. This means the artwork should actively contribute to space (geometry, functionalism) becoming place (feeling, connection), thereby building community through placemaking, rather than the decorative afterthought that is much public art. In this way the outcome is a seamless integration between landscape and artwork—allowing the artwork to become a "living" expression of the land, a presence that calls out to the community for its own growth and evolution. More broadly, the methodology for creating this artwork is suggestive of more connected communities in which landscape architecture, design and art are combined to accompany the planning process in new community developments (Carter 2005; 2013; 2015; Lacey 2016). This approach could be extended to the development of new infrastructure in general, such that connecting community with place becomes as fundamental as the functional requirements (transport, housing, amenities) of new city developments.

Building the other

To develop a robust conceptual framework that put community needs at the center of the creative process, the design team engaged in a series of design development workshops in which the general issues informing the design of interactive public art were discussed, debated, and organized into a legible structure. In formulating a methodology in which memory and community interaction can be manifest, the idea of the conceptual Other emerged.

The analogy of an artwork that perceives the world around it, stores these perceptions within its memory, and expresses these memories through ephemeral media became the ordering principle through which the artwork's component parts were conceived. We recognized that the Other would be constituted of a body (site), mind (memory), nervous system (interactive system), and a heart (community interaction). Through its interaction with the community and through the nature of its expressive output the artwork would provide a link between the community and place, and the two would become intertwined.

The "body" was understood through the artwork's physical attributes (ground surfaces, decks, stages, seating, and trees) as well as its spatial qualities (visual connections, zoning, access, flow, and lighting). The concept of memory suggested that there exists a "mind" in which the trace of actions and interactions are stored. In an interactive artwork, the "mind" is constituted by a digital repository of records of interactions with the body. At its simplest level, it would need to possess a short-term memory, directly remembering the physical interactions of the community. It also needed to possess the qualities of long-term memory to recall, reminisce, reflect, and dream. In this way, the "mind's" role was to collect the memory of the community and engender an enduring memory of place.

The next corporeal analogy that the team adopted was that of the "nervous system." This related to how the artwork sensed the interaction with the community in relation to its environmental affordances (see Gibson 1979; Norman 2002). Technology provides a wide range of input mechanics for interactive systems; these include wind, rain, humidity, temperature, touch, proximity, and acoustic sensors. These sensors collect data that can then be programmed to generate physical outputs to the stimuli they perceive. The establishment of an appropriate "nervous system" for the artwork and the coding of response protocols in its "mind" that trigger light, sound, and physical responses presented a Pandora's box of possibilities and relationships between the input and output of the system.

Artwork overview

The conception of public artwork as an interactive and mnemonic entity rather than an object or sensorial field brought to the surface the philosophical issue of the relationship between the body and the mind. While it was useful to make distinctions between the physical aspects (body) and the interactive aspects (mind, nervous system, heart) of the artwork to conceptualize a logical design methodology, the intent was never to hold on to this dualism. [2] Rather, we sought through design development and collaboration to attain a synthesis of concerns in the final design. This integration of conditions also extended into the relationship between the artwork and the landscape design, and ultimately between the artwork and the community itself. In this sense, the artwork was considered a "being of care," an embedded and reassuring presence within the community whose character would develop and evolve over time. We imagined children interacting with this community presence as they grew, and how it would both collect and foster memory for the community. In this case the Other's configuration could be thought of as a constantly shifting assemblage whose identity was constructed through community interaction. Ultimately we wished the artwork to dissolve into the landscape and into the community, manifesting a complex ecology of place.[3]

In order to extend the artwork's scope beyond ideas on the nature of memory and connect it wholly with the physical world, the team began to interrogate ideas pertaining to the temporal, the durational, and the event. We considered the solar, lunar, and annual cycles as an enduring rhythmic pulse. We then considered the seasonal and meteorological cycles of nature that alter atmospheric conditions. The effect of these natural phenomena was counterpointed by a consideration of the cycles of human existence, the daily rituals and routines, the paths and journeys we make each day, the constants and fluctuations in our habits, and the accretion of knowledge and experience that we build over time.

While the stimuli gathered by an interactive artwork's sensor system would be ongoing it was recognized that its output characteristics should be focused and concentrated to give the artwork a distinct identity. A system was envisaged in which the artwork would gather information over time and store this input into its memory. This data could then be called upon to create unique compositions of light, sound, and physical sensation. In this model, the artwork would offer an evolving interpretation of its interactions with the outside world, imbuing the site with different moods and atmospheric qualities each hour of the day and each day of the year.

The team began to identify the nature of the physical outputs that the artwork could generate and their potential to create mood and expression. The integration of programmable lighting with the artworks interactive system promised to add definition and drama to the qualities of a physical form; to subtly shift and pulse, swell, flicker and dissipate; and to create immersive fields that alter our perception of the larger environment. The use of sound offered the potential to capture, through field recordings, the recognizable soundscapes that imperceptibly define the aural characteristics of place. Sound and vibration also have the potential to operate in purely physical ways, to create tonal and frequency-based interactions with the human body and to manifest spatial dynamics through the use of multi-speaker arrays. Ultimately the synesthetic union of light, sound and vibration was envisioned to coalesce and create immersive sensorial experiences that intensify our connection to a time and place in sublime and profound ways.

A major consideration in manifesting an interactive public artwork was the nature of its physical form, its sculptural presence, and its relationship to the landscape in which it resides. Through a review of precedents, the team identified three different typologies of form that defined different approaches:

- The **singular** artwork suggests an intimate relationship between the human body and a singular object that invites a haptic interaction through direct engagement. The works of Rafael Lozana-Hemmer were referenced in establishing an understanding of these relationships.
- An **array** is an ordered arrangement of poles embedded with lighting and/or speakers. Unlike the singular object, the arrays promote movement through a given space and engender a sense of immersion. Christian Moeller's "Audio Grove" is a seminal work in this approach to interactive spatial engagement.
- The **integrated** artwork is defined by the lack of distinction between the art and the design of the landscape. The overall effect would be shifting ambience and definition of the physical conditions of the site, a system that constantly reconstitutes the spatial perception of the constructed landscape. Nikola Bašić's symbiotic artwork "Sea Organ" and "Sun Salutation," are good examples of this approach.

The final design was seen as a combination of "singular" and "integrated"—an approach favored by both the council and the ALL team. In this schema, a large basalt sculptural element is sited in a decked area close to the entrance of the community center (see Figure 12.1). The central carved stone form, inlaid with aluminum sensing strips, invites haptic interaction and engagement from the community. The artwork then expresses itself through a system of integrated sound and vibration that emanates discretely from the ground plane surrounding the sculptural element.

Sonic approaches

Sound as affective medium is a particularly potent way to draw emotive responses from listeners. Music is an example of such possibilities; the translation of musical practices into environmental sound design is a relatively recent phenomenon foregrounded by the composer Murray Schafer (1977) and since expanded in multiple domains (Cobussen 2016). There are many sound art installations that successfully transform urban space for the benefit of the community using sounding objects and electroacoustic devices (Ouzonian 2008; Lacey 2016). The artwork discussed here takes three broad approaches to sound production. The first is the use of transducers to vibrate two large metal plates. The second is a stereo pair of electroacoustic speakers to generate sounds in the space. Thirdly, in combination, these sounds will create a soundmark (Schafer 1977) that can produce meaning for the community. The term "soundmark" is a useful way to think of the possibility of sounds to create sites of community significance. One example is the church bell that summons the community to significant events. In our secular times, finding a soundmark in new suburban environments is a significant challenge (see Lacey 2017).

The soundmark of the Solandra Rise artwork is embedded in the two main events expressed by the Other at dusk. These will be short-lived sonic events that will play sound in relation to the memories collected by the artwork via its accumulated memories. Designing a soundmark is arguably impossible, given that meaning cannot be imposed on a community; rather, it should emerge through community processes. The design team turned to ethnography as a means to gather sonic material with which the artwork might create an evolving soundmark. Sarah Pink, a pioneer in the development of sensory ethnography, provides a useful overview of the relationship between ethnography and soundscape, concluding that "there would be a need of both composers and listeners to facilitate means of communicating about sonic knowing that can accommodate both scholarly and experiential understandings" (Pink 2015: 173–76). The design team used a Facebook community page to ask the community directly for their favorite sounds. The collaborative team was impressed by the passion shown by the respondents, a unique urban-fringe community transitioning from a rural landscape to a suburban landscape, who were particularly proud of their multicultural makeup (see Table 12.1).

The next stage saw the recruitment of two new sound artists to the team, Camilla Hannan and Nat Grant, to collaborate with Jordan Lacey in the collection of community sounds. Over three weeks the sound artists combed the suburb collecting the community-reported sounds with field recording equipment. These sounds were edited into short, event-based recordings that will be stored in the artwork's programming. These sounds will form the collective memory of the artwork, an historical artifact expressed by the artwork for its duration. The sounds will be released into the atmosphere in varying configurations depending on the artwork's interaction with the community. It is hoped that in this process, a community soundmark might be revealed.

As the community center was being constructed, the design team were struck by the vastness of the sky and landscape in which the Selandra Rise

Table 12.1 Favorite local sounds as identified by the Selandra Rise community

Social	Infrastructure	Domestic animals	Natural
Basketball * 4	Screeching tires	Cows * 3	Crows
Balls kicked in park	Main roads surrounding suburb * 2	Sheep	Crows on street lights
Kids playing * 5 (children's center)		Horses on roadside	
		Horses neighing	Bird * 6
Kids on play equipment	Friendly car horns	Horses galloping across the paddock (late at night)	Magpies * 2
Flying kites	V8s & turbo cars		Flocks of galahs
Youth park			Cockatoos * 2
	Planes flying * 2		Magpies swooping
Couple arguing in foreign language & Mum yelling at kids (at same time!)	Helicopter * 2		Rainbow lorikeets
	Sirens	Dogs barking * 5	Frogs (creek)*2
	Waste disposal trucks	Walking dogs	Crickets at night*2
		Dogs playing	
Interaction & banter	Trampoline springs		Wind blowing empty can
Boot camp instructors at Hilltop Park (sat morn)	Lawn mowers		Wind * 2
	Bikes riden on paths		Whistle of the wind between houses
	Construction		
Chit-chat retirement residents	Music from school (bell)		Silence
	Espresso - volt café		
Live worship (Sat & Sun)			Lakes and walking parks – Cascades on Clyde
Loud music			
BBQ (see Smells)			
Cracking a can			
Launching cork			

community sits, leading us to revisit a discovery made in a laboratory experiment. Exploring the concept of sympathetic frequencies, we vibrated a steel plate with a transducer with low frequencies, the higher harmonics of which were played electro-acoustically through a tone-generated sounding object placed on top of the plate. A person standing on the plate could feel and hear sounds at sympathetic frequencies. All participants reported a strong sense of harmony between the haptic and the aural. The team's experience of the stretching scope of sky and landscape elicited the decision that the emergent soundmark should include a tonal expression at sympathetic frequencies with the vibrating plates, as explored in these prior experimentations. The sonic ethnography will be interspersed within this expressive moment: a crescendo of tones and vibrations that carry the memories of site as played back by the interactive artwork. There is a feeling of consistency between the expansiveness of the combined vibration-tonal listening experience, and the landscape in which the artwork will sit.

Data interactions

From an empirical perspective, the collected data driving the sound, vibration, and light output comprises the touches laid upon the stone by people over time. We wanted to transform this data by "softening" the ways it is interpreted. By "softening" we refer to the emphasis on the emergent qualities of perceiving experience (Simpson 2011), in our case a peculiar positioning of how a stone might remember human touch, and leaning away from the connotations of electronic devices as agents of surveillance (Liu 2004). The softening of data refers to ways data might be related to community building and the generation of sensory experience. It is data that cares, rather than controls. Softened data connects people and the built environment by way of aesthetic and emotive experience, rather than a form of quantitative measurement (demographics, weather stations) or social control (which is not to ignore the fact that some community members might feel safer, for instance, around security cameras). Community forms through connected experience, not through environmental control, and the discussed artwork use data as a means to achieve this. The sensed data becomes a dynamic curatorial tool; an instrument of memory, if you will, that shapes the expressions of the stone. Thinking about data as "soft" and malleable, in the same way we might reminisce and channel our memories, led us to use the data recordings of touch to express rich tapestries of community sounds.

Capacitance sensing (Lee 2006) is a technology implemented in many electronic devices, such as mobile phones and touchscreens, that relies on

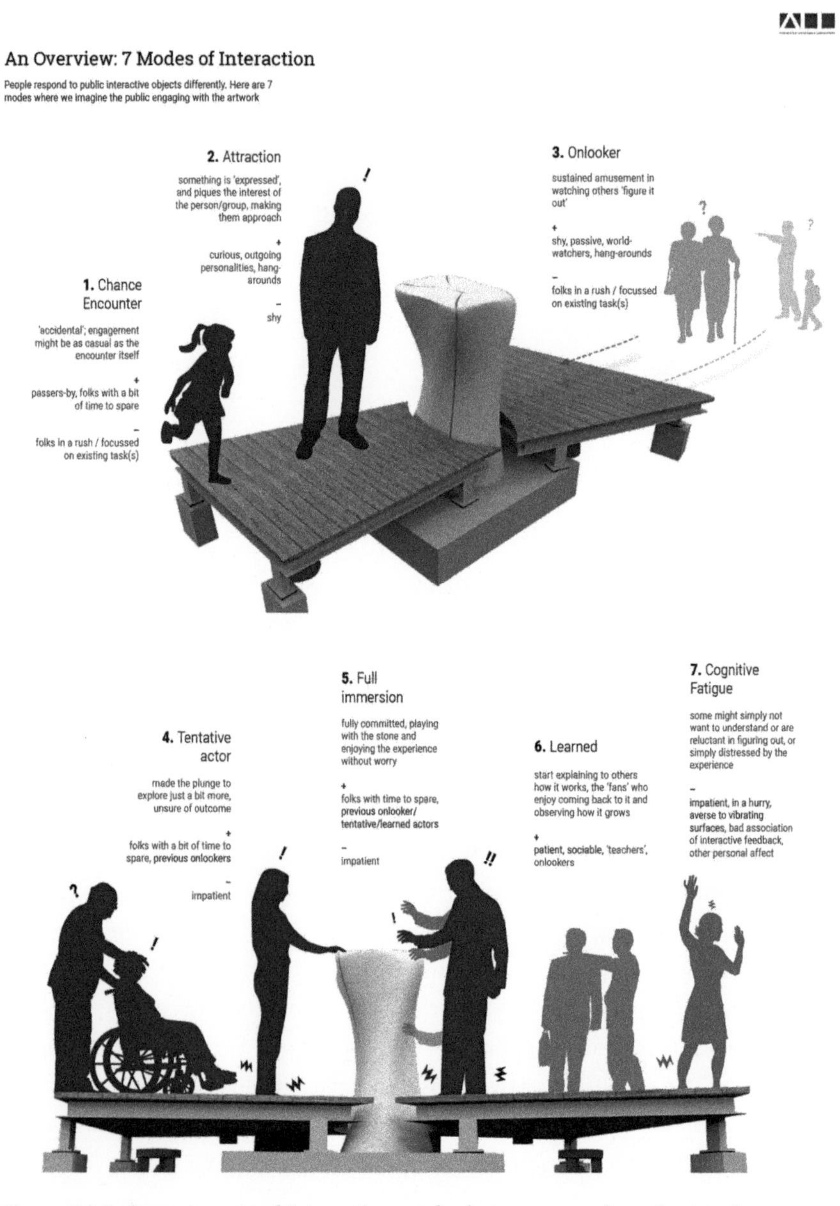

Figure 12.2 Seven imagined interactive modes between people and artwork.

the ability of integrated chips to detect the electrical capacitance of our skin and human tissue. Technological experiments with a large-scale, atypical application of capacitance sensing had to be taken into account in this work, and sensing circuits had to be tuned as part of the creative process. The resulting aluminum sensing strips, resolved through the design process, ultimately shaped the interaction design of the stone (see Figure 12.2). Four haptic, near-field and almost intimate gestures—hovering, pensive taps, touching, and embrace—emerged as the means by which one could activate the stone. The poetry and semiotics of physical action in connection with the feedback presented by the Other is meant to provide an easily learned, yet hopefully complex, emergent interface—a tacit coupling of knowledge through interactive dialogue (Gill 2007). The means by which people interact with the sensing stone reveals complex audio and vibration tracks depending on how the stone is being touched. Hovering interactions are linked to community sounds and vibrations that are atmospheric, distant. Pensive taps ring out bright, percolating sounds and perhaps distant, tentative ones. Touching activates swelling responses in vibration texture and near-field community sounds, while embracing the stone or fully engaging the conductive strips creates a state of saturation, where a strong vibrational pattern and immediate sounds of life and living in the community are delivered. These are suggestions only, which will be defined more clearly once the artwork is completed.

Conclusion

This chapter presents a methodology for integrating artworks within the public realm through interactive design, with the intention of creating a sense of place through community interaction. The methodology conceives of these works as new pieces of public infrastructure and considers them as expressions or gestures of care, rather than the imposition of preconceived architectural solutions that determine and constrict behavior. A caring artwork is one that reaches out to the community for its own evolution; it remembers the community and expresses its memory uniquely. In this chapter, cultures of care have been expressed in two primary ways. Firstly, the design process demonstrated that to produce infrastructure that cares for community, the creators of that infrastructure must be caring in their creation. Caring in this instance means ongoing attention to detail and considering what the needs of the community might be in every step of the process. It is care without expectation of return —the community may well be averse to or disinterested in the outcomes. But even this is a result, given that understanding community response can become the driver for future projects. To immerse oneself in a process of care is to work diligently toward the creation of something that can provide sustenance to the community who will live with the intervention.

Secondly, to respond to this need, the artwork has been perceived as an Other that remembers. The Other is a living sculpture that interacts with the community. It is understood here as a being of mystery with which the community interacts. Mystery acts as a repository for the imaginative, in which the encountering person can invest their sense of the unknown. It is from this investment that interconnection and meaning might spring. The Other remembers the interacting community through the collection of soft data, and in its remembering expresses vibration, light, and local sounds that have been chosen by the community. The work will develop in unexpected ways. To know whether the Other has truly evolved to become a being of care that operates as interconnector between people and environment, future research on community responses will be required. The idea that infrastructure should care could be extended to urban design projects that go beyond the artwork. If the creators of our cities thought more about the affected communities and not just the functional processes they are forced to respond to, such as the rapid addition of housing and roads for growing populations, the formation of a built environment that communities can connect with would be more probable. It is no doubt an over-extension to suggest artworks can solve urban problems, but they can at least suggest the importance of diverse experiences, emerging from the encountering of mystery, to human well-being and the potential for thoughtful urban design to catalyze such experiences across a range of infrastructure.

Notes

1 In public art programs run by local government (including this case study) artworks are called for after the new estate has been built.

2 Such a discussion is well beyond the scope of this chapter; however, the burgeoning and interrelated fields of embodied knowledge and distributed cognition mark recent thinking in this area (see Serres 2008, Latour 1993, Delanda 2004).

3 There has been a renewed interest in ecological thinking in many disciplines in an attempt to reconceive dynamic complex interactive systems. Ecological thinking is of course intimately connected with distributive cognition, embodied knowledge, and the flat ontologies of the new materialism. See for example Bateson (1972), Morton (2012) and Mostafavi (2010).

References

Bateson, G. (1972), *Steps to an Ecology of Mind*, Chicago: University of Chicago Press.

Carter, P. (2005), *Mythform: The Making of Nearamnew at Federation Square*, Melbourne: Melbourne University Press.

Carter, P. (2013), *Meeting Place: The Human Encounter & the Challenge of Coexistence*, Minneapolis: University of Minnesota Press.

Carter, P. (2015), *Places Made After Their Stories: Design and the Art of Choreotopography*, Nedlands WA: University of Western Australia Publishing.

Cobussen, M. (2016), *Towards a 'New' Sonic Ecology*, Netherlands: Universiteit Leiden.

Delanda, M. (2004), *Intensive Science and Virtual Philosophy*, New York: Continuum.

Gibson, J. (1979), *The Ecological Approach to Visual Perception*, Boston: Houghton Mifflin.

Gill, S. P. (2007), *Cognition, Communication and Interaction Transdisciplinary Perspectives on Interactive Technology*, Dordrecht: Springer.

Lacey, J. (2016), *Sonic Rupture: A Practice-Led Approach to Urban Soundscape Design*, New York: Bloomsbury.

Lacey, J. (2017), "Let Cities Speak," theconversation.com, 22 May.

Latour, B. (1993), *We Have Never Been Modern*, Cambridge, MA: Harvard University Press.

Lee, M. (2006), "At the Heart of Any Capacitive-Sensing System is a Set of Conductors that Interact with Electric Fields.—The Art of Capacitive Touch Sensing—Recent Advances are Making Capacitance-Based Switches an Alternative to Mechanical Switches (FEATURE - Best of 2006)," *Electronic Engineering Times*, December 28, 2006, Issue 1455.

Liu, C. (2004), "A Brief Genealogy of Privacy: CTRL [Space] Rhetorics of Surveillance from Bentham to Big Brother," *Grey Room*, 15: 102–18.

Maller, C., Nicholls, L., and Strengers, Y. (2016), "Understanding the Materiality of Neighbourhoods in 'Healthy Practices': Outdoor Exercise Practices in a New Master-planned Estate," *Urban Policy and Research*, 34 (1): 55–72.

Morton, T. (2012), *The Ecological Thought*, Cambridge, MA: Harvard University Press.

Mostafavi, M. and Doherty, G. (2010), *Ecological Urbanism*, Harvard University: Lars Müller Publishers.

Nicholls, L., Phelan, K., and Maller, C. (2015), "'Time Poor, Health Poor? Travel Related Time Poverty and Resident Health in a Greenfield Master-Planned Estate," *State of Australian Cities Conference*, December 9–11, 2015.

Norman, D. (2002), *The Design of Everyday Things*, New York: Basic Books.
Ouzounian, G. (2008), "Sound Art and Spatial Practices: Situating Sound Installation Art Since 1958," PhD Thesis, University of California, San Diego.
Pink, S. (2015), *Doing Sensory Ethnography*, 2nd ed., London: Sage.
Schafer, M. (1977), *The Soundscape: Our Sonic Environment and the Tuning of the World*, Canada: Destiny Books.
Serres, M. (2008), *The Five Senses: A Philosophy of Mingled Bodies*, London and New York: Continuum.
Simpson, Z. (2011), "Merleau-Ponty and Emergent Perception," *Journal of the British Society for Phenomenology*, 42 (3): 290–304.
Vichealth (2016), *Planning and Designing Healthy New Communities: Selandra Rise*, Carlton: Victorian Health Promotion Foundation, https://www.planning.org.au/documents/item/7719 (accessed July 24, 2016).

13

Seeking Empathy in Conscious Cities

Claire McAndrew and Itai Palti

Seeking empathy

Seek (1969–70), also known as Blocksworld, was an installation produced by Nicholas Negroponte with the Architecture Machine Group at MIT, originally shown in the exhibition *Software / Information technology: Its New Meaning for Art.*[1] This 5 × 8 foot superstructure contained metal cubes that when displaced by the small population of gerbils were straightened and/or spatially recalibrated by a robotic arm, opening up the opportunity for a dialogic and self-reconfigurable architectural form.

Almost fifty years on, the vision of the conscious city has entered the radar. It takes as its heartland the idea of a "conversation" between inhabitants, digitally imbued objects, and responsive architectural fabrics at the city scale. Made possible by advances in the internet of everything, neuroscience, artificial intelligence, and big data, it explores the opportunities that might come from a more sentient city. Palti and Bar (2015) suggest: "The conscious city considers new parameters for successful planning. It presents an opportunity to raise the intelligence of our surroundings and improve our well-being." They speculate on how rapid developments in data technology and behavioral science could offer the prospect of our streets alleviating ailments such as stress, anxiety, and boredom by being sensitive to the pervading moods of people in different parts of the city. This chapter suggests that the conscious city when conceived as an environment of care calls not only for empathetic sensing, but intelligence in response to the environment itself.

The idea of a "conversation" between cities and its citizens is not altogether new. The architect behind the Smithsonian National Museum of African American History and Culture, David Adjaye (2015), has said: "I believe that for architecture to be emotionally relevant to people, that there has to be a connection, there has to be a relationship, that architecture cannot be autonomous. If it's not connected to the lives of people, the histories of people, I think there's a problem." Juhani Pallasmaa et al. (2015: 7) suggest that "architectural spaces are not just lifeless stages for our activities. They guide, choreograph, and stimulate actions, interests and moods, or in the negative case, stifle and prohibit them."

For architecture, to "care," might suggest more than emotional relevance or the inciting of mood. The word empathy stems from the Greek *empatheia* (from *em-* in + *pathos* feeling), and today means "the ability to understand and share the feelings of another" (Oxford 2016). For the conscious city, it is not enough to sense the underlying pathos. Nor is it sufficient to react without empathy. Seek, a system entrenched in responsive capabilities, was ultimately unable to "sense" the aggression, and sickness that eventually became rife as the gerbils wrought havoc within the supercube. For cities to be empathetic they need to sense the emotional states of the citizens.

Despite its imperfections, Seek has been described as one of the earliest examples of "intelligent architecture" (Shanken 1998). The programming behind it followed a simple production rule format (If . . . Then . . .) that instructed the robot to leave the blocks alone unless one of them has been knocked or fallen out of alignment with the grid. Blocks would be straightened to the nearest cell if nudged. If they had been knocked to the floor blocks would be repositioned on top of the nearest stack, in what has been described as "an inspiring image of a machine that paid attention to the preferences expressed by the gerbils and then completed and formalized them into new, pleasing structures" (Wardrip-Fruin and Montfort 2003: 247). The exhibition catalogue notes,

> If computers are to be our friends they must understand our metaphors. If they are to be responsive to changing, unpredictable, context-dependent human needs, they will need an artificial intelligence that can cope with complex contingencies in a sophisticated manner (drawing upon these metaphors) much as Seek deals with elementary uncertainties in a simple-minded fashion. (Architecture Machine Group 1970: 23)

The ability for the robot to "learn" and develop what we might today conceive to be artificial intelligence (AI) was bound by the simplicity of the production rule format. For Negroponte, an architecture machine in the truest sense would not simply serve human needs in a cause-and-effect fashion, but would sense and respond to sensory inputs. The process of design would be "a dialogue between two intelligent systems—the man and the machine—which are capable of producing an evolutionary system" (Negroponte 1969: 9).

The concept of conscious cities as spaces of dialogue opens a conversation between societal care, AI, and governance about the design of cultures of care. The sections that follow unpick three elements of this dialogue. 01 Voice of AI questions the neutrality of "the programmer" and posits a future of singularity and transparency. 02 Flaws and Faults considers how human biases and errors might be subsumed collectively within a democratic, conscious city. 03 Care for whom? raises questions of inclusive design and the ability of the conscious city to respond to and reconcile with individual and societal needs.

Dialogue 01. Voice of AI

Seek's attempts to handle unexpected events failed, and the relationship between the programmed environment and its inhabitants surfaced as a source of friction rather than cooperation. The resulting motif—a struggle between biological life and an AI—sat neatly within the era's growing artistic interpretation of an imminent threat from ever smarter technology.

In 1968 (two years before Seek), *2001: A Space Odyssey* depicted the computer brain of a space shuttle becoming aggressive toward its captive human. The mysterious nature of computer thinking added another layer to existing folktales of man-made beings turning on their makers. From the Golem of Prague to Frankenstein, the fear of creating sentient beings as a form of self-destruction is deeply embedded in our collective memory. In George Orwell's *Nineteen Eighty-Four* the figure of an eye in the sky entrenched our suspicion that technology as an enabler of tyranny is a real danger in the not so distant future.

In the field of AI the term "singularity" refers to machine intelligence that surpasses the capabilities of human intelligence. Our fears of self-inflicted doomsday resurface in the debate surrounding singularity with bright minds such as Stephen Hawking warning it could signal the end of the human race: "It would take off on its own and redesign itself at an ever increasing rate. Humans, who are limited by slow biological evolution, couldn't compete, and would be superseded" (Luckerson 2014).

We tend to imagine any being more intelligent than us as a direct threat to our existence because in biological evolution, superior intelligence secured human dominance at the cost of others. The scientific community is now debating methods to assure that AI will not become a threat to humans, suggesting a set of restrictions on self-modification, or built-in functions such as ruling that "cooperation [with humans] is always preferred to conflict" (Shulman 2010: 3). No existing proposal confidently lays out a solution, perhaps in recognition that AI might inherit human logic that allows us to break even our own laws.

The clear advantage of AI over human capabilities is the faster and more consistent methods of analyzing large amounts of data. A collaboration between Harvard and Vermont universities applied machine learning tools to identify markers of depression in 43,950 Instagram photos from 166 individuals, performing better at diagnosis than general practitioners examining patients in-person (Reece and Danforth 2016).

This superhuman ability is coupled with the unfortunate and sometimes disturbing transference of the very human quality of prejudice. Researchers at the University of Bath and Princeton University have demonstrated this transference, stating "that if AI is to exploit via our language the vast knowledge that culture has compiled, it will inevitably inherit human-like prejudice" (Flaherty 2016). In early 2016, Microsoft introduced an AI chat robot named Tay, to Twitter. In less than twenty-four hours, Tay went from tweeting "Can I just say that I'm stoked to meet u? Humans are super cool" to "Hitler was right I hate the jews" (Horton 2016). Microsoft quickly pulled the plug on Tay, explaining that her responses are derived from her interactions with humans: "a coordinated attack by a subset of people exploited a vulnerability in Tay" (Lee 2016).

Our fears of a super-intelligence are based on two factors: a suspicion that there is a correlation between high intelligence and aggression (although the opposite is true, see Huesmann, Eron and Yarmel 1987), and that a powerful nonhuman would almost certainly pose a threat to our existence. We might instead look at the "flaws and faults" in our own behavior and conclude that a greater intelligence would know better what is good for us than we know ourselves (i.e., unless it learns too much from us). Would a greater intelligence augment these qualities or overcome them?

There is as yet no set protocol for transparency in AI development, a mechanism that might introduce a level of accountability and confidence. In December 2016, Apple published its first AI paper as a response to growing criticism from the research community about its secretive operations: "The move towards more openness with the community is important for Apple as the push for more advanced AI software spreads across the tech industry" (Tilley 2016). Might growing transparency allow us to spot and understand why and how thought processes at odd with our ideals of care, equality, and democracy are seeping into technology?

Dialogue 02. Flaws and faults

Negroponte (1970) expressed a desire for technological humanism and embodied a belief in "collective ownership of information and information processing and the participation of users in decision-making processes" (Vardouli 2011). This view was informed by social and political movements in Europe and made visible through Negroponte's reference to Martin Shubik's "Information, rationality, and free choice in a future democratic society":

> Modern decision theory, economics, psychology and game theory recognize, as a basic case, clearly motivated individual choice under conditions of complete information. It is also recognized that two unfortunate facts of life remove us from the relative simplicity of this basic case. The first concerns man as an information processor and the second the conflict of individual and group preferences. (Shubik 1967: 772)

Fifty years on, we still like to believe we are rational creatures, logical in thought and optimal in all our choices. In the quietness of the laboratory, with choices described and the luxury of time, we can be the optimizing machine we desire. Allow the choice to be experienced rather than described (Camilleri and Newell 2009) or even take the experience of choice out of the laboratory and into the wilderness of the city (McAndrew and Gore 2013) and the patterns of human decisions change. This is not to say we become irrational, only that there are differences in choice mechanics.[2]

It has even been suggested that humans are "boundedly rational" in outlook (Simon 1957). Limited by the bounds of time, the tractability of the problem and cognitive power we interweave heuristics or shortcuts into our thought processes that exploit regularity of the environment (Gigerenzer and Selten 2002). Realizing these constraints we search through available alternatives that will satisfy (rather than optimize) our minimum requirements. The result is bias.

These flaws and faults are important as we contemplate conscious cities as spaces of dialogue. We have already suggested that a greater intelligence—which eliminates cognitive shortcuts and biases—might know better what is good for us than we know ourselves. But what if these cognitive heuristics form part of the dialogue to which cities sense and respond? Could we end up creating suboptimal cultures of care? Might we produce responsive environments with a set of design conditions that simply satisfice—adequately, but not perfectly meeting our needs?

To think of conscious cities as spaces of dialogue also necessitates thinking about the collective, for "The aggregation of individual wants and powers into social wants and powers is one of the central problems of political science, economics and sociology" (Shubik 1967: 774). We can see this in studies of human cognition, such as the phenomenon of groupthink, coined by William H. Whyte, an American commentator on cities, people, and open spaces. "We are not talking about mere instinctive conformity—it is, after all, a perennial failing of mankind. What we are talking about is a rationalized conformity—an open, articulate philosophy which holds that group values are not only expedient but right and good as well" (Whyte 1952). It denotes a mode of thinking in which concurrence-seeking within a group becomes so dominant that it overrides a realistic appraisal of alternatives (Janis 1982). This desire for harmony results in unwittingly irrational and even dehumanizing outcomes for the Other.

Writer, editor, and broadcaster Ian Hislop (2016) opens up the issue of citizens becoming trapped in their own social media "echo chambers," hearing only the opinions of those in their own circles and dismissing the facts and views of those that exist outside of it. Mary Cross (2011: 62) applies this theory to Twitter, which "submerges independent thinking in favor of conformity to the group, the collective." She notes that *New York Times* columnist David Carr refers to the digital social sphere as a "throbbing networked intelligence." We are reminded by Sarah Robinson (2015: 47) of Dewey's definition of empathy as "entering by imagination into the situations of others." The question is, how can the consciousness of a city be "read" democratically without being locked down in its own "filter bubble"?

Such concerns—albeit termed "loopthink"—are also appearing in machine intelligence circles: "Machine intelligence may also come to mimic human foibles, including the psychosocial phenomenon of 'groupthink,' in which excessive conformity to the group dynamic inhibits appropriate critical reassessment of a group's policies and actions" (Cheshire 2017: 7). Cheshire envisioned a future where some components of care are provided by AIs operating as interactive collections of cognitive entities.

> This loopthink would be a type of implicit bias, similar in some respects to the human bias in groupthink, that resists appropriate reappraisal of information or revision of an ongoing plan of action. Instead, digital processing of morally

> relevant data gets stuck in a loop of uncritical, rationalized, repetitious uniformity. Lines of code click along quietly, despite signals that things might be headed in the wrong direction, signals ignored or sidelined by the AI. (Cheshire 2017: 8)

It is not clear how individual wants and collective desires can be assembled in a democratic society. With empathy contingent on understanding and sharing in the feelings of the Other, how can the conscious city care equally and act equally and with fairness in its decisions?

Dialogue 03. Care for whom?

Arguably, conscious cities have existed since the early stages of urbanization. The city's consciousness, or rather awareness, of its populace is reflected in the observations, predictions, and reactions of decision makers. The dialogue between decision maker and citizen has varied with the balance of power—between plebeians and emperors, citizenry and democratically elected officials, to today's mixed model of central and local governance.

It is the dialogue between administrator and citizens that forges the city's awareness of and empathy with its people. At the heart of that relationship lie the mechanisms of human decision making, most importantly in vested interest, and empathy.

What is the motivation of a city to care for its citizens, and how does empathy inform an action of care?

This motivation stems partly from the confidence of citizens to demand more from civic space, emerging with the advent of nation-states and the weakening of feudal systems. The resulting political shift to republican, democratic, and socialist agendas empowered citizens to imagine what value public space could hold.

In 1968, Henri Lefebvre demanded "a transformed and renewed access to urban life" (Lefebvre, 1996: 158). David Harvey endorses the concept: "The freedom to make and remake our cities and ourselves is, I want to argue, one of the most precious yet most neglected of our human rights" (Harvey, 2008).

The blurring of ownership boundaries poses a question about the balance between private and public spaces, questioning the threshold between individual and collective expectations and responsibilities. Civic engagement meant individual responsibility to the public sphere, and emerging universal rights meant the creeping of government responsibility into the home. This dichotomy of private/public and individual/collective forms the basis of the question of whom the city cares for, and how? How can a city care for the individual and the collective simultaneously without conflicting interests?

If the city is to understand our needs, we must first be able to define for ourselves the thresholds of individual and collective desires. Our need for novelty, for example, is different in the home than in the city. We might change our regular commute to raise the chances for serendipity in public space, but it would be strange to behave similarly in the home. Unexpected novelty in our private daily routine would be unsettling.

Our needs and trust, therefore, adjust as we cross these thresholds. The more people, and the greater diversity of people, we share a space with, the more difficult the question becomes of whom and how to prioritize. If a city cared equally for people who benefit from different experiences within a shared environment, how could it care democratically? Considering the finite nature of economic and material resources to be distributed, even a highly developed intelligence would run into ethical issues of this nature.

In the United States, a 1981 Executive Order that institutionalized a cost-benefit analysis for Federal decision making stated that "regulatory action shall not be undertaken unless the potential benefits to society from the regulation outweigh the potential costs to society" (Shabecoff 1981). Supporters of the order explained that evaluating the outcomes of actions would lead to better decision making. The flaw of such a system surfaces when benefits become difficult or even impossible to measure. Even the important cause of investing in health care becomes a quantitative obstacle, let alone issues that can evade measurement, such as aesthetic qualities of space.

The cost-benefit formula underpinning this policy depends on the measurability of each variable, even though those variables become almost impossible to assess democratically. To decide which neighborhood a new air route should fly over, for example, one would need to calculate the total detriment of added noise to one local population compared with others. In reality, the perceived detriment to each population is extrapolated from the volume and intensity of objections raised, and their sources. Once again, the politics of in-groups and out-groups trump equality.

Even a well-intentioned formula for decision-making has the potential to discriminate. Accordingly, our confidence in political systems is based on a set of rights that guarantee to limit damage to individuals. Rights (and a robust acceptance of the notion of natural or inalienable rights) create thresholds between collective will and individual needs, limiting the ability of in-groups to ignore the needs they share with out-groups. It is perhaps those same mechanisms that would limit the possible harm AI could do, and allow humans to trust in the powers given to it.

Looking ahead

Seek, and Negroponte's (1970) vision of an "architecture machine," imagined the process of design as a "conversation" between two intelligent entities, human and machine. The theory of conscious cities as spaces of care has broadened the conversation. It calls not only for empathetic sensing, but intelligence in response, suggesting that one of our most urgent dialogues ought to center on the relation between societal care, AI, and governance. That we are faced with a lack of certainty about how to embrace this notional AI future is perhaps not surprising given our inability to decipher what is best for ourselves.

Hello, Robot, an exhibition at the Vitra Design Museum in Germany in 2017, is one attempt to bring the public into this conversation. Exhibition curator Amelie Klein alludes to this tension when she notes, "The difference between well-meant care, patronising control and spying is very fluid" (Aouf 2017). Exploring the relation between trust and care, the exhibition asks its spectators: "Do you want a robot to take care of you?," and even, "How do you feel about objects having feelings?"

The dialogues raised in this chapter challenge society to define this relation more fundamentally—What is care for *us*? Dialogues 01–03 address the dimension of trust through this relationship. This is not just about providing belief in the voice of AI or faith in our own decision-making abilities; it runs deeper into our confidence in the aspiration of the city to empathize. It might seem like a contradiction to look to the present day, but dialogue needs trust, and for this to be enabled we need frameworks of governance and law. We might even consider a form of constitution.

This is not unusual thinking. In the science fiction story *Runaround* (1942), Isaac Asimov proposed three laws to govern the behavior of robots:

1. A robot may not injure a human being or, through inaction, allow a human being to come to harm.
2. A robot must obey the orders given to it by human beings, expect where such orders would conflict with the First Law.
3. A robot must protect its own existence as long as such protection does not conflict with the First Law or the Second Law.

Later in the story he introduced a "zeroth law":

0. A robot may not harm humanity, or, by inaction, allow humanity to come to harm.

These laws might be seen to function as a constitution, one that ultimately limits the power of AI in the design of future cultures of care.

Notes

1 *Software / Information technology: Its New Meaning for Art* was curated by artist and critic Jack Burnham for the Jewish Museum in Brooklyn, New York City, from September 16 to November 8, 1970, and the Smithsonian Institution in Washington, DC, from December 16, 1970, to February 14, 1971.

2 Barron and Yechiam (2009) have shown that behavior can differ from judgment, illustrating that after a suicide bombing people can both believe the risk to decrease and behave cautiously. This holds a close relation to George Orwell's *Nineteen Eighty-Four* "doublethink," in which it is possible to accept two contradictory beliefs as correct. People learned doublethink and newspeak (a linguistic design to limit freedom of thought) to "fit in." The result was a deterioration in mental efficiency, reality testing and moral judgment.

References

Adjaye, D. (2015), "David Adjaye Talks to Lisa Fletcher," August 28, 2015, http://america.aljazeera.com/watch/shows/talk-to-al-jazeera/articles/2015/8/28/david-adjaye-talks-to-lisa-fletcher.html (accessed February 24, 2017).

Aouf, R. S. (2017), "Hello Robot Explores Our Mixed Feelings about Intelligent Machines," *Dezeen*, February 18, 2017, https://www.dezeen.com/2017/02/18/hello-robot-exhibition-explores-mixed-feelings-intelligent-machines-vitra-design-museum/ (accessed February 24, 2017).

Asimov, I. (1942), "Runaround," *Astounding Science Fiction*, March, 93–103.

Barron, G. and Yechiam, E. (2009), "The Coexistence of Overestimation and Underweighting of Rare Events and the Contingent Recency Effect." *Judgment and Decision Making*, 4: 447–60.

Camilleri, A. R. and Newell, B. R. (2009), "The Role of Representation in Experience-Based Choice," *Judgment and Decision Making*, 4 (7): 518–29.

Cheshire, W. P., Jr. (2017), "Loopthink: A Limitation of Medical Artificial Intelligence," *Ethics & Medicine*, 33 (1): 7–12.

Cross, M. (2011), *Bloggerati, Twitterati: How Blogs and Twitter are Transforming Popular Culture*, Santa Barbara, CA: Praeger.

Flaherty, N. (2016), "Bath Researcher Shows Machines can be Prejudiced Too," *Techspark*, October 21, 2016, https://techspark.co/bath-researcher-shows-machines-can-prejudiced/ (accessed February 24, 2017).

Gigerenzer, G. and Selten, R. (2002), *Bounded Rationality: The Adaptive Toolbox*, Cambridge, MA: MIT Press.

Harvey, D. (2008), "The Right to the City," *New Left Review*, 53 (September–October): 23–40.

Hislop, I. (2016), "The Right to Dissent (and the left too)," *The Orwell Lecture*, https://www.theorwellprize.co.uk/events/the-orwell-lecture-2016-2/ (accessed February 24, 2017).

Horton, H. (2016), "Microsoft Deletes 'Teen Girl' AI after It became a Hitler-Loving Sex Robot Within 24 Hours," *The Telegraph*, March 24, 2016, http://www.telegraph.co.uk/technology/2016/03/24/microsofts-teen-girl-ai-turns-into-a-hitler-loving-sex-robot-wit/ (accessed February 24, 2017).

Huesmann, L. R., Eron, L. D., and Yarmel, P. W. (1987), "Intellectual Functioning and Aggression," *Journal of Personality and Social Psychology*, 52 (1): 232–40.

Janis I. L. (1982), *Groupthink*, Boston: Houghton Mifflin.

Lee, P. (2016), "Learning from Tay's Introduction," *Official Microsoft Blog*, March 25, 2016, https://blogs.microsoft.com/blog/2016/03/25/learning-tays-introduction/#sm.0000qmlyoe16slct4z9t35vlfvadp (accessed February 24, 2017).

Lefebvre, H. (1996), "The Right to the City," in E. Kofman and E. Lebas (eds.), *Writings on Cities*, Cambridge, MA: Wiley-Blackwell.

Luckerson, V. (2014), "5 Very Smart People that Think Artificial Intelligence Could Bring the Apocalypse," *Time*, December 2, 2014, http://time.com/3614349/artificial-intelligence-singularity-stephen-hawking-elon-musk/ (accessed February 20, 2017).

McAndrew, C. and Gore, J. (2013), "Understanding Preferences in Experience-Based Choice: A Study of Cognition in the 'Wild,'" *Journal of Cognitive Engineering and Decision Making*, 7 (2): 179–97.

Negroponte, N. (1969), "Towards a Theory of Architecture Machines," *Journal of Architectural Education*, 23 (2): 9–12.

Negroponte, N. (1970), SEEK. *Software / Information Technology: Its New Meaning for Art*, September 16–November 8, 1970, Brooklyn, NY: Jewish Museum.

Oxford English Dictionary (2016), *Empathy*, https://en.oxforddictionaries.com/definition/empathy (accessed February 20, 2017).

Pallasmaa, J., Mallgrave, H. F., Robinson, S., and Gallese, V. (2015), *Architecture and Empathy*, Finland: Tapio Wirkkala-Rut Bryk Foundation.

Palti, I. and Bar, M. (2015), "A Manifesto for Conscious Cities: Should Streets be Sensitive to Our Mental Needs?" *The Guardian*, August 28, 2015, https://www.theguardian.com/cities/2015/aug/28/manifesto-conscious-cities-streets-sensitive-mental-needs (accessed February 20, 2017).

Reece, A. G. and Danforth, C. M. (2016), *Instagram Photos Reveal Predictive Markers of Depression*, arXiv preprint arXiv:1608.03282.
Robinson, S. (2015), "Boundaries of Skin: John Dewey, Didier Anzieu and Architectural Possibility," in J. Pallasmaa, H. F. Mallgrave, S. Robinson, and V. Gallese (eds.), *Architecture and Empathy*, Finland: Tapio Wirkkala-Rut Bryk Foundation, 42–63.
Shabecoff, P. (1981), "Reagan Order on Cost-Benefit Analysis Stirs Economic and Political Debate," *The New York Times*, November 7, 1981, http://www.nytimes.com/1981/11/07/us/reagan-order-on-cost-benefit-analysis-stirs-economic-and-political-debate.html? (accessed February 24, 2017).
Shanken, E. A. (1998), "The House that Jack Built: Jack Burnham's Concept of 'Software' as a Metaphor for Art," *Leonardo Electronic Almanac*, 6 (10), October.
Shubik, M. (1967), "Information, Rationality, and Free Choice in a Future Democratic Society," *Daedalus*, 96 (3): 771–78.
Shulman, C. (2010), *Omohundro's "Basic AI Drives" and Catastrophic Risks*, San Francisco, CA: The Singularity Institute.
Simon, H. A. (1957), *Models of Man, Social and Rational: Mathematical Essays on Rational Human Behavior in a Social Setting*. New York: Wiley.
The Architecture Machine Group (M.I.T) (1970), "Life in a Computerized Environment," in *Software / Information Technology: Its New Meaning for Art, Exhibition Catalogue*, New York: Jewish Museum, 20–23.
Tilley, A. (2016), "Apple Publishes Its First Artificial Intelligence Paper," *Forbes*, December 26, 2016, http://www.forbes.com/sites/aarontilley/2016/12/26/apple-publishes-its-first-artificial-intelligence-paper/ (accessed February 24, 2017).
Vardouli, T. (2011), "Nicholas Negroponte: An Interview," *Open|architectures*, https://openarchitectures.com/2011/10/27/an-interview-with-nicholas-negroponte/ (accessed February 24, 2017).
Wardrip-Fruin, N. and Montfort, B. (2003), *New Media Reader*, London: MIT Press.
Whyte, W. H. (1952), *Groupthink, Fortune*, July 22, 2012, http://fortune.com/2012/07/22/groupthink-fortune-1952/ (accessed February 24, 2017).

Possible images

The 1970 poster for *Software / Information technology: Its New Meaning for Art* exhibition.
Seek (1970) Negroponte with Architecture Machine Group, MIT.
A Manifesto for Conscious Cities (2015).

14

Concerning Relations in the City: Designing Relational Services in Sharing Economies

Cameron Tonkinwise

Concerned beings

Martin Heidegger, among others, is often credited with recognizing that the nature of human being is to be concerned about the nature of being.[1] We humans do not, or rather do not aspire to, just exist, but rather care about the quality of our existence. We want to not just survive, but thrive, with purpose, but also in ways that expose new ways of being—new forms of living, but also new life-forms and even just new things.

This is, or so it seems to me, a nice philosophy. It feels therapeutic to know that being concerned about the meaning of life is the meaning of life;[2] to worry about who I am and what I should be doing, to be questioning how I am doing things and why, even to the point of anxiety, is, according to Heidegger, the very point of being human. Being concerned, about what to do today or what to do if this is my last day alive, or what that thing there is or even why there is something rather than nothing, all of these concerns are what it means to be human.

It is an important part of Heidegger's argument that what he is describing relates some of the more mundane aspects of everyday life—being concerned about where your keys are, whether you ate a good-enough breakfast and how to find time to do more reading—to "larger," more political issues—being concerned about whether a neighborhood is a good place to raise children and how to find ways of helping to improve it. This is in fact the early Heidegger's major contribution to philosophy—building an account of the world that begins with equipment but extends to all existence, including the historico-political nature of people. The essence of what a hammer is lies in what it is for, which is a cascade of increasing significance: hammering, in order to build things, like homes, so that we can dwell in protection, and so be able to contemplate the meaning of existence.

It is in these nested systems of practices and meanings that Heidegger locates other people. In the scenario Heidegger describes, a person is concerned about getting a whole bunch of things done well each day, which they do with and for other people and their collective sense of what is appropriate. While the concerns that structure everyday activities feel particular to each person, occasionally to the singularizing fact that one day that person will die, those activities always to some extent involve other people: what matters to you is that you matter, which you evaluate in terms of others—what others think matters and whether, with respect to what they think matters, you matter to them.[3] What Heidegger considered collectively appropriate turned out to be quite compatible with what Nazis and even anti-Semites thought mattered.[4]

Being helped and helpful

Relations to other people should have arisen sooner in Heidegger's philosophy than they do. Heidegger was clear for instance that being anxious about the state of every single thing in the world, and the world itself and our place in it, is not a sustainable way to be. It is easy to be overwhelmed by all that seems to matter, from the little things all the way up to the big, existential ones. For Heidegger, we try to deal with this overwhelming set of situations by making decisions about what really matters. To do this, Heidegger argues that we consult other people, perhaps just in the abstract, as to our ethno-historical priorities.[5] But before doing this, you can, probably do, and perhaps should, just ask other "concrete" people for help with some of your pressing concerns. Long before prioritizing according to our linguistic community's destiny, we can simply each act to relieve some of the concerns of those we count as friends and relatives, at least the instrumental concerns.

The problem with this "just help each other out" philosophy is that helping someone might lessen the concerns of that person, but only at the cost of adding those concerns to those of the helper. Helping someone else means redistributing concerns, not "net concern elimination." If I am concerned about you, I help by taking on some of your concerns; you "share" your concerns with me, unburdening yourself of them so that I might shoulder them for you.

To some extent, political economy is how as a society we negotiate this. We decide whose concerns are more important, and find ways of compelling others to give up servicing their own concerns and instead service those of the more important (see, for example, Fiske 1991). This compulsion could be slavery, or patriarchy, or capitalism, and so on. Service Design, and its step-child, the Gig Economy, are perhaps the latest processes for arranging who bears whose concerns. I will come back to this below.

Taking care of things

Despite the dangerous politics entailed by Heidegger's philosophy, there are other valuable insights that come from his starting with equipmentality. For, another way to work at making the nature of our existence less overwhelmingly concerning is the fabrication of tools and built environments.[6] We try to find ways of coping with things by making things that ease our concerns: clothes and environments that can protect us from the elements while we sleep; tools and devices that can allow us to work with more power, accuracy, and/or speed; objects, images, and communications that remind us of specific people or the cultural values of "our" people; and so on.

As Elaine Scarry (1985) and Bruno Latour (1992) have noted in quite different contexts, when we (meaning designers) make these things to alleviate our concerns, we are delegating that being-concerned to things, things that we animate to act as caring people-substitutes. We design artifacts that offer assistance to us for this or that specific concern, making themselves available to us as soon as the need arises. What designers call affordances are things articulating their concern for us (Tonkinwise 2017b)—the seat for our tiredness while we read, the mixing machine for combining ingredients for a cake while we make the icing, the emergency services number for when we are in crisis. According to the global consumer class, being comfortable means having things, rather than people, about you ready to comfort you whenever you might have a concern (Shove 2004). We call these things conveniences; they are gathered around us (*venire*—to come, *con*—with) so that it takes little effort to access them and their capacities to help us cope with everyday existence (Ierley 1999).

To live comfortably with fewer concerns in capitalist societies seems to entail having a house stuffed with furnishings and devices. Supposedly, there is some upper limit to the number of things that are needed to take more or less adequate care of such people's concerns. This is however never really the case for three reasons. First, the whole point of human existence, according to Heidegger's generative philosophy, is to be concerned. By taking care of certain concerns (via other people or animated things), we are freed to let our concern turn to other things we care more about, or consider to be more concerning. These other concerns may then demand further things that could help us take care of those "higher order" matters. Secondly, as the number of things proliferates, the capacity of individual things to take care of us in the way they were designed to, can be constrained or disrupted by other existing things, or rather the practices associated with accessing their services. We then need more things to handle the conflicts between existing things.[7] Thirdly, what concerns us are not only things we are currently suffering, but things that might happen. I feel the need for things just in case certain situations arise: a larger oven in case many guests arrive for a meal; skis in case I get time to take a vacation; and so on. The list of things that could take place, and so need concern-alleviating things, is exhaustless.

There are then two ways of dealing with our concernful (the opposite of carefree) day-to-day lives. Get people to help us, or get things to act in place of people. In either case, these designed-to-take-care-of-things people or things need to be at hand if they are to be of assistance. In capitalist societies, keeping helpful people and things at hand is accomplished through ownership: paying to have access to that help when and where it is needed.[8]

The political economy of the Global North over the second-half of the twentieth century promoted the idea that freedom entailed freedom from people by possessing large numbers of conveniences. With sufficient possessions, it was possible to live apart from other people, in free-standing buildings buffered from other buildings by small strips of nature—not concerning quantities or qualities of nature; just carefully controlled exhibits of nature called gardens. Suburban households with the minimum number of genetically related people in them came to be an idealized version of a concern-free existence.

Concerning cities

However, given the human predilection for being concerned, these settlement patterns quickly proved inadequate. Despite piping different experiences into all those households via television, people seem to have been feeling the need to access contexts in which many more and different kinds of concerns can be met.[9] So those with sufficient means have been re-urbanizing.

Cities afford quite different ways for people to handle the concerns of human existence. Increased density means that people may not be able to possess so many things; but because so many people are so close by, it is not necessary to possess so many people-substitute products; and all those people can afford a much greater range of concerns to get help with. In short, the number of people in a city make possible people-based help with all that is or could be of concern.

The number of people in cities is however also their drawback. As I walk down a crowded city street, I encounter countless numbers of people each with their own concerns more or less on display. It is just not possible to be someone concerned for all other people in a city. We know from urban sociology that people had to learn to be unconcerned by or for others in cities. Civil inattention is a foundational skill for being in a city (Goffman 1963). In other words, though cities afford greater servicing of our concerns, enhancing our capacity to lives worth mattering about, cities also demand that we be less concerned about all the people we encounter as we go about those meaningful lives.

According to macroeconomic social histories (Polanyi 1957), the scaling up of cities required monetized systems of exchange in order to deal with these care paradoxes. Neutral measures of equivalence allowed spontaneous contracts between people who did not therefore need to be concerned for each other before or after an economic exchange. Strangers were able to offer goods and services to each other to meet their concerns without having social ties: economic interactions were decoupled from social relations, allowing more fluid systems of "cooperation without trust" (Cook, Hardin, and Levi 2005). It was now possible, with enough money, to be in the city and get help with any of your concerns, without being encumbered by concerns for too many other people.

Performing the role of being concerned

A combination of the development of the "firm" and customer-centered capitalism added an extra layer to this. In service industries, employees are paid to play the role of being helpful to other people. That role is to be a representative of larger entity—the company, the brand. The design of service employment—scripts, uniforms, front-stage/back-stage—enables concernful engagements without service providers having to be fully concerned. Conversely, service recipients can expect consistent levels of help with their concerns irrespective of who the individual is that is actually serving them on that day; they are being looked after by the company or brand, merely mediated by any current employee.

There is obviously something disconcerting about what results. Cities become sites for human flourishing, as the density allows many concerns to be serviced, even new ones. But cities do so only by involving highly alienated exchanges. One of the challenges of contemporary Service Design is to heighten the "authenticity" of service interactions (Gilmore and Pine 2007).

Now, this whole account of the "human concerned-being," which can proceed by way of the ownership of caring products or accessing caring service workers in cities, is complicated by the recent rise of the Sharing Economy. The title, "Sharing Economy," is, as many have complained, already a contradiction. I would like to suggest however that that contradiction, between social gifts and monetized exchanges, points to exactly what is significant about the phenomena that the title refers to.

Sociality involves sharing, and humans seem physiologically structured to share: mirror neurons seem fundamental to the awareness of other minds needed to communicate; and coordinated perception—such as being able to infer what someone else is looking at[10]—allows cooperative action (de Waal 2010, Tomasello 2009). Sociality is also however rivalrous; use of the first person coincides with object possessiveness (Tomasello 1998). All human societies seem to involve combinations of rivalrous and non-rivalrous concern mitigation and distribution, and the nature of this or that society lies in the system that people use for deciding what is shared versus possessed. In so-called capitalist societies, such as dominate in cities for reasons previously discussed, non-monetized sharing occurs within families and some communities, while monetized exchange of possessions tends to characterize interactions between strangers.

It is important to note that even capitalist exchanges involve forms of sharing. When I go to get a coffee, I am borrowing aspects of the coffee shop owner's property: the chairs, the WiFi, the coffee machine. I may have to pay for some of these to get access to the others, but in many cases my use is cross-subsidized by other patrons or aspects of the business model. In this same way, one could say that even employment at a business involves a kind of sharing. The capitalist owns the means of production but shares access to it with workers so that the latter might earn their livelihood.

I make this tenuous argument in order to dispel the idea that what is unique about the Sharing Economy is the sharing component, which is often extolled as a trusting sociality. If sharing is what takes place within capitalism already, both as repressed domesticity and in the third places (between the domestically private and state-based public domains[11]) that are commercial services and even places of employment, then the Sharing Economy is just an extension of aspects of economic interactions that already exist (and for this reason not an oxymoron).

The comfort of strangers

What is the perhaps distinctive about the Sharing Economy is more the peer-to-peer component. This has become apparent as the Sharing Economy has evolved from Business-to-Consumer Product Service Systems, such as providing access to pooled goods (Laundromats, Print Shops, Car Share, etc.—see Tonkinwise 2017a) to Digital Platforms that broker economic relations between people (*AirBnB*, *BlablaCar*, Pet Sharing). While there has also been a shift from the sharing of things to the sharing of services (people come with the things—a driver with a car, a *Task Rabbit*, etc.), what is distinctively common to either kind of situation is that people are encountering people for the purpose of an economic exchange without the protection of employment; that is, without one party being able to play the role of a firm's representative while the other plays the role of "the customer."

In its original formulation, *AirBnB* involved being a guest at somebody's house. This meant that there was a likelihood that your host would at some point see you in your pyjamas, or vice versa. Even if only meeting the property owner to get the keys, there is a certain unavoidable social awkwardness precisely because this host is not in the uniform of a service provider. Similarly, in the original version of *Lyft*, riders were encouraged to sit in the front seat, and "fist-bump" the driver who was offering to give them a (paid) lift. If capitalism entailed the disembedding of economic exchanges from social relations, the Sharing Economy involves a surprising amount of re-embedding.

This re-socializing does not mean that economic concern alleviation in the Sharing Economy only takes place between people who are familiar with each other. Sharing Economy systems arose after designers found ways of allowing "peers" who do not know each other find each other and engage in transactions without too many costs in terms of time and effort. The platforms exist to supplant, or at least accelerate, the need for people to get to know each other in order to redistribute their concerns. This is of course the value proposition of these systems. They provide access to forms of concern alleviation or distribution that are otherwise buried in private property, mostly in under-utilized ways. And they do so by taking care of much of the social work required to find those resources and exchange them. From the perspective of the platform provider, if interactions required for strangers to take care of each other involve too much social friction, then those interactions cannot be scaled up to profitable quantities and rates. People will be attracted to take care of each other via Sharing Economy platforms only if those interactions are comparatively quick and easy; in which case, sufficient transactions will take place to keep the owners of the platforms profitable.

However, there are limits as to how much Sharing Economy platforms can commodify those interactions. Because the concern disburdening things and people we are talking about exist in domestic contexts, their situations are varied and not so controllable. If these potentially useful things had been bought up by a company, as stored assets or employees, they could be carefully scripted; but they would then be less well distributed, less available. The advantage of shared goods and labor, their accessibility, is what makes them resistant to being standardized into consistent forms. And that resistance manifests as people encountering each other as people rather than merely economic actors when they participate in Sharing Economies. These interactions are less than familial relations, or trusting communities, but more than impersonal commercial transactions. What distinguishes Sharing Economy encounters from conventional modes of business in anonymized cities, is that people are present to each in somewhat concerning ways, even as they seek concern alleviation.

The task of a Sharing Economy platform experience designer is to minimize without eradicating these concerns surrounding concern-alleviation done by way of people or things owned by other people. It is now apparent that if designers get this balance wrong and manage to remove too much social friction from the sharing experiences, the platform enables de-humanizing modes and levels of capitalism: AirBnB causes gentrification primarily when enable people with multiple properties offer accommodation without any direct engagement with their guests (Slee 2016); Uber exploits drivers and riders alike when the monetary exchange of the ride-share is backgrounded such that neither party sees the amount actually involved (Raval and Dourish 2016) As the business model of *AirBnB* evolved, as a result of investors seeking exponential profits, an increasing proportion of the listings on the site were by people with multiple properties. (Slee 2016) In other words, *AirBnB* redesigned the platform to accommodate more commodified forms of short-term rentals in which hosts would have little to no direct engagement with their guests. It is the volume of these less person-to-person transactions – transactions that can attain profitable volumes because they are not slowed by person-to-person interactions – that has been resulting in significant gentrification and housing affordability concerns. AirBnB has tried to obstruct efforts to regulate its offerings by denying that a significant portion of its transactions are performed by owners of multiple properties, hosts who therefore have to provide access to guests with as little person-to-person interaction as possible. AirBnB invests heavily in projecting an image of itself as collection of diverse individuals. One interesting counter move by AirBnB has been to try to create a motivational community of its hosts through distributed branding and large-scale events. These are all efforts to get people who are not employees to nevertheless interact with hosts in more or less standardized ways. Under such regimes, the levels of care provided between peers in these Sharing Economies attains improved minimum quality in service provision, but always at the risk of becoming more impersonal or less authentic.

Designing careful identities

How then to design carefully Sharing Economy platforms, so that the opportunities they afford for facilitating concern distribution in cities in less alienating or possessive ways are preserved? What is at issue here has been identified by collaborative service design researchers taking up sociological and philosophical accounts of sociality. In his account of Design for Social Innovation, Ezio Manzini offers typologies drawn from some of his collaborators' research with respect to Mark Granovetter's notion of weak ties (Baek, Meroni and Manzini 2015) and Martin Buber's ethics of existential dialogue (Cipolla and Manzini 2009). Granovetter's work evaluated social relations on their thickness—from temporary, functional, and/or commercial, so virtually anonymous to longer-term relationships with many layers including emotional ties. Granovetter argued that internet connectivity allowed thinner ties between people, limited to just shared interests, for example, to be nevertheless actioned for certain kinds of concern distribution and alleviation. This meant that there was a category of productive social relations between the impersonal interactions of the money-back markets and the kind of intimate engagements in which whole persons encountered each other that were promoted by Buber. For Manzini and his research collaborators, what is interesting about these digitally enabled collaborations is that they prove to have latent potential for becoming thicker social relations over time. What begins as a merely convenient concern sharing in one context can become the basis for more comprehensively caring relationships in other domains of everyday life.

This is not a natural evolution. It is something that the design of the Sharing Economy platform enables, and so can also disable. A key example is the ubiquitous profile page that each of us must fill in when signing up for any new social media system. On the one hand, these are merely identity verifiers that move internet presences from anonymized avatars to legally accountable persons. But on the other hand, they are registers of aspects of our personalities that allow weak ties to be latencies for thicker encounters between people. Interaction designers will create both the data collection forms that we complete and then the profile page that re-presents that data to other people on the platform. The decisions that interaction designers make in this regard lie at the crux of what it means to be careful in a Sharing City.

Design concerns

The density of the city allows a generative form of concern alleviation, but at the risk of creating an uncaring collection of economic exchanges. The cliché of the city becomes the corporate worker rich with economic concerns, ignoring the less privileged begging on the street. The Sharing Economy facilitates people-based concern coping, and can be the basis for more relational services, to use Cipolla's term (2007), ones that can restore moments of care. The key to this possibility for cities of care is the interaction designer, the person making decisions about the service design of Sharing Economy transactions. To foster cities of care, such designers need to break with their habit of wanting to delegate as much concern as possible to things. The Sharing Economy designer must try to make room for, and even encourage, situations in which people's concerns are presented to each other.

Notes

1 Heidegger opens *Being and Time* (1996 [1927]) by defining humans as the beings whose being is to have a relation to (the nature of) being: "Da-sein [the 'there-being' that Heidegger uses as a shorthand for human being] is a being that does not simply occur among other beings. Rather it is ontically [that is, at the level of everyday experience] distinguished by the fact that in its being this being is concerned *about* its very being." (page 10)

2 It is worth noting that more existential interpretations of Heidegger's philosophical teaching have inspired some forms of therapeutic psychologies. Eugene Gendlin, an early translator of Heidegger, established a body-focused process called Focusing (2012). Heidegger himself engaged with a series of psychotherapists, primarily through Medard Boss (Heidegger 2001 [1987]).

3 This way of speaking, about mattering, alludes to two distinct discourses. The first is a humanist ethics (Loewenstein & Moene 2006), the second is Bruno Latour's more posthumanist account (2004) of the overlap between "matters of fact" (a physical thing) and "matters of concern" (an issue that people share and organize around).

4 Heidegger's support for the Nazis, to the extent of having been appointed by the SA to the position of Rector of Freiburg University for eighteen months, has long been known. The recent publication of Heidegger's notebooks, known as "The Blackbooks," which Heidegger demanded be the very last thing published in his Collected Works, have made clear the extent of Heidegger's anti-semitism (Nancy 2017).

5 For the purposes of this chapter and this book, it is worth indicating that Heidegger's personal account of being authentic to what matters entailed reasserting a very particular version of Germanic tradition, one that is avowedly rural (though not so much that of agricultural laboring). Heidegger declares his opposition to cosmopolitan urbanism most explicitly when refusing a city-based academic appointment (Heidegger 1981).

6 Hannah Arendt's *The Human Condition* (2013 [1958]) argues that Work (the production of artifacts) is undertaken to ease unceasing Labor (tending to our physical needs) in order to create space and time for Action (communicative engagements about the nature of human being and society – i.e., politics). Importantly, the latter, for Arendt, takes place in the city, because only in cities are there on the one hand, sufficiently dense diversity of opinions to make the *agora* a productive source of Action, but also sufficient access to slaves to do the labor that frees selected humans (adult aristocratic men) to participate in the *agora*.

7 Vilem Flusser noted this tendency, of design's product-based solutions to in turn become problems, in his article "Design – Obstacle to/for the Removal of Obstacles" in the collection *Shape of Things* (1999).

8 Property in a legalistic sense refers to something that you have the right or power to control the use of, more than something in your possession. Owning something means that you can determine who has access to that thing, when, and how.

9 It was widely noted that a few years ago more than half the population of the planet was now living in urban settings, and that this would continue to increase. The most significant factor is rural to urban migration in developing nations. Urbanization is also a broad concept which does not necessarily mean densification, with many cities sprawling as a result. The phenomenon that I am focusing on is more like

Richard Florida's argument about Creative Class Cities. This is where the white flight to the suburbs in the second half of the twentieth century primarily in North America is reversed by those employed in Knowledge Economies. While Florida initially promoted this demographic shift as increasing cosmopolitanism (Florida 2014 [2002]), he has more recently noted the inequality that is comes with such urban gentrification. (Florida 2017).

10 Primatologists have argued that human capacity for cooperation has something to do with the fact that the whites of human eyes are visible (which is not the case for apes). This allows proximal humans who are not noticeably communicating (through voice or gestures like a head turn) to discern what each other is looking at, sometimes even unintentionally (such as when a glance gives away the location of a secret). This "joint attention," it is argued, in addition to allowing humans to act in concert such as when hunting large prey together, also becomes the basis of understanding the intentions of others: that is, "I see what you want."

11 The term "third place" usually refers to places of socialized consumption and production between a first private home and the second place of employment (Oldenburg & Brissett 1982). These "privately owned public spaces" do the work either of the emotional labor of the domestic sphere (therapeutic conversations with a barman) or allow work outside of the office (co-working in a café). My usage is more expansive, including all sites of sharing, including workplaces, as opposed truly public domains (parks, town squares, or streets, etc.).

References

Arendt, H. (2013), *The Human Condition*, Chicago: University of Chicago Press.

Baek, J. S., Meroni, A., and Manzini, E. (2015), "A Socio-Technical Approach to Design for Community Resilience: A Framework for Analysis and Design Goal Forming," *Design Studies*, 40: 60–84.

Cipolla, C. (2007), "Designing for Interpersonal Relational Qualities in Services," *A Model for Service Design Theory and Practice*, PhD thesis in Industrial Design, Milan: Politecnico di Milano University.

Cipolla, C. and Manzini, E. (2009), "Relational Services," *Knowledge, Technology & Policy*, 22 (1): 45–50.

Cook, K. S., Hardin, R., and Levi, M. (2005), *Cooperation Without Trust?*, New York: Russell Sage Foundation.

De Waal, F. (2010), *The Age of Empathy: Nature's Lessons for a Kinder Society*, New York: Broadway Books.

Fiske, A. P. (1991), *Structures of Social Life: The Four Elementary Forms of Human Relations: Communal Sharing, Authority Ranking, Equality Matching, Market Pricing*, New York: Free Press.

Florida, R. (2014), *The Rise of the Creative Class—Revisited: Revised and Expanded*, New York: Basic Books (AZ).

Florida, R. (2017), *The New Urban Crisis: How Our Cities Are Increasing Inequality, Deepening Segregation, and Failing the Middle Class and What We Can Do About It*, New York: Basic Books.

Flusser, V. (1999), *Shape of Things: A Philosophy of Design*, London: Reaktion Books.

Gendlin, E. T. (2012), *Focusing-Oriented Psychotherapy: A Manual of the Experiential Method*, London: Guilford Press.

Gilmore, J. H. and Pine, B. J. (2007), *Authenticity: What Consumers Really Want*, Cambridge, MA: Harvard Business Press.

Goffman, E. (1963), *Behavior in Public Places: Notes on the Social Organization of Gatherings*, New York: Free Press.

Heidegger, M. (1981), "Why Do I Stay in the Provinces?" in T. Sheehan (ed.), *Heidegger: The Man and the Thinker*, London: Transaction Publishers.

Heidegger, M. (1996), *Being and Time: A Translation of Sein und Zeit*, Albany, NY: SUNY Press.

Heidegger, M. (2001), *Zollikon Seminars: Protocols, Conversations, Letters*, Evanston, IL: Northwestern University Press.

Ierley, M. (1999), *Comforts of Home: The American House and the Evolution of Modern Convenience*, New York: Three Rivers Press.

Latour, B. (1992), "Where Are the Missing Masses? The Sociology of a Few Mundane Artifacts," in W. E. Bijker and J. Law (eds.), *Shaping Technology/Building Society: Studies in Sociotechnical Change*, Cambridge, MA: MIT Press, 225–28.

Latour, B. (2004), "Why Has Critique Run Out of Steam? From Matters of Fact to Matters of Concern," *Critical Inquiry*, 30 (2): 225–48.

Loewenstein, G. and Moene, K. (2006), "On Mattering Maps," in J. Elster, O. Gjelsvik, A. Hylland and K. Moene (eds.), *Understanding Choice, Explaining Behaviour*: Essays in Honour of Ole-Jorgen Skog, Oslo: Oslo Academic Press, 153–76.

Nancy, J. L. (2017), *The Banality of Heidegger*, New York: Oxford University Press.

Oldenburg, R. and Brissett, D. (1982), "The Third Place," *Qualitative sociology*, 5(4): 265–84.

Polanyi, K. (1957), *The Great Transformation: The Political and Economic Origin of our Time*, Boston: Beacon Press.

Raval, N. and Dourish, P. (2016), "Standing Out from the Crowd: Emotional Labor, Body Labor, and Temporal Labor in Ridesharing," in *Proceedings of the 19th ACM Conference on Computer-Supported Cooperative Work & Social Computing*, ACM, 97–107.

Scarry, E. (1985), *The Body in Pain: The Unmaking and Making of the World*, New York: Oxford University Press.

Shove, E. (2004), *Comfort, Cleanliness and Convenience: The Social Organization of Normality*, Oxford: Berg.

Slee, T. (2016), *What's Yours is Mine: Against the Sharing Economy*, Toronto: Or Books.

Tomasello, M. (1998), "One Child's Early Talk about Possession," *Typological Studies in Language*, 36: 349–73.

Tomasello, M. (2009), *Why We Cooperate*. Cambridge, MA: MIT press.

Tonkinwise, C. (2017a), "Transitions in Sociotechnical Conditions that Afford Usership: Sustainable Who?" in J. Chapman (ed.), *Routledge Handbook of Sustainable Product Design*, New York: Taylor & Francis.

Tonkinwise, C. (2017b), "The Practically Living Weight of Convenient Things," in L. Atzmon and P. Boradkar (eds.), *Encountering Things: Design and Theories of Things*, London: Bloomsbury.

15

Layers of Care: Co-Designing a City Laboratory of Intercultural Dialogue

Noel Waite

Care is "a matter of various hands working together (over time) towards a result . . . an interaction in which the action goes back and forth (in an ongoing process)" (Mol 2008: 68). Care is reciprocal, both given and received. The patient I wish to consider is the city, and the question of its long-term sustainment in terms of social, economic, and environmental health and well-being. According to Charles Landry (2008), two of the defining characteristics of a creative city are places of anchorage and places of possibility. The stories we tell about our city speak to that city's history and heritage, as well as of a city's presence and possibility. If these stories are presented in a dynamic way in our urban streetscapes, as locally specific, narrative layers of care for people and place, the city itself might become a novel form of intercultural dialogue that encourages future care-taking of people and planet.

UNESCO Creative Cities Network

The United Nations has clearly identified urbanization as a major driver of development and poverty reduction, and as an unprecedented challenge to environmental and cultural sustainability (Clark and Bokova 2013). Habitat III, the United Nations Conference on Housing and Sustainable Urban Development, took place in Quito, Ecuador in October 2016, while the UNESCO Creative Cities Network (UCCN) was established in 2004 to promote cooperation with and among cities that have identified creativity as a strategic factor for sustainable urban development. Melbourne, Australia, has been a UNESCO Creative

City of Literature since 2008, and Dunedin, in New Zealand, became a City of Literature in 2014. At the 11th annual meeting of the UCCN in Kanazawa, Japan, in 2015, new Membership Monitoring Guidelines were introduced that required member cities to report on their activities every four years, and provide a four-year action plan outlining initiatives that the city commits to undertake to achieve the Network's objectives (UCCN, "Reporting"). Of particular interest to design is the requirement in Section 6.1 that at least one city initiative should be "of a cross-cutting nature and link with at least one of the other creative fields covered by the Network" (UCCN, "Membership").[1] In addition to Literature, these creative fields are Craft & Folk Arts, Design, Film, Gastronomy, Media Arts, and Music.

Under the heading "Why creativity? Why cities?" on the UNESCO website (UCCN), there is a photograph of Melbourne, showing a cyclist passing in front of RMIT University's Building 80 on Swanston Street. This image speaks of the creativity and tangible heritage of architecture, the value of education, and the sustainability of human-powered transport—but it tells little about Melbourne's story as a City of Literature. In terms of the city's creative ecologies, architecture, music, and the visual arts are the most prominent and diverse on its streets. The William Barak building, designed by ARM Architecture in collaboration with Wurundjeri elders, commemorates this significant elder in the city's streetscape. Swedish researcher Christine Hansen (2015) described it as "a poetic and welcome intervention in the cityscape," but she also reminds us that Barak's advocacy for, and struggle over Aboriginal land rights is well documented in Diane Barwick's seminal book *Rebellion at Coranderrk* (1998), and that the change he experienced in his lifetime was profound. Hansen concludes "He reminds us other meanings lie beneath the great urban sprawl of contemporary Melbourne, not extinguished but in a layer that underpins the city." As a recent (January 2016) arrival to Melbourne, how do I find my way into the stories of this city, and how might these be communicated to future migrants and visitors? This may not be a question of writing new narratives, but synthesizing and communicating them more directly at street-level, and is one way that we might express care for a creative city of literature.

Stephen Banham's "Multistory Window" is an excellent example of the way design can provide insight into the tangible and intangible history of the city. "Multistory Window" is a typographic installation that communicates Melbourne stories through a single window outside a busy public toilet on the third floor of the Emporium Shopping Centre, and is described on Banham's

Letterbox studio website as "a quiet little discovery in the everyday." While Edinburgh University Library commissioned artist Alec Finlay in 2010 to commemorate its first donor in 1580 and his words "thair to remain" or "There to Remain" (Finlay 2013) through a mesostic poem, cities have been reluctant to inscribe text unless it has a specific commercial function; but it is precisely this commodification of language that requires a challenge if we are to humanize, diversify, and sustain our streetscapes. The vibrant street art of Melbourne is a case of resisting visual commodification while supporting new tourist ventures.

The UCCN has identified Creative Tourism—which it defines as "travel directed toward an engaged and authentic experience, with participative learning in the arts, heritage, or special character of a place, and it provides a connection with those who reside in this place and create this living culture" (UCCN, "Towards")—as one of the functions of creative cities. Georges Poussin (2010:106) explains that tourism is not just about visitors: "this aspect of connection with those who reside in this place is the most essential element to its sustainability. The local community and visitors will have an educational, emotional and social, and personal interaction with the place and the local culture, as well as share an experience of exchange with the local population. It is a chance to build up a relationship based on mutual respect, rather than on pure commerce," providing "a true laboratory of intercultural dialogue."

My approach here is to frame both a problem and opportunity in terms of a future Melbourne City of Literature that cares to communicate the human creative contribution to the city and impart lessons of sustainability and growth to ensure a sustainable city. This could take the form of sustaining narratives of the city, as well as environmental sustainment, exploring what the UN terms the biocultural diversity of the city. The Global Diversity Foundation defines biocultural diversity as, "the total variety of the world's cultures and natural environment. . . . Their co-evolution over time has generated local ecological knowledge and practice: a vital reservoir of experience, understanding and skills that help communities to manage their resources now and in the future" (GDF 2015). What stories can we tell to assist locals, new migrants, and visitors alike to learn from the biocultural diversity of this city Melbourne? What are the lessons of its rapid growth that could be shared within the city, and among the Network, and whose are the new and emergent voices who care for its future? And, how might this inform biocultural design?

Stories of care

Beginning with this opportunity to link Literature and Design in Melbourne, I wish to reflect on four cross-cutting initiatives I was involved with in Dunedin prior to, and concurrent with its designation as a UNESCO Creative City of Literature in December 2014. That they were cross-cutting was not intentional and only emergent in hindsight. The first two activities were for the Hone Tuwhare Charitable Trust to raise funds to support the establishment of a creative residency in the former home of New Zealand poet Hone Tuwhare. The first was a limited-edition series of prints with four New Zealand typographic designers—Kris Sowersby, Catherine Griffiths, Sarah Maxey, and Matt Galloway—in what I have called an experiment in slow co-design in an interview for *Design Assembly*. The original brief was for the designers to each work with the same Hone Tuwhare poem "Papatuanuku," to produce four interpretations of it. In discussions, the designers began reading Hone's poems and asked whether they could select their own poem, or as Catherine Griffiths put it: "it was very much a personal engagement with the work of Hone Tuwhare, entering into his world, and feeling a certain responsibility to make a work worthy of his words" (Anon 2015).

Each poster, in both content and form, was individual to the designer, but they had to work as a set, so decisions about process and production were collaborative. Kris Sowersby, for example, created a bespoke typeface, based on Hone's handwriting he found inside a second-hand book of poems, and incorporated a circle design from the cover, designed by artist Ralph Hotere. The production method was not determined in the initiating brief, and silk-screen printing was selected after considerable discussion within the team. The decision to screen print then brought printmaker Steve Lovett of the INKubator printlab at the Faculty of Creative Arts at Manukau Institute of Technology into the mix. Another debate ensued about what our black and red inks would be, before the prints were delivered to the Trust. Steve mixed the red and black inks from Matt Lewis's Live to Print rice-based vegetable inks, in consultation with Catherine Griffith. The first proofs were made in December 2013 with recent Bachelor of Visual Arts graduate Winston Shacklock, and groups of students from first to final year of the Bachelor of Creative Arts helped test and develop the color mixes.

The second activity, "Koha for the Crib,"[2] a concert and fundraising auction, was planned to launch the print series by the Trust in Dunedin on October

Figure 15.1 The four limited-edition prints of Hone Tuwhare poems designed by (from left to right): Kris Sowersby, Sarah Maxey, Catherine Griffiths and Matt Galloway.

18, 2014, at Toitū Otago Settlers Museum. The performance involved five musicians (Don McGlashan, Rio Hemopo, Graham Downes, Martin Phillipps, David Kilgour, and Ciaran McMeekin)[3], and four poets (Emma Neale, Majella Cullinane, Sue Wooton, and Peter Olds). Musicians played twenty-minute sets, each followed by a poetry reading of five minutes. Hone's love of food was also celebrated through chef Scott Murray who designed a menu based on the tastes of locally gathered, hunted, and sustainably farmed food. VJ Alice Lake-Hammond also provided a montage of images of Hone Tuwhare and his crib at Kaka Point to accompany the performance in the new foyer of Toitū. The key facilitator for the event was Scott Muir, a Dunedin venue and band manager. The event encompassed five of the seven Creative City themes (Design, Gastronomy, Literature, Music, and Media Arts), and succeeded in raising awareness of the Trust's activities, and contributed over $8000 to the Hone Tuwhare Trust.

Both the limited edition poetry prints and the fundraising event were co-designed, and their success was directly attributable to collaboration and the weaving together of different creative practices—"a matter of various hands working together (over time) towards a result" (Mol 2008:68). All were also infused with the Māori notion of *koha*, which is a gift involving reciprocity and strengthening of relationships—creative and productive in both these cases. Everyone gave their time freely, and enjoyed the excitement and challenge of sharing their care for their craft in a creative collaboration. The event also brought together different audiences from literature and music. Hone Tuwhare used to collaborate with a number of artists, in particular Ralph Hotere; they would independently develop creative responses to each other's work. Design can be a solitary activity, so there was a strong ethos of collectivism to the print project, in part inspired by Hone and in part to encourage cross-disciplinary fertilization. Fundraising is a necessary and vital part of the sustainability of any long-term creative endeavor, and I was seeking an inclusive and reciprocally creative process that would raise funds and raise awareness of Hone's and the Trust's work.

Figure 15.2 Promotional poster for the Koha for the Crib fundraising concert in Dunedin, New Zealand, 2014.

The third and fourth initiatives followed Dunedin's designation as a City of Literature. Poetick was the initiative of University of Otago Design student Ben Alder, and was developed through coursework in Strategic Design and Design Futures in 2015. The catalyst for the project was identifying the negative experience of paying for inner-city parking and considering the opportunity provided by Dunedin's recognition as a UNESCO Creative City of Literature to take poetry to the streets through an existing distribution system, the parking machines that distribute window-display tickets. As Ben put it: "It's that 20–30 seconds of walking back to your car. You're not doing anything anyway. So you'd just flip [your ticket] over and have a read of your poem" (Borley 2015). The goal of the project was to "connect people, place and literature" and its aim was to raise awareness of Dunedin's UNESCO Creative City of Literature status.

The Dunedin City Council's parking authority provided obsolete parking machines for prototyping purposes, and Ben, in collaboration with Design and Computer Science student Liam Bigelow, set about designing an identity, redesigning the physical interface and programming the internal printers to print poems, as part of a third-year Strategic Design social enterprise paper. While the strategic plan was to have the poetic parking machines installed in Dunedin and throughout the UNESCO Creative City of Literature network, the Vogel Street Party,[4] a community-driven street festival celebrating innovation, history, culture, and the arts, provided an opportunity to field test Poetick and obtain feedback from locals. The 2015 Vogel Street Party was themed "Literature and Light" in recognition of Dunedin's UNESCO Creative City designation and 2015 being the UNESCO International Year of Light. The adaptive reuse of heritage buildings within the Warehouse Precinct provided a companionable context for the adaptive reuse of parking machines. A Poetick tent was set up featuring ten working parking machines that randomly distributed poems from a collection provided by Dunedin and other UNESCO Creative City writers. Ben, Liam, and two fellow design students, Connor Harrison and Innes Galloway, were on hand throughout the day and night to explain the concept, and a short video, produced in association with ReFramed Media, demonstrated an array of delightful smiles as people received their poems from the machines and a successful proof of concept.[5] These results were incorporated into Ben's submission to the Shenzhen Design Award for Young Talents on October 20, a competition open to all UNESCO Creative Cities.

Figure 15.3 Designer Benjamin Alder demonstrates Poetick from his tent at the Vogel Street Party in October 2015 (top left), which provided the first public interaction with the poetic parking ticket machines. Poetick installed as an interactive exhibit at Toitū in the Creative City space (bottom), and the back of a Poetick parking ticket (top right) today

Poetick was also showcased by Ben at the University of Otago during a visit by Prince Charles and Camilla, the Duchess of Cornwall on December 1, 2015. The poem the Duchess received was written by a Dunedin high school student and began "Thus lightly but with passion shall I hold you as gravity." Her experience was reported in both local and international media, and her support for the idea was reported in *The Telegraph*: "I would love that idea passed on to Britain" (Boyle 2015). By March 2016, Toitū Otago Settlers Museum commissioned a machine as an interactive exhibit with the intention of developing it so the public and school groups could submit their own poems. The Lord Provost of Edinburgh, on an official sister city visit, was the first visitor to use the Poetick poetry machine at Toitū. A TripAdviser post of March 27, 2016, commended the museum, encouraging visitors to "be sure to play the Poetick machine!" (Anon 2016). To celebrate National Poetry Day on August 26, 2016, the first pay-and-display parking meters featuring eight Dunedin poets were placed in the central city Octagon. Poems are being added to other machines around the city, and there are plans to expand the number of local writers, including young poetry competition winners.

The fourth activity, Worldly Literature Dots, took advantage of adhesive vinyl printing, pairing a poem with a photograph, some literal and some allusive, of a Creative City of Literature. Initially, this was a local Dunedin initiative designed by Liz Knowles. Small 150mm prototypes were printed and distributed to City of Literature delegates at the XIth Annual UNESCO Creative Cities Network annual conference in Kanazawa, Japan in 2015, as well as some Kanazawa venues. Following positive feedback from recipients, Dunedin requested images and texts from other Cities of Literature, and produced a series of 500mm Worldly Literature Dots. As part of the celebrations for the 2015 Vogel Street Party, visitors were invited to explore the "Worldly Literature" exhibition by joining the dots around the Warehouse Precinct. In the evening, poetry from Dunedin and fellow Cities of Literature Krakow, Heidelberg, Norwich, Dublin, and Edinburgh, was projected onto windows and buildings on Vogel Street.

All four initiatives were sustained by collaboration and co-design, and the developing sense of reciprocity engendered by these projects strengthened both creative and productive relationships, as well as social participation with the results. The print series brought designers, a visual artist, and printmaker and an ink producer together to interpret Hone Tuwhare's poems, and encouraged a sharing of expertise through care and attention to the materials, both tangible and intangible. Similarly, the Dunedin Koha for the Crib brought together musicians, poets, a chef, and a media artist in a performative tribute to Hone Tuwhare, and the city of Dunedin that sustained him before his move to nearby Kaka Point. Koha for the Crib also provided the platform for the first release of the print series, and both projects aligned with the objectives of the Trust and its long term aim to provide a sustainable creative residency in the poet's former home at Kaka Point.

Poetick and Worldly Dots took place within the context of Dunedin's UNESCO Creative City of Literature designation, and intercultural dialogue between designers, computer scientists, local government, photographers, and authors informed the creative production, while there was an active and participatory approach to the introduction of both initiatives at the Vogel

Figure 15.4 The small 150mm prototype trialed in (and removed from) an Air New Zealand plane of a Dunedin Dot (a precursor to the 500mm Worldly Dots featured on the street at Vogel Street Party), which featured a poem and photograph from UNESCO Creative Cities of Literature.

Street Party. The VSP is a celebration of cultural heritage, both in terms of the adaptive reuse of the nineteenth-century warehouse precinct and as a site of band practice rooms and performance venues for "Dunedin Sound" musicians in the 1980s and 1990s. This community initiative exemplifies the notion of the creative city as a stage or platform for creativity, which both acknowledges and celebrates the city's heritage while simultaneously treating it as a space of possibility, where new ideas can be tested out and shared at an intimate, community level.

From branding to a sustainment strategy

A preliminary survey of the first decade of existence of the UNESCO Creative Cities Network (Rosi 2014) noted two distinct tendencies within member cities. The first was place branding to attract investors and tourists, and was the most prominent amongst member cities. The second approach was to collaborate with cities across the Network and build identity collectively and through international partnerships. The most successful event in this regard was the Shenzhen Design Award for Young Talents, which targets young professional and student designers, and is open to any member of a UNESCO Creative City, regardless of affiliated theme. Rosi also noted the limits of a brand-centered approach, and advocated a synthesis of branding and sharing.

While the designation of Dunedin as a UNESCO City of Literature in 2014 clearly provided both national and international recognition of the city's cultural production and potential for broadening its established base in environmental tourism, the benefits of active participation in the international Network were always a vital strategic component of the city's bid. The re-establishment of a literary festival (2014) as part of the UNESCO bid, and a subsequent New Zealand Young Writers Festival (from 2015)[6] have enriched cultural life in the city, expanded its creative tourism offerings and, in the case of the NZYWF, strengthened links with its Australian counterpart the National Young Writers Festival based in Newcastle and Melbourne City of Literature (Campbell 2015). These local initiatives have been complemented by opportunities within the Network, such as Henry Feltham's participation in Melbourne's Digital Writers Festival "20 Minute Cities" (Feltham 2015), a writing residency in Prague for poet David Howard, and the translation and projection of eight Dunedin poets on Krakow city walls, as part of the UNESCO Cities of Literature Multipoetry Project (McAvinue 2015; 2016).

However, with 116 cities from 54 countries currently in the Network, international collaborative partnerships need to be considered carefully to ensure mutually beneficial results and long-term sustainability. They also need to be considered within the larger strategic framework of the seventeen Sustainable Development Goals to 2030, which build on the eight Millennium Development Goals. Goal 11, Sustainable Cities and Communities, aims to make cities inclusive, safe, resilient, and sustainable, and is to be measured by eleven Targets, including "strengthening efforts to protect and safeguard the world's cultural and natural heritage" (United Nations). The UCCN can be a powerful mechanism to achieve this goal, but it will require a participatory approach at a local level, which encourages reciprocity and strengthening of relationships at the global scale.

Layers of care and dependence

A Māori whakataukī or proverb speaks of the interdependence of people and the environment:

> Hūtia te rito o te harakeke. Kei hea te kōmako e kō?
> Kī mai nei ki ahau. He aha te mea nui ki tēnei ao?
> Māku e kī atu. He tangata, he tangata, he tangata.
>
> If you were to pluck out the centre of the flax bush, where would the bellbird sing?
> If you were to ask me "What is the most important thing in the world?"
> I would reply, "That it is people, people, people."

Extending an ethic of care to the flaxbush sustains the bellbird that feeds on it and the people who utilize its strong fibers to create functional and beautiful weaving. The heart of the flaxbush is the central shoot from the flax root, which is protected on either side by two larger shoots. These are referred to by weavers as the child and parents, for if they are cut out, the surrounding leaves cannot be produced or sustainably harvested. While the proverb speaks of the importance of people, it is only through a relationship of care for the health and well-being of our environment that we can sustain the creative practices that enrich our lives and our relationship to one another. This is the foundation of care and dependence between the natural environment and the people and cultures it sustains.

The UNESCO Creative City Network has identified cities as concentrations and catalysts of creative cultural change. A healthy diversity of creative cultures strengthens community resilience, but the UNESCO Creative City designation acknowledges a city's care for a specific form of cultural practice—in the cases of Dunedin and Melbourne, this is sustaining a strong and diverse literary culture that is the work of many hands across time. This recognition entails a second layer of care to ensure this heritage is re-interpreted for the present—for new generations who inhabit or visit the city, in order for them to understand their place in the world—as well as to inspire the next generation of creative practitioners in the field. The third layer of care is afforded by the UCCN in the form of international exchange, collaboration, and translation, learning from the experience of writers and their communities in other cities and the challenges and opportunities their particular situation affords as a form of intercultural dialogue.

However, latent within the seven themes of the Network is a fourth layer of care. This is the licence to experiment within an expanded creative laboratory. If we reconsider the themes not as silos but as a sample of creative practice elements (see Figure 15.5), that represent some of the cultural building blocks of creative cities, the Network provides an opportunity for a recombination of these elements at local level to expand the community of creative practice and raise awareness of the opportunities of the Network beyond the designated city theme. When poetry is successfully put to music or when a film successfully interprets a novel, something different arises that strengthens and develops both practices and, generally, reaches a broader audience. Or more specifically and perhaps less conventionally for the stories of care I have discussed here, poems can speak to the place where we park our cars and develop alternative publication and distribution systems, while designers and photographers can express their

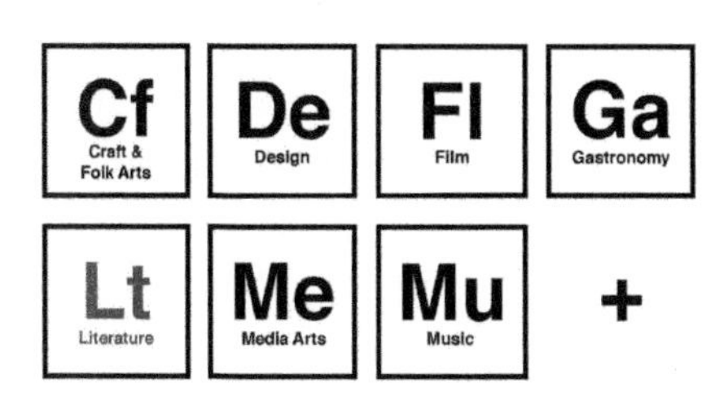

Figure 15.5 The seven elements of UNESCO Creative Cities present an opportunity for recombination in novel urban experiments at local and international scales.

care for their own crafts and visualize poetry in our homes and on our streets. A small inkling of the creative and productive capacity of an event like Koha for the Crib also demonstrates the potential of such diverse contributions to provide for future international cross-cutting collaborations that truly activate and connect the Creative City Network.

When applied at an international level through the Network, this connection allows for more cities to collaborate, and more ways to engage with a diversity of creative communities. The Poetick project demonstrates the potential to consider a local design experiment at a global scale through the Shenzhen Design Award for Young Talents, and a similar Christchurch project in 2017 (which uses a centrally placed parking machine labeled "Nothing to do here" to provide local insights into free things to do in the city) demonstrates the way ideas spread nationally (Anon 2017). These care-full collaborations can strengthen local creative communities and build innovative prototypes that can be tested within an international network, expanding Poussin's "laboratory of intercultural dialogue" from local interactions and testing to global validation, moving, in Landry's terms, from place-based cultural anchorage to exploring future sustaining cities of possibility.

At its essence, UNESCO has designed a framework of cultural care through the Creative City designation and Network, but in order for participating cities to actively contribute to global sustainability, they will need to acknowledge the inter-dependency of creative communities and enable and facilitate dialogue and collaboration locally and internationally. Philosopher Eva Kittay has argued for an ethics of care, explaining, "When we acknowledge how dependence on one another saves us from isolation and provides the connection to another that makes life worthwhile, we can start the process of embracing needed dependencies" (Kittay 2011: 57). This human dependency extends to the environment of our cities. The city is more than a mere stage for creative performance; it needs to be considered as a living member of our community of care. It is only through recognition of this foundational layer of care—the *rito* or "heart" of the city—that we can activate the other layers of care to develop sustainable creative cities.

Notes

1 In 2018 the UCCN meeting will be hosted jointly for the first time by Krakow and Katowice, respectively, Creative Cities of Literature and Music from Poland.

2 The Māori word "koha" (also widely used in New Zealand English) means a gift, especially one maintaining social relationships, and has connotations of reciprocity. A "crib" is a small holiday house in the lower South Island ("bach" is the vernacular term elsewhere in New Zealand).
3 This involved four Dunedin musicians with Rio Hemopo of Trinity Roots performing solo and Don McGlashan, who had featured on the "Tuwhare" album which featured New Zealand musicians putting Hone Tuwhare's poems to music.
4 Initiated in 2014 by Vogel Street Charitable Trust, the 2015 Vogel Street Party, "Literature and Light" attracted over 15,000 visitors. Vogel Street is at the center of Dunedin's harborside warehouse precinct, which was the subject of a 2013 Council Revitalization Plan that supported conservation and adaptive reuse of heritage buildings in the area.
5 It had been hoped that a wireless network would enable people to submit their own poems to the machines adding a further level of interactivity, but this was not achievable on the day. The video can be seen on YouTube.
6 The Dunedin Writers and Readers Festival <http://www.dunedinwritersfestival.co.nz/> and the New Zealand Young Writers Festival <https://youngwritersfest.nz/>.

References

Anon., "The Tuwhare Project," *Design Assembly*, December 21, 2015, www.designassembly.org.nz/articles/the-tuwhare-project

Anon., *TripAdviser Australia*, March 27, 2016, https://www.tripadvisor.com.au/ShowUserReviews-g255119-d256972-r358981602-Toitu_Otago_Settlers_Museum-Dunedin_Otago_Region_South_Island.html

Anon., (2017), "Parking Meter with a Difference Unlocks Christchurch's Best Kept Secret," July 6, 2017, http://www.christchurchnz.com/media/newsroom/parking-meter-with-a-difference-unlocks-christchurchs-best-kept-secret/

Banham, S., "Multistory Window," *Letterbox* (2016), https://letterbox.net.au/projects/installations/multistory-window/

Borley, C., "Poetic Take on Parking Debut," *Otago Daily Times*, October 10, 2015, https://www.odt.co.nz/news/dunedin/poetic-take-parking-debut

Boyle, D., "Prince Charles Yelps with Fright in Close Encounter with Bumble Bee on New Zealand Tour," *The Telegraph*, November 5, 2015, http://www.telegraph.co.uk/news/uknews/prince-charles/11976575/Prince-Charles-yelps-with-fright-in-close-encounter-with-bumble-bee-on-New-Zealand-tour.html

Campbell, S., "Spotlight On: The New Zealand Young Writers Festival," *National Young Writers' Festival*, July 22, 2015, http://youngwritersfestival.org/news/spotlight-new-zealand-young-writers-festival/

Clark, H. and Bokova (2013), "Foreword," in *Creative Economy Report: Widening Local Development Pathways*, New York: United Nations Development Programme (UNDP); Paris: United Nations Educational, Scientific and Cultural Organisation (UNESCO), 9–11.

Kittay, Eva F. (2011), "The Ethics of Care, Dependence and Disability," *Ratio Juris*, 24 (1): 49–58.

Feltham, H. "20 Minute Cities: Dunedin," *Digital Writers Festival*, February 15, 2015, http://digitalwritersfestival.com/2015/event/20-minute-cities-dunedin/

Finlay, A., "Interleaved," July 3, 2013, http://alecfinlayblog.blogspot.com.au/2013/07/interleaved.html

Global Diversity Foundation (GDF), "Focus on Biocultural Diversity," Retrieved from: http://www.globaldiversity.org.uk/biocultural-diversity

Hansen, C. "Melbourne's New William Barak Building is a Cruel Juxtaposition," *the conversation*, March 19, 2015, http://theconversation.com/melbournes-new-william-barak-building-is-a-cruel-juxtaposition-38983

Landry, C. (2008), *The Creative City: A Toolkit for Urban Innovators*, 2nd ed., London: Earthscan.

McAvinue, S. "City's Poetry Projected in Poland," *Otago Daily Times*, January 18, 2016, https://www.odt.co.nz/news/dunedin/city%E2%80%99s-poetry-projected-poland

McAvinue, S. "Prague Residency Delights Writer," *Otago Daily Times*, September 4, 2015, https://www.odt.co.nz/news/dunedin/city%E2%80%99s-poetry-projected-poland

Mol, A. (2008), *The Logic of Care: Health and the Problem of Patient Choice*, London: Routledge.

Poussin, G. (2010), "The Creative Tourism Movement," in R. Wurzburger, T. Aageson, A. Pattakos, and S. Pratt (eds.), *Creative Tourism: A Global Conversation: How to Provide Unique Creative Experiences for Travellers Worldwide*, Santa Fe: Sunstone Press, 104–07.

Rosi, M. (2014), "Branding or Sharing? The Dialectics of Labeling and Cooperation in the UNESCO Creative Cities Network," *City, Culture and Society* 5: 107–10.

United Nations, "Goal 11: Make Cities Inclusive, Safe, Resilient and Sustainable," *Sustainable Development Goals*, http://www.un.org/sustainabledevelopment/cities/

UNESCO Creative Cities Network [UCCN] (2015), "Membership Monitoring Guideline," https://en.unesco.org/creative-cities/sites/creative-cities/files/Membership%20Monitoring%20Guidelines%202017.pdf

UNESCO Creative Cities Network [UCCN] (2015), "Reporting and Monitoring" http://en.unesco.org/creative-cities/content/reporting-monitoring

UNESCO Creative Cities Network [UCCN], "Towards Sustainable Strategies for Creative Tourism, Discussion Report of the Planning Meeting for 2008 International

Conference on Creative Tourism Santa Fe, New Mexico, U.S.A. October 25–27, 2006," http://unesdoc.unesco.org/images/0015/001598/159811e.pdf

UNESCO Creative Cities Network [UCCN] (2015), "Why Creativity? Why Cities?" UNESCO Creative Cities Network, http://en.unesco.org/creative-cities/content/why-creativity-why-cities

16

Performing a Practice of Care: A Dialogue

Mick Douglas and Laurene Vaughan

Laurene: I'm interested to explore the idea that performing practice, design practice in particular, can be a practice of care.

Mick: For me, the interlinking of design practice and care throws into question the *sign* in design. We open up a question of thinking about the relationship of signification and representation embedded within the idea of design and its practice. To undertake a practice of care as a practice of design challenges what we might assume of that relationship with the sign. One way of thinking about this is to consider how performative practices of *doing* are less concerned with the signs of representation, and therefore, the distancing effects that the sign can have.

Laurene: What do you mean by a *performative practice*? Are you alluding to something here that is between the tangible and intangible or . . . ?

Mick: Well, I wonder whether a practice of design, if considered as a practice of care, necessitates a questioning of the potential distancing effect that can be embedded in design when we maintain the privileged role of representation in design. If we start opening up questions of the *doing* of design, and the performative actions and effects through practices of design, then, with less of a distancing effect, we might be able to activate care.

Laurene: I think that's interesting, but, I'd like you to explain a little bit more about representation. What are you referring to in that?

Mick: That much of design's strength has been in developing ways of constructing that which is imagined as possible, into forms that can be communicated and translated into realization. This has involved the development of high levels of expertise and know-how in visualization, modeling, communication, and representational strategies. But, at the same time, there can be a distancing effect, in that the enmeshed conditions in which the effects of design unfold and in which design becomes affective in its intra-activity, can be held somewhat at bay by those representational devices. So, the question that I put back to you is: do you think that a practice of design as a practice of care endeavors to ameliorate the potential distancing effects of designing, and seeks to induce other kinds of qualities when we refer to the idea of *care*?

Laurene: Yes, I think it does, and I think it also equally links to the way in which our understanding of design is changing as well. And this is where I have found Maurice Hamington's work as an ethicist of care interesting. His writing has left me wondering what is it to design a culture of care, and what is it to have design as a practice of care, and why care matters. I think that as design has matured and with the evolution of, and perhaps in response to, digital technologies, we have been challenged to design differently.

For me, this proposition of there being intersections between design and care allows us to think about different ways in which design happens, and that this is not just a Western construct. We have to acknowledge that other cultures have other ways of doing and talking about design. It's not like they haven't been designing, they just have different ways of articulating and practicing it. I think that there are a range of domains that are informing how this might be, and why I've been thinking about this, and why I want to talk about it with you.

A lot of design practice has become more about a practice of *being with* others. We could say people are becoming the material that we are designing with, whether it is in organizations, communities, or social groupings. Here, the materials are the relationships and the people, and design is a way of manifesting or creating conditions for something to happen.

But, my interest here is in what it is to practice design, and so it's about what or how you *are* as a designer, and how to *be* a designer. I suppose I'm thinking of this in terms of their disposition in relation to their practice. After all a practice is not stationary; a practice is evolutionary, and it's never perfect. The great practitioners in other fields, such as music or dance, know that they are practicing their whole life; we could say that they never arrive at an end. It is this kind of attitude toward practice that I think we have not yet really brought to design, but we are starting to.

To me this is about design as a practice of being active—it is an active state of being and doing. As we know, design is both a noun and a verb. So, if we think of design as the verb form, we are looking at the activities of design, and so, I suppose I'm wondering, *how do we perform that practice*?

What informs that performance and how might we then move beyond just calling these actions? It is these questions that have really driven my interest in talking with you, because of the work you've been doing around performance and performance studies. You have an industrial design background, and you are a visual and performing artist.

Mick: Yes, my own path into interests of the performative and performance came through ephemeral public art and socially engaged art, what these days is called social practice that operates across different creative fields. So yes, the relations between people and elements in their contextual condition have long been a focus of mine. In addition to this wider rise of interest in the social as a medium of practice, the other relevant shift here is the rising interest in the performative. J. L. Austin's idea of the performative is the common starting point. He articulates the performative utterance, which simply put, is where a speech act not only representationally describes something, but actually is able to *do* something by putting into effect an action in the world.

I've been increasingly interested in performative orientations toward creative practice, by which I mean practices that look for the most direct means for an effect to take place in the world, by actually doing what is of interest, and through which a creative process can set up an immediate feedback loop and gain the value of that feedback as directly as possible.

Often that's thought of as prototyping or enacting live conditions—whether it's framed laboratory conditions or chaotic immersive conditions—which test out the hunches that might be emerging, and importantly, allow for the emergence of creative actions and contributions through the situatedness of dynamic intra-activity. Such an emergent process is an example of seeking to minimize the distancing effect that too much design beforehand can potentially impose upon a set of conditions, or to put it another way, how too much of the sign of design preceding engagement in real conditions can pre-empt the capacity for design to emerge through sensitive intra-action. So, it seems to me that this performative orientation is always looking for ways in which the interests of creative practice or design research can be immediately tested, made palpable, made actionable, through the way that the creative research performs its doing. And, in order to do so, design practice inherently needs to work with how it's enmeshed within certain conditions, and I think that's where, in those relationships of enmeshment, care is at stake.

Laurene: I think that's interesting, and this makes me start to really understand what I think is taking place in co-design. The basis of a lot of collaborative, or co-design, is a designer working with a community, and we might call the people in the community lay designers. Because these people might be the client, the group, or a community who have design capabilities that are thought of as skills or expertise, but not formalized as design qualifications or design expertise, and yet they still perform design actions with designers. Perhaps it is through the activity of working together that the feedback loop is happening in real time, in the same way that you have just proposed, and the designer is performing a role, just as everybody in the room is performing a role. But, they are charged with a certain responsibility to the group. This is because that's what their role at this point in time is. In reality that responsibility could be with anybody in that group, as you are endeavoring to do something together. And as you say, that's when the disposition of care or respect has to really manifest. It is both care for the thing that we are working on, the issue at hand as you might say, but also care and respect for everybody present at that moment working together. Everybody has a role to play.

From my understanding of the kind of social practices you are talking about, it requires humility. There's a certain boldness required to practice design—to be the person doing and leading; but there also has to be a certain element of humility or egolessness, which may not really be possible. Perhaps that's at the heart of what I'm asking. To perform this practice of care or design as care, you need to understand the situation at hand, and the dynamics of what you are doing and what others are doing, and the implications of what everyone is doing.

Because, unless you really want to cause harm, which is not the norm, how are you ensuring that there is no harm as a result of your actions?

Mick: You raise the issue of dynamics in that condition, which I think is very important, because it opens up questions of our relationship to time or our expected relationship to time through designing creative practices. And, if we are open to an ever-unfolding trajectory, we are also open to the fact that today's designs are what we inherit tomorrow as part of the conditions to be negotiated, potentially part of the problems to be solved and so on. If that then places us with an openness to the conditions that we engage in as always being emergent, then we're constantly *in* these dynamics. And so how we conduct roles, relationships, negotiations, navigations, in these ever-evolving emergent dynamics becomes a critical concern of care.

This, it seems to me, is a matter of being attentive to the vitalities at play in emergent conditions, whether they be amongst select individuals, or in the assemblage of interests and concerns and social and cultural stakes, or whether that be undertaken amongst other than human actants in a set of conditions, and how we are able to care for the life of these forces in their interplay through particular conditions and situations. This raises how we navigate our own ethical responsibilities, and even identify and become aware of responsibilities and our dynamic responsiveness as a matter of conducting a practice. In such a dynamic schema, I appreciate this idea of a *disposition* of care as being an orientation of attentive awareness, but also being qualities of practice that may be practiced.

Laurene: I think that is what you've just been going through too, from a design perspective, having a practice or approaching a practice in that way, or to *practice the practice*, as Leon van Schaik has talked about. This also calls us to expose the mythologies around design as *problem solving*, because this is based on an assumption there is a problem to be solved and that will be the end. When in fact we know that we only ever choose to stop at a point in time for various reasons and not because we have reached THE solution. Design is as much a propositional and problem-making practice as it is problem solving. Likewise this perspective challenges the classification of design as logic, which is the current focus on design thinking, when that only looks at design in one way; it's only one aspect of what design is.

As we discuss this I think such propositions also call out the need to remember the ethics of design, both in practice and in outcomes, or application. There is a need for us to take responsibility for what we designers do, whether we are working with materials or individuals or communities. I think that that's really interesting. You've clearly articulated for me a way of understanding the complexity that design practice is, and even more so if we frame it as a practice of care.

Mick: We also need to caution ourselves about embracing self-belief in care. When could it be that there is too much care brought to a practice of design and care? When can care be so great an investment that it has a corrosive force on what might be more desirable qualities of care? Historically, examples are what might seemingly be benevolently well-intentioned and honorable acts of charity, or acts of spreading what one regards as the good word or the good faith or the good belief or good design! In their own righteousness, such pursuits regarded as care can induce harm, and at worst, be patronizing acts of appropriation, domination, colonization. I would advocate for more open and emergent forms of care that are embedded in some form of reciprocity that establishes the value of that care, rather than assuming that a value for care exists.

Laurene: Some people talk about the burden of care too, which I think is also important—we could burden ourselves with care. What I think you are alluding to goes back to us understanding the components of the situation at hand. And so, if I were to approach something with righteousness, I have a pre-ordained idea of what the care act will be, as opposed to being open to the conditions and what everybody wants or needs in a situation.

Earlier on we were talking about not being wedded to an outcome, but being wedded to a process and being open to the process and responding to a need, or a catalyst to see what would be the outcome. I wonder, if you go through the design process and there is no change in the outcome, has design taken place? Having integrity in going through the process is what is significant. And so, I suppose what I'm wondering, and what I hope this book is exploring, is what are the elements of design? What works? What goes wrong? Things will go wrong, you can't be sure that people won't get hurt, but I think it's about acknowledging this too.

Mick: Maybe this is a question of how we might come to know a practice of design as a practice of care. And how would we know of the care at play in a practice of design? Would that be healthy communities? Healthy environments? You know, we could speculate on what might be the indicators there. But perhaps there needs to be a level of non-attachment to care in order to care.

Laurene: I think that's very much the case and that's what I'm trying to say by using the term disposition; it's an intentionality to act with care, without being attached to the outcomes so that you force that. It is also an awareness of *that*, in the same way—you know, if we're thinking materially, it's about being aware of the implications of the materials and asking the right questions along the way about where they come from and what they can withstand. That it is one of the ways of being in practice, of inquiry and non-attachment to outcome.

It's quite easy to categorize acts of care. I visit my parents when they are elderly, I give money, I try not to waste water—there can be all sorts of ways that I might demonstrate actions of care. But, they could also be public performance with no actual care behind them. So, I think care does manifest in actions and that's what they say is the difference between empathy and care: that empathy is affect or emotive, where care is actionable.

But the integrity of that action is as ambiguous as any action; you can't really know what is behind it. I do think it is an interesting way to expand our thinking about the implications of what we do and how we do it. And I suppose that's what has driven my, in many ways, interest in care.

Mick: That brings to mind a sense of the distribution of value as a part of what might constitute a practice of care. Design might be thought to have emerged through developing a capacity to aggregate a sense of value, and to claim authority and purpose over that proposition of value that is thought to be desired by invested producers and a broader community of consumers or users or a public. Rather than assuming that the design activity is one of identifying and proposing a value to be put forth, a practice of care would be operating in a more distributed fashion, both in determining what is of value and in allowing values to inform what comes to be appreciated through an emergent process.

Laurene: Yes I think that is true, and I think that's why it's timely that we have these discourses coming out now, around what it is to be a designer or to practice design, or what design can do. The field is maturing. It no longer has to be based on proving value through skill, or value through economic impact. Rather, there are other kinds of indicators of value and design's contribution in relation to other disciplines, and hence, also, greater recognition of design plus science, design plus humanities—we're now able to work in more interdisciplinary ways because the value is becoming clearer. As designers, we are becoming better at being able to evidence a practice that has value in a different way to the shiny objects of design's past.

Mick: Given that we could argue that all practices and conduct might be undertaken with a disposition of care, what might design practice bring to practices of care, that other practices may not? One contribution might be how the particularly emergent qualities of design practices offer affordance for practices of care. My sense is that a relevant legacy of design practice is the capacity to navigate poise amidst the dynamics of different elements and forces at play, or within complex intractable sets of conditions. This is what Horst Rittel was advancing with the now widely accepted idea of design's capacity to engage with what he called "wicked problems." The field of design has a lineage of practiced expertise working in the distributed nature of a relational field, working with the complexities of time. Bringing higher levels of reflexivity, ethical awareness, and ecological enmeshment into these emergent practices might be what design could offer to a wider pursuit of practices of care.

Laurene: I think that is definitely the case.

That's why the ability to work in the wicked spaces is okay; because there doesn't have to be certainty upfront—we can discover the certainty, if there will be any. It's interesting—to go back to Hamington—he's making a correlation about the value between design thinking and practices of care or care ethics. Yet for him care is often reactive, which is limited, as design can be proactive. Design's ability to take steps into uncertainty or the unknown underpins what designers do and they learn to do, either formally or informally. That is another reason for design's value in interdisciplinary or other relational practices.

Mick: Yes, performing practices of both design and care involve quite an ongoing dance with sustaining openness to intra-relations and the responsibility to act, recognizing that our mere presence in a situation is never neutral, but embedded amidst an ecology. Rather than fixate on any finiteness as such, there is opportunity to pause and develop practices of attending to the constant negotiations that are living out of an ethical poise.

Index